INTERACTIONS II
A Reading Skills Book

SECOND EDITION

INTERACTIONS II
A Reading Skills Book

Elaine Kirn
West Los Angeles College

Pamela Hartmann
Los Angeles Unified School District

McGraw-Hill, Inc.
New York St. Louis San Francisco Auckland Bogotá
Caracas Lisbon London Madrid Mexico City Milan
Montreal New Delhi San Juan Singapore
Sydney Tokyo Toronto

This book is printed on acid-free paper.

This is an EBI book

Interactions II: A Reading Skills Book
Second Edition

0 DOC/DOC 9 5 4

ISBN 0-07-557538-8

Cover illustration: Frantisĕk Kupka: *Lines, Planes, Depth,* c. 1920–22. Oil on canvas, 31½ × 28½″. Albright-Knox Art Gallery, Buffalo, New York. Charles Clifton and George B. and Jenny R. Mathews Funds, 1977.

Sponsoring editor: Eirik Børve
Developmental editor: Mary McVey Gill
Project editor: Cathy de Heer
Production supervisor: Renée Reeves
Copyeditor: Stacey Sawyer
Proofreader: Karen Kevorkian
Illustrations: Sally Richardson
Photo research: Judy Mason
Interior and cover design: Cheryl Carrington
Composition: Graphic Typesetting Service
Color separation: Color Tech
Printing and binding: Rand McNally

Grateful acknowledgment is made for the following material.

Readings   *page 212,* adapted from Knud Rasmussen, "Report of the Fifth Thule Expedition," 1921–1924, v. VII, no. 1, *Intellectual Culture of the Iglulik Eskimos; page 213,* adapted from Carol Laderman, "Trances That Heal: Rites, Rituals, and Brain Chemicals," *Science Digest,* July, 1983, pp. 80–83

All dictionary entries except that on page 31 are from *The Longman Dictionary of American English: A Dictionary for Learners of English.* White Plains, N.Y.: Longman, Inc., 1983.

Realia   *pages 33–36* Vancouver Tourist Board; *89* 1. © The Venice Beach House; 3. © Joseph Simms; 5. © ZCLA Zen Mountain Center; 6. © Bret Lyon; 7. © Voter Hotline; *116–118* Four Winds Travel; *144–145, 146* Metropolitan Toronto Convention and Visitors Association; *170* 1. © Waxing by Larisa; 2. © Donna's Hair and Nails; *171* 3. © Sun Lovers; 5. © Laura Gray Fortuné Beauty Workshop; *172* 6. © Perfect Body; 7. © Camp del Mar; *221–222* from *Faith Healing* by Louis Rose, Penguin Books, 1971; *237, 238, 239 The Los Angeles Times; 261* Legal Action Workshop

CONTENTS

PREFACE
to the Second Edition

INTERACTIONS: THE PROGRAM

Interactions consists of ten texts plus two instructor's manuals for in-college or college-bound nonnative English students. *Interactions I* is for high-beginning to low-intermediate students, while *Interactions II* is for low-intermediate to intermediate students. Within each level, I and II, the books are carefully coordinated by theme, vocabulary, grammar structure, and, where possible, language functions. A chapter in one book corresponds to and reinforces material taught in the same chapter of the other three books at that level for a truly integrated, four-skills approach.

Each level, I and II, consists of five books plus an instructor's manual. In addition to *A Reading Skills Book,* they include:

A Communicative Grammar I, II: Organized around grammatical topics, these books include notional/functional material where appropriate. They present all grammar in context and contain a wide variety of communicative activities.

A Writing Process Book I, II: These books use a process approach to writing, including many exercises on prewriting and revision. Exercises build skills in exploring and organizing ideas, developing vocabulary, using correct form and mechanics, using coherent structure, editing, revising, and using feedback to create a final draft.

A Listening/Speaking Skills Book I, II: These books use lively, natural language from a variety of contexts—dialogues, interviews, lectures, and announcements. Listening strategies emphasized include summarizing main ideas, making inferences, and listening for stressed words, reductions, and intonation. A cassette tape program with an instructor's key accompanies each text.

A Speaking Activities Book I, II: These books are designed to give students the opportunity to practice their speaking and listening skills in English by promoting realistic use of the language through individual, pair, and small-group work. Task-oriented and problem-solving activities simulate real-life situations and help develop fluency.

Instructor's Manual I, II: These manuals provide instructions and guidelines for use of the books separately or in any combination to form a program. For each of the core books except *Speaking Activities,* there is a separate section with teaching tips, additional activities, and other suggestions. The instructor's manuals also include sample tests for the grammars and readers.

The grammatical focus for the twelve chapters of *Interactions II* is as follows:

1. Review of basic verb tenses
2. Nouns, pronouns, and articles
3. Modal auxiliaries and related structures
4. The perfect tenses; *Would/used to, was/were going to*
5. Phrasal verbs and related structures
6. Compound and complex sentences; Clauses of time, condition, reason, contrast, and purpose
7. Transitions; The past perfect continuous tense
8. Adjectives and adverbs; Clauses and phrases of comparison
9. The passive voice
10. Adjective clauses
11. Common uses of infinitives, gerunds, and related structures
12. *Wish, hope,* and conditional sentences

INTERACTIONS II: A READING SKILLS BOOK

Rationale

Interactions II: A Reading Skills Book is based on the idea that people learn to read by *reading.* If the material is interesting and not too difficult, students will enjoy reading and will be encouraged to read more; the more they read, the better they will be at it. The problem for academic nonnative students is that they want to read sophisticated material but lack the skills with which to do so.

The solution is twofold: (1) to give students readings that are intellectually stimulating but not beyond their lexical, grammatical, or syntactic understanding; and (2) to teach strategies that make reading easier. The reading selections in *Interactions* contain sophisticated material; however, vocabulary and grammar have been very carefully controlled for the students' level of comprehension. In addition, the exercises guide students toward acquiring the skills of good readers, skills that make reading both easy and fun.

Vocabulary items presented in one chapter of *Interactions* are recycled in subsequent chapters to prevent students from forgetting them. This constant recycling enables students to make rapid progress; their vocabulary will increase dramatically as they use the book, and yet the process won't be perceived as difficult.

One of the biggest obstacles to comprehension in many academic readers is that the grammar is too difficult for nonnative, low-level/intermediate students. They simply haven't learned it yet. In the reading selections of *Interactions,* however, the grammar points have been carefully sequenced and appear only as students are likely to learn them. This text is not only coordinated with *Interactions II: A Communicative Grammar* but is also compatible with the sequencing in most grammar syllabi for nonnatives.

It should be noted that since this is a *reading* book, grammar is not taught for the sake of grammar. Instead, it is seen as an aid—one of many—to comprehension. Other such aids, or strategies, taught in this text include guessing meaning from context, increasing reading speed, understanding stems and affixes, making predictions before actually reading, learning to accept some uncertainty, making inferences, and distinguishing fact from opinion.

Because the material in the *Interactions* readers *looks* difficult but *isn't,* students can read easily and with a growing sense of confidence and accomplishment. Academic students won't feel that their intelligence is being demeaned by puerile material.

Chapter Organization

Because its primary purpose is to provide instruction in the reading process, *Interactions* offers a large variety of exercises and activities directed toward that end. It is left to individual teachers to choose those sections suited to the specific needs of their students. The following outline lists the different kinds of activities in the four parts of each chapter.

Part One

Getting Started: a prereading exercise consisting of a picture and accompanying questions; sets the tone for the chapter

Preparing to Read: prereading questions for the students to keep in mind as they read the selection

Reading Selection: a controlled reading on the theme of the chapter, usually nonfiction, giving practical information and divided into lettered paragraphs

Getting the Main Ideas: a postreading exercise to help students check their general understanding of the reading selection

Guessing Meaning from Context: specific suggestions followed by exercises on words from the reading selection

Understanding Reading Structure: exercises focusing on organization of ideas or relationships between ideas

Making Inferences (Chapters 6, 7, and 8): exercises to help students read between the lines

Distinguishing Facts from Theories (Chapters 9 and 10): a list of words associated with facts and others associated with theories, followed by exercises to help students distinguish them

Discussing the Reading: questions that relate the reading selection to students' lives and that allow for conversation

Part Two

Skimming for Main Ideas: an activity that guides students in recognizing the main idea of a paragraph

Reading Selection: the second controlled reading of the chapter, similar in theme to the first but often somewhat lighter, divided into lettered paragraphs

Understanding Idioms (Chapters 6 and 7): an exercise in which students apply their skill of guessing meaning from context to idioms as well as to individual words

Making Inferences (Chapters 6, 7, 8, 9, 10, and 12): more practice; similar to the section in Part One

Distinguishing Facts from Opinions (Chapter 11): practice in distinguishing fact from opinion

Discussing the Reading: as in Part One, questions that relate the reading to students' lives through in-class conversation

Part Three

Building Vocabulary and Study Skills: a variety of exercises to help students expand their passive and active knowledge of vocabulary, followed by activities to aid students in acquiring essential skills for academic reading—using a dictionary, marking a book, increasing reading speed, and accepting some uncertainty

Part Four

Scanning for Information: a section of "realia" (a city map, classified ads, charts, movie reviews, etc.) accompanied by a short glossary and questions for scanning

Teaching Suggestions

The following suggestions are designed to help teach the reading strategies used by good readers, skills essential to students' academic success.

Part One

Prereading: The skill of anticipation—forming predictions about what is to be read—is an important part of active reading. This skill may be encouraged through the *Getting Started* and *Preparing to Read* sections. First, have students discuss the picture, answering the questions in the *Getting Started* section. Then read through the *Preparing to Read* questions. Tell students that they aren't expected to be able to answer these questions before reading. Instead, they should keep them in mind as they read.

Initial Reading: Each student should read the selection silently, as this is the most common form of academic reading. The selection should be read quickly, without a dictionary. Encourage students to guess the meanings of new words. Emphasize the importance of simply getting the main idea, the most basic of reading skills.

Have students complete the *Getting the Main Ideas* section, which checks comprehension of general themes and important ideas in the reading. Students should complete these exercises quickly, without looking back at the reading selection. The answers can be checked later, after students reread the selection.

The *Guessing Meaning from Context* section is self-explanatory. It contains specific hints and step-by-step exercises on *how* to guess meanings of new words, thereby avoiding tedious and time-consuming trips to the dictionary.

Rereading: Students reread the selection, this time more carefully, focusing on details. Although they might occasionally use a dictionary this time, they should still be encouraged to apply the skills they have learned in the *Guessing Meaning from Context* section.

When they finish the reading selection, students should check their answers in the *Getting the Main Ideas* section before completing the exercises that follow.

Postreading Exercises: As they do the exercises in the *Understanding Reading Structure* section, students will need to look back at the reading selection to better understand its organization.

Students can actively practice their newly learned vocabulary words as they express their opinions and share ideas in the *Discussing the Reading* section. There are a number of ways in which the questions in this section may be answered. Among them:

1. Ask questions of the entire class. The advantage of this technique is that the teacher can control the discussion and encourage students to expand on their ideas. The disadvantage, though, is that few students may volunteer to speak.

2. Have students discuss the answers in small groups (three to four people). A representative from each group can then report that group's ideas to the whole class.

3. Have students discuss the answers with just one partner. This technique is conducive to the participation of students who are usually too shy to speak in a larger group.

4. Choose one of the questions and organize a debate on it. Divide the class into two teams, each of which will prepare arguments.

Part Two

Have students skim (read quickly) the paragraphs in the reading selection and find the main ideas. They should not use a dictionary; instead, they should guess meaning from context, without worrying about details.

The techniques suggested for the *Discussing the Reading* section in Part One also apply here. In addition, you might try a role-play activity where appropriate: Students can play the parts of different characters from the reading selection.

Part Three

Although the *Building Vocabulary* exercises can be assigned as homework, the *Study Skills* activities should be completed in class, particularly those dealing with increasing reading speed.

Part Four

The ability to find specific information quickly is an important skill for academic students and is the focus of Part Four, *Scanning for Information*. Briefly go over the short glossary with the students. Then have them answer the questions individually or in small groups, from the information found in the realia. Discourage them from reading every word as they hunt for the answers. Instead, they should run a finger over the page until the answer "pops out" at them.

In the *Going Beyond the Text* section, as homework, students find a map, brochure, etc. on the theme of the chapter. They bring it to class and share it with the other students, in small groups or as a class. This activity is meant as a brief recap of the ideas and vocabulary from the chapter.

Teachers who want to give their students additional reading practice in a certain chapter might choose to forego the quiz (found in the instructor's manual) for that chapter and copy the reading selection for students to do either as a group exercise or as a home-work assignment.

Changes to the Second Edition

1. The readings have been updated and/or revised; there are also new readings in sev-eral chapters.
2. Many exercises have been revised, and new ones have been added.
3. The instructor's manual contains new quizzes for each chapter, which can be dupli-cated and distributed to students. Also, exercises from the *Understanding Details* and *Interpreting Sentence Structure and Meaning* sections are included in the instructor's manual for selected chapters.
4. The new edition has a clearer design and layout. New photos and artwork have been included as needed to accompany exercises and readings.

ACKNOWLEDGMENTS

The authors would like to thank Eirik Børve, who inspired the *Interactions* program, and Mary McVey Gill, who undertook the monumental task of coordinating it. Thanks also to our versatile artist Sally Richardson, the organized and supercapable Lesley Walsh, and the production crew led by Cathy de Heer. A word of thanks as well to Margaret Segal and Lois Locci, two reviewers whose comments, both favorable and critical, were of value in refining certain portions of the text. Appreciation goes to Judy Guitton for help with quizzes in the instructor's manual. And for their help with research, we'd like to thank Susana Cox, William de la Torre, Beatrice Hartmann, Cherry Vasconcellos, and Armin Shimerman.

Also, thanks to the following first-edition reviewers for their help in shaping the second edition: Barbara Flaharan Aghai, Tacoma Community College; James Burke, El Paso Community College; Daniele J. Dibie, California State University, Northridge; David Fein, UCLA Extension; Pam Greene, Springfield Technical Community College; Judy

Guitton, San Jose State University; Matthew Handelsman, St. Michael's College; Monica Kapadia, El Paso Community College; Cathy McDade, Mountain View College, Dallas; Kay Ritter, Laney College; Simin Rooholamini, County College of Morris; Lydia Samatar, Upsala College; and Webster J. Van De Mark, Valencia Community College.

Finally, we'd like to acknowlege each other for a productive and pleasant coauthoring experience.

E. K.
P. H.

SUMMARY OF READING SKILLS

CHAPTER	PART I Guessing Meaning from Context	PART I Understanding Reading Structure	PART I Additional Skills	PART II Skimming for Main Ideas
1 Education and Student Life	punctuation (parentheses, dashes, commas) clues in another sentence or sentence part	paragraph form		topic sentences
2 City Life	examples opposites details	the main idea		topic sentences
3 Business and Money	clues in phrases abbreviations (*i.e., e.g.*)	the main idea		topic sentences
4 Jobs and Professions	review	the main idea		topic sentences
5 Lifestyles	review	the main idea		the main idea rephrased
6 Travel and Transportation	words with basic and secondary meanings meanings of words in phrases finding words in definitions (scanning)	understanding structure through outlines	inference	the main idea rephrased
7 North America: The Land and the People	summary of context clues	outlines: arrangement of topics, subtopics	inference	the main idea rephrased
8 Tastes and Preferences	writing definitions finding words that fit definitions	outlines: summaries	inference	details that imply the main idea
9 The Sky Above Us	writing definitions	outlines: definitions, reasons, examples	facts versus theories	writing the main idea
10 Medicine, Myths, and Magic	tolerating ambiguity of meaning	outlines: comparison	facts versus theories	writing summarizing statements
11 The Media	tolerating ambiguity of meaning	time relationships (chronological order)		
12 Prejudice, Tolerance, and Justice	writing definitions	writing an outline		listing main ideas

SUMMARY OF READING SKILLS (continued)

CHAPTER	PART II Additional Skills	PART III Building Vocabulary	Study Skills	PART IV Scanning for Information
1 Education and Student Life		words with similar meanings words in phrases	reading and following instructions	enrollment forms
2 City Life		parts of speech (words with two) related words (same stem)	using the dictionary: parts of speech	city map list of attractions
3 Business and Money		words in categories parts of speech: suffixes (nouns, adjectives)	increasing reading speed: reading in phrases	banking forms
4 Jobs and Professions	viewpoint	adjective and noun phrases compound words	increasing reading speed: left-to-right eye movements	classified newspaper ads
5 Lifestyles	viewpoint	suffixes (nouns, verbs, adverbs) prefixes	using the dictionary: words with more than one meaning; examples	newspaper ads (services and events)
6 Travel and Transportation	understanding idioms inference	expressions and idioms	using the dictionary: expressions and idioms increasing reading speed	a travel brochure
7 North America: The Land and the People	understanding idioms inference viewpoint	categories of words prefixes and suffixes word roots	vocabulary learning methods	a city magazine (local events)
8 Tastes and Preferences	inference	words with similar meanings	using the dictionary: exact definitions; connotations; usage increasing reading speed	advertisements
9 The Sky Above Us	inference	words with similar meanings categories of words word roots and affixes	marking a book summarizing	sky charts
10 Medicine, Myths, and Magic	inference	categories of words word forms word roots and affixes	prediction	reading an index
11 The Media	facts versus opinions	hyphenated words figurative language	accepting ambiguity	movie reviews
12 Prejudice, Tolerance, and Justice	writing inferences	categories of words	prediction	legal brochure

INTERACTIONS II
A Reading Skills Book

1

EDUCATION

METHODS OF EDUCATION: EAST VERSUS WEST

Getting Started

Look at the pictures and discuss them.

1. Where is each scene taking place? What is happening?
2. Compare the methods of education in the two pictures on the left with the methods in the two pictures on the right.
3. Which type of class do you prefer? Why?

Preparing to Read

As you read the following selection, think about the answers to these questions.

1. How is the educational system in most Asian countries different from the system in many Western countries?
2. Why do different countries have different methods of education?
3. What are the advantages and disadvantages of different teaching methods?

Read the selection quickly. Do not use a dictionary. Then answer the questions that follow the reading selection.

Methods of Education: East Versus West

A
A teacher from a Western country recently visited an elementary school in an Asian country. In one class, she watched sixty young children as they learned to draw a cat. The class teacher drew a big circle on the blackboard, and sixty children copied it on their papers. The teacher drew a smaller circle on top of the first and then put two triangles on top of it. The children drew in the same way. The lesson continued until there were sixty-one identical cats in the classroom. Each student's cat looked exactly like the one on the board.

B
The visiting teacher watched the lesson and was surprised. The teaching methods were very different from the way of teaching in her own country. A children's art lesson in her own country produced a room full of unique pictures, each one completely different from the others. Why? What causes this difference in educational methods? In a classroom in any country, the instructor teaches more than art or history or language. He or she also teaches culture (the ideas and beliefs of that society). Each educational system is a mirror that reflects the culture of the society.

C
In a society such as the United States or Canada, which has many national, religious, and cultural differences, people highly value individualism—the differences among people. Teachers place a lot of importance on the qualities that make each student special. The educational systems in these countries show these values. Students do not memorize information. Instead, they work individually and find answers themselves. There is often discussion in the classroom. At an early age, students learn to form their own ideas and opinions.

D
In most Asian societies, by contrast, the people have the same language, history, and culture. Perhaps for this reason, the educational system in much of the Orient reflects society's belief in group goals and purposes rather than individualism. Children in China, Japan, and Korea often work together and help one another on assignments. In the classroom, the teaching methods are often very formal. The teacher lectures, and the students listen. There is not much discussion. Instead, the students recite rules or information that they have memorized.

E
There are advantages and disadvantages to both of these systems of education. For example, one advantage to the system in Japan is that students there learn much more math and science than American students learn by the end of high school. They also study more hours each day and more days each year than North Americans do. The system is difficult, but it prepares students for a society that values discipline and self-control. There is, however, a disadvantage. Memorization is an important learning method in Japanese schools, yet many students say that

after an exam, they forget much of the information that they have memorized.

F   The advantage of the educational system in North America, on the other hand, is that students learn to think for themselves. The system prepares them for a society that values creative ideas. There is, however, a disadvantage. When students graduate from high school, they haven't memorized as many basic rules and facts as students in other countries have.

Getting the Main Ideas

Answer the questions according to the reading selection. Which statements apply to which systems of education? Write W (*Western*) or A (*Asian*) on the lines. Don't look back at the reading.

1. *a*   The teacher draws pictures that the children copy exactly.

2. *W*   Each child draws a different picture; the teacher helps individuals.

3. *W*   The society values individualism highly.

4. *W*   Students have to find information themselves, and there is a lot of discussion.

5. *A*   Most of the people in the country have the same language, history, and culture.

6. *A*   Students listen to the teacher and memorize information and rules.

7. *A*   The system prepares students for a society that values discipline.

Guessing Meaning from Context

You do not need to look up the meanings of all new words in a dictionary. You can guess the meanings of many new words from the context—the other words in the sentence and the other sentences in the paragraph.

Sometimes a sentence gives a definition of a new vocabulary item or information about it. This information may be in parentheses ( ), after a dash (—), or after a comma (,).

Example: There were sixty-one <u>identical</u> cats in the classroom, each one exactly like the one on the board. (What does <u>identical</u> mean? It means "exactly alike.")

A. Find the meanings of the underlined words in the sentences. Write them on the lines.

1. A children's art lesson produced a room full of <u>unique</u> pictures, each one completely different from the others. *completely different*

2. The instructor also teaches the <u>culture</u> (the ideas and beliefs of society). *ideas and beliefs of society*

3. People highly value <u>individualism</u>—the differences among people. *the differences among people*

4. Most Asian societies value <u>discipline</u>, or self-control. *self-control*

Sometimes the meaning or a clue to the meaning of a new vocabulary item is in another sentence or sentence part.

Example: A teacher from a Western country recently visited an elementary school in an Asian country. In one class, she watched sixty young children. (What is an <u>elementary</u> school? It's a school for young children.)

B. Write the meanings of the underlined words on the lines.

1. The teacher drew a big circle on the blackboard, and the children <u>copied</u> it. Then she drew a smaller circle, and the class drew it the same way. *It's a child who imitates another*

2. The <u>teaching methods</u> were very different from the <u>way of teaching</u> in her country. *systematic arrangement (process for accomplishing something*

3. Students <u>memorize</u> information; they learn and <u>remember</u> basic rules and facts. *To commit to memory*

4. They work <u>individually</u> and <u>find answers themselves</u>. *It's a single person or organism as opposed to a group*

5. Each educational system is a mirror that <u>reflects</u> the values of the society. In the Orient, it <u>shows</u> society's beliefs in group goals rather than individualism. *To throw or bend back*

6. People in Western cultures <u>value</u> individualism highly. Teachers place <u>a lot of importance</u> on the qualities that make each person special. *worth in importance*

C. Read the selection at the beginning of the chapter again carefully. Try to guess the meanings of new words from the context. Use your dictionary only when absolutely necessary.

Check your answers in the "Getting the Main Ideas" section, which follows the reading selection. Correct your errors.

Understanding Reading Structure

A. Paragraphs divide reading material into topics. In the selection at the beginning of the chapter, there are letters next to the six paragraphs. One paragraph is usually about one topic. Match the paragraphs with their topics and write the letters of the paragraphs on the lines.

1. _C_ How Western school systems reflect the value of individualism

2. _F_ The advantages and disadvantages of the North American system

3. _B_ Reasons for differences in educational systems

4. _D_ How Asian school systems reflect group goals

5. _A_ Introduction: A classroom in an Asian country

6. _E_ The advantages and disadvantages of Asian methods of education

B. A reading may express one main idea. The main idea is the most important idea of the reading: It sums up the topics and ideas of all the paragraphs. Circle the number of the main idea of the reading selection at the beginning of the chapter.

1. In elementary schools in Asia, children copy pictures of cats from the blackboard.
2. There are advantages and disadvantages to different educational systems, which reflect culture.
3. In a society such as the United States or Canada, teachers value individualism highly.
4. Students from Japan can memorize information better than students from the United States can.

C. Turn back to the beginning of the chapter and answer the questions in the "Preparing to Read" section.

Discussing the Reading

Talk about your answers to these questions.

1. What is the system of education like in your country? How is it different from the North American system?
2. Which system do you prefer? Why?
3. What other educational methods are there? Describe them and tell some of their advantages and disadvantages.

PART TWO

COLLEGE LIFE

Skimming for Main Ideas

A paragraph usually tells about one topic. Often one sentence is the *topic sentence*. It tells the topic and the main idea of the paragraph. It sums up the ideas of the other sentences, which give details about the main idea.

Example: Dong Kyu is a Korean teenager; his family moved to Canada a year ago. After ten years in the Korean school system, he entered a Canadian high school. By the end of the school year, Dong Kyu was one of the best students in his class. He explained his success: "I've had the best possible education. In the Korean schools, I memorized a lot of basic information, and I learned self-discipline. Then in the Canadian school, I learned to form my own ideas and opinions. The combination of the Eastern and Western systems is the best possible kind of education."

(The topic sentence is "The combination of the Eastern and Western systems is the best possible kind of education." The topic of the paragraph is the two systems of education. The main idea is that both methods have advantages, and the other sentences give examples of those advantages.)

Read the following paragraphs quickly. Do not use a dictionary and don't worry about the details. Then underline the topic sentence of each paragraph, the sentence that gives the main idea.

College Life

A   In many countries, such as France, Greece, and Japan, it is often more difficult for students to pass the college entrance exams than to do the course work when they are actually in college, and students who don't have much money are at a disadvantage. Students prepare for these tests for years in advance. Often, students attend a private school at night (for instance, a *juku* in Japan or a *frontisirion* in Greece) to get ready for them. These private schools are usually expensive. If their families don't have much money, students can't attend, and they might not pass the entrance exams without this extra preparation.

B   In contrast, students can easily get into an American or Canadian college—at least more easily than in other countries. American students take an entrance exam called the S.A.T. (the Scholastic Aptitude Test). However, colleges do not consider only S.A.T. scores. They also consider a student's grades and activities throughout high school. A student who has done well in high school will probably get into college.

C   What happens when a student finally enters a college or university? Students in China, Korea, or Japan might find their college studies easier than high school work. On the other hand, when American or Canadian students begin college, many of them discover that they need to work very hard and study seriously for the first time in their lives—especially if they plan to go to graduate school. If college tuition is high, they may need to work part-time to help pay for their education. College education in many countries (such as Saudi Arabia, Kuwait, and the United Arab Emirates), by contrast, is free. Because of the combination of studies and a job, college life may be more difficult for students in North America than it is for students in other countries.

D   In the 1960s and 1970s, many students in Europe and North America demonstrated against the government and hoped to make big changes in society. College life has been changing since then, however, and students are not paying much attention to politics these days. Instead, most students are interested only in their studies and future jobs. Twenty years ago, many college students chose a major in sociology, anthropology, or another social science. Courses in the humanities (literature, art, philosophy, and so on) were also popular. But these days, students all over the world are majoring in more practical subjects such as business administration, computer science, and engineering.

Read the selection on college life again. Use your dictionary only when absolutely necessary, and try to guess the meanings of new words from the context.

Discussing the Reading

Talk about your answers to these questions.

1. What kind of school are you studying in now? What schools have you studied in in the past? Where were they?
2. How did you get into the schools? Tell about entrance exams and preparation for them, school records, applications, and so on.
3. Compare college life in your country to college life in the United States or Canada. Talk about costs, jobs, and academic work.
4. In your opinion, has college life been changing? How and why?

PART THREE

BUILDING VOCABULARY AND STUDY SKILLS

Synonyms ~same~

Match the words with their meanings. Write the letters on the lines.

1. _g_	instructor	6. _d_	recite	a. learn and remember
2. _e_	method	7. _fe_	discipline	b. conversation
3. _j_	reflect	8. _c_	examination	c. test
4. _a_	memorize	9. _i_	prepare	d. say aloud
5. _b_	discussion	10. _hf_	enter	e. control
				f. get into
				g. teacher ✓
				h. way
				i. get ready
				j. show

Words in Context

Write the missing words in the blanks. Choose from these words:

graduate   society   combination   value
elementary   demonstrate   tuition   formal

1. Children often have art lessons in _elementary_ school.

2. National and religious differences are part of the culture of American _society_.

3. In a _formal_ college classroom, the teacher lectures and the students listen.

4. Some people _demonstrate_ against the government to express their political opinions.

5. Many students attend college after they _graduate_ from high school.

6. Some societies _value_ individualism and original ideas.

7. At expensive schools, students must pay high _tuition_ for their education.

8. There are advantages and disadvantages to any educational system; the best system probably uses a _combination_ of methods.

Reading and Following Instructions

Textbooks, quizzes, and exams often use special words in instructions. Follow the instructions for these exercises carefully.

A. Which words show examples of which instructions? Match the instructions on the left with the words on the right. Write the letters of the words on the lines. Pay special attention to the verbs.

1. Circle the word. *m*

2. Underline the word. *d*

3. Put a box around the word. *A*

4. Put a check by the word. *C*

5. Cross out the word. *b*

6. Count the words and write the number. *f*

7. Fill in the blank. *j*

8. Complete the word. *h*

9. Divide the word; draw lines. *K*

10. Change the word. (Write the past tense.) *i*

11. Match the words; connect them with lines. *e*

12. Cross out the mistakes and correct the word. *L*

13. Choose the correct word and circle it. *g*

14. Number the words in alphabetical order. *n*

15. Write the words in order. *O*

a.   attention

b.   C̶a̶n̶a̶d̶ian

c.   ✓ activities

d.   politics

e.   social administration business science

f.   high, free, popular *3*

g.   major in a ____ subject consider (practical) anthropology

h.   diffi *culties*

i.   study *studied*

j.   an *Asian* country

k.   memorization

l.   e̶j̶u̶c̶a̶s̶h̶u̶n̶ *education*

m.   (original)

n.   *2* society
     1 school
     3 system

o.   OFTEN TOGETHER WORK IN SCHOOL STUDENTS
     Students often work together in school.

B. Follow the instructions carefully.

1. Circle the college subjects.

   (anthropology)   contrast   (sociology)   (art)   tuition

2. Put a check by the nouns. Underline the verbs.

   methods   facts   choose   happen   idea   consider

3. Draw lines to match the words with opposite meanings.

   advantage   free   enter   difficult   forget

   expensive   disadvantage   remember   easy   graduate

4. Cross out the incorrect words, correct the spelling mistakes, and write the correct words above them.

   entrance   *exam*   *extra preparation*
   It's difficult to pass the intrance egzam without ekstra prepareashun.

5. Count the words that name shapes. Write the number here. ___*3*___

   smaller   circle   identical   triangle   box   relatively

6. Draw lines to separate the words from each other.

   Readtheseparagraphsquicklywithoutadictionary.

C. Write instructions for the groups of words.

1. *Underline the adjectives and put a check by the adverbs.*

   poor   ✓probably   original   basic   ✓relatively   ✓seriously

2. *put in each box of the school*

   instructor   [university]   [private school]   [college]   exam

3. *draw lines to match the words with belong together*

   (graduate   aptitude   pay   computer   basic   self
   school   science   test   attention   control   rules

4. *correct the mistakes spelling*

   A children's art lesson in this country produces (yunik pitchers.)
   unique pictures

D. Write instructions for each sentence and/or group of words. (There may be several possibilities.) Then exchange books with a classmate and follow the instructions.

1. *correct the words*

   At an early age, students form their own ideas and *options*___ .

   information   opinions   differences   individualism

2. _____*matches the same word*_____

teacher   system   different   instructor   goal   identical

3. _____

Saudi Arabia   China   North America   Europe   Korea

4. _____*underline the verbs and circle*_____

Children have lessons in elementary school.

E. Write your own page of exercises with instructions. Exchange papers with a class-mate and follow the instructions.

PART FOUR

SCANNING FOR INFORMATION

Sometimes you want to find information quickly. In this case, you don't read every sentence. Instead, you "scan" the material—you look quickly for the important words.

A. Read the explanation and study the following vocabulary.

In the United States, a student from another country needs to have a student visa. This visa is called an "F-1." To get an F-1 visa, a student must get an I-20 form from an American school.

community adult school = a school where students over 18 can get free education

residents = people who have their home in a certain place

Immigration and Naturalization Service = a government agency

requirements = necessary conditions

a minimum of = at least

questionnaire = a form that asks questions

submit = offer; send; give a paper to a school or government office

sponsor = a person who is responsible for an immigrant

transcripts = a list of all courses that a student has taken and his or her grades in the classes

verification = proof; evidence that something is true

financial status = a person's "money situation"

recommendation letter = a letter that says good things about a person

fees = money for something

application = a written request to do something

prerequisite = something that is necessary before something else can happen

status = position

objective = purpose; plans

post- = after

absence = not being in a place

work permits = government permission to get jobs

B. Read the letter on page 15. Find the answers to the questions below, and write them on the lines.

1. What can students learn at E. Manfred Evans Community Adult School? _____
   _____ specializing, English _____

2. Who goes to this school? _E-1 student_____

3. How old must a student be to get an I-20 form? _18_____

4. Which of the following must a student send along with his or her question-naire? Put checkmarks on the lines.

   a. __✓__   a medical form from a doctor

   b. _____   a letter from the student's parents

   c. __✓__   a paper from the student's sponsor

   d. _____   four big pictures

   e. _____   a $500 check for tuition

   f. __✓__   high school and/or college transcripts

   g. __✓__   information about his or her sponsor's financial situation

   h. _____   a list of reasons that the student needs to study English

   i. __✓__   a letter from the student's present school or job

Los Angeles Unified School District

E. Manfred Evans Community Adult School

717 North Figueroa St., Los Angeles, California 90012-2196

Telephone: (213) 626-7151

Date:

Dear Prospective Student:

E. Manfred Evans Community Adult School is a Los Angeles City School specializing in teaching students to communicate in English. Although designed for residents of the Los Angeles area, it has also been approved by the United States Immigration and Naturalization Service for admittance of nonimmigrant F-1 visa students. F-1 visa students' class hours are 1:30-6:40 p.m., Monday through Friday, from September to June.

REQUIREMENTS FOR THE I-20 FORM ARE AS FOLLOWS:

1. Must be a minimum of eighteen years of age.

2. Complete and submit the attached questionnaire.

3. Submit medical form completed, signed, sealed, and dated by a medical doctor. Chest x-ray results must also be included.

4. Submit the signed sponsor statement.

5. Submit one passport-type photograph.

6. Submit copies of transcripts of high school and/or college records in English (for the last three years).

7. Submit verification of sponsor's financial status.

8. Submit a recommendation letter from the school currently attending or from an assigned work unit.

The required forms constitute an application to Evans Community Adult School, not an acceptance. After the completed forms reach this school, if all is satisfactory, an I-20 form, a prerequisite for F-1 student visa status, will be issued.

Sincerely,

Counseling Staff

C. Find the answers to these questions about the application form on page 17. Write the answers on the lines.

1. What is the student's first name? _Carlos_

   His last name? _de menezes_

2. In what country is he living right now? _Brazil_

3. Where was he born? _portugal_ Is he a citizen of that country? _Brazil_

4. How much money will he probably spend in one year in the United States?
   _$ 8000.00_ Where will he get the money? _Brother_

5. How many years did he spend in elementary school? _9_ Did he finish high
   school? _3_ Has he gone to college? _3_

6. What does he plan to do after he finishes his courses at Evans?
   go back to his country

7. What will his field of study probably be? _film direction_

8. What must he do to stay in school? Check the answers.

   a. _✓_   go to class at least 25 hours a week

   b. ___   get a job after school

   c. _✓_   study and get good grades

   d. ___   live with an American family

D. Work in pairs. Ask and answer questions like those above about the letter and the application form.

Going Beyond the Text

Bring to class things to read about college life. Some examples are catalogs, course schedules, school newspapers, orientation information, and so on. Share them with the class. Discuss the important information and learn new vocabulary.

E. Manfred Evans Community Adult School

717 North Figueroa St., Los Angeles, California 90012-2196

Telephone: (213) 626-7151

In Country: _____

Out of Country: _____✓_____

Date: _1/12/XX_____   Counselor: _____

PERSONAL   DATA

de Menezes   _Carlos_   _E._
PRINT - LAST NAME   FIRST   INITIAL

PRESENT ADDRESS: _R. Almirante   32_   _São Paulo_   _Brazil_
                         STREET   CITY   COUNTRY

BIRTHDATE: _3 / 19 / 67_   _Portugal_   _Brazil_
          MONTH DAY YEAR   COUNTRY OF BIRTH   COUNTRY OF CITIZENSHIP

FINANCIAL STATUS: The estimated cost of living in the United States is approximately $8,000 per year. Who will provide your financial support? _Brother_____

EDUCATION: Please indicate number of years of school in your country at each level.
Elementary: ___9___ Secondary: __3____ University or college: _3_____ Total: _15_

EDUCATIONAL OBJECTIVE: Do you plan to return to your country as soon as you
have completed your English course of studies at Evans? Yes: _X_____ No: _____
If your answer is "NO," please indicate your post-Evans educational plans:
Community College: _____   University: _____   Trade School: _____
Business College: _____   Graduate School: _____
Other: _____

What field of study would you like to pursue (example: business, engineering, medicine, education, etc.)? _film direction_____

GENERAL INFORMATION:

1. Student MUST be at least 18 years of age.

2. Student will attend assigned F-1 visa classes for a minimum of 25 hours
   per week. Excessive absence is a cause for dismissal from the F-1 visa program.

3. Work permits are not granted by the Immigration and Naturalization Service to students enrolled in a language school.

4. Students are to exhibit satisfactory academic progress and good citizenship.

5. The status of F-1 visa students is considered to be a contract between student
   and school. IT IS ESSENTIAL FOR STUDENTS TO FULLY UNDERSTAND THE
   REQUIREMENTS OF THE F-1 VISA PRIOR TO ACCEPTING THIS STATUS.

6. Class hours are 1:30 p.m. to 6:40 p.m., Monday through Friday, from September through June.

STUDENT ACCEPTANCE:

I have read (or had translated for me) the information on this page, and I agree
to follow school requirements.

Student's Signature: _Carlos E. de Menezes_ Date: _1/12/XX_____

2

CITY LIFE

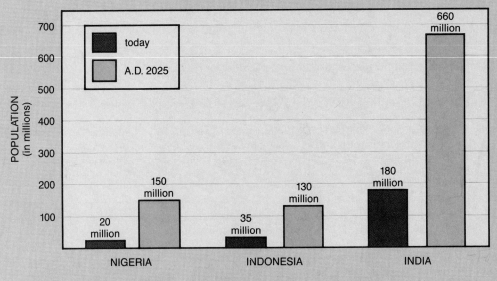

PEOPLE LIVING IN CITIES

THE URBAN CRISIS

Getting Started

Look at the pictures and discuss them.

1. Where do you think these pictures take place?
2. What might be some of the problems in these cities?
3. How many people now live in cities in Nigeria? In Indonesia? In India?
4. How many people will be living in cities in these countries in the year 2025?

Preparing to Read

As you read the following selection, think about the answers to these questions.

1. Why do many North Americans want to move out of cities?
2. Why do people in many countries want to move *to* cities?
3. What is the population of the world today? What will it be in the year 2025?
4. What are some problems of overpopulation?

Read the selection quickly. Do not use a dictionary. Then answer the questions that follow the reading selection.

The Urban Crisis

A   One goal of many Americans and Canadians is to move out of a busy urban area such as New York, Los Angeles, or Toronto. They say that they want to escape from pollution (for example, smog and noise pollution). They want to get away from crime. They're tired of the crowds of people each day on the mass-transit systems—buses, commuter trains, and subways. Or, if they have cars, they would like to avoid the traffic that they get into when they commute daily from their homes to their offices and back. These people believe that life would be better in the suburbs—that is, the areas just outside the city—or even farther away, in the countryside.

B   This dream of a better life in another place is certainly not unique to North Americans. However, this dream may take various forms in different parts of the world. In some areas there is a movement to the countryside; in contrast, millions of people are moving away from rural areas in other countries. In other words, in much of the world there is an exodus from the countryside to the cities. The urban population in most developing countries such as India and Nigeria is increasing very fast.

C   The statistics are not pleasant. In 1987, the world population reached five billion. One billion of these people lived in cities in the developing nations. People who study population growth predict that by the year 2025, the population of the world will be more than eight billion. These experts say that cities in developing countries, where overpopulation will be especially serious, will be home to almost four billion of these people.

D   There are several reasons for this enormous population growth. Of course, there is a general increase in the world population because modern medicine and new methods of food production allow adults to live longer and babies to survive, not die soon after birth. In Latin America, where seven out of ten people already live in cities, most future growth will be from this natural increase. But in many other countries millions of people are moving to urban areas because they must find work. There simply aren't jobs in the countryside. There isn't enough good farmland for large families in rural areas. In addition, farming methods are not always modern. These out-of-date methods cause farms to be unsuccessful. These problems are worsening, not getting better, so more and more people are leaving their homes to find a better life in cities.

E   Is life better in cities? Probably not. There is little space for each person, and this overcrowding causes problems—sickness, traffic, and crime. There isn't enough water, transportation, or housing. And there aren't enough jobs. One-third to one-half of the people who are now living in many cities in developing nations cannot find work or can find only part-time jobs. Millions of these people are hungry, homeless, sick, and afraid for the future. The crisis is worsening daily; that is, this time of terrible difficulty is just beginning. Population experts tell us that by the year 2025, the population in cities in developing nations will increase to *four times* its present size.

Getting the Main Ideas

Write T on the lines before the statements that are *true,* according to the reading.
Write F on the lines before the statements that are *false.*

1. __T__   Many Americans would like to move out of cities.

2. __F__   The population of cities in developing nations is getting smaller.

3. __T__   Eight billion people will be living in cities by the year 2025.

4. __T__   Millions of people in many countries are moving to cities because they need to find work.

5. __F__   The situation in most cities will be better in the future.

stat-istics = numbers

enormous = huge - big

Guessing Meaning from Context

You do not need to look up the meanings of new words if you can guess them from the context.

Sometimes there are examples of the meaning of a new vocabulary item in another sentence or sentence part. The words *for example, for instance,* and *such as* or punctuation marks such as parentheses ( ), dashes (—), and commas may introduce examples.

A. Find examples of the underlined word(s) in each sentence and write them on the lines.

Example: One goal of many Americans and Canadians is to move out of a busy urban area such as New York, Los Angeles, or Toronto.

New York, Los Angeles, Toronto

1. They want to escape from <u>pollution</u> (for example, smog and noise pollution).

2. They're tired of the crowds of people each day on the <u>mass-transit system</u>—buses, commuter trains, and subways.

3. The urban population in most <u>developing countries</u> such as India and Nigeria is increasing very fast.

> Sometimes another word or words in another sentence or sentence part has the opposite meaning from a new vocabulary item.
>
> *Example:*   In some areas there is a movement to the countryside; in contrast, millions of people are moving <u>away</u> from rural areas in other countries. In other words, in much of the world there is an <u>exodus</u> from the countryside to the cities. (An <u>exodus</u> is a movement <u>away</u> from a place.)

B. Write the words from each item that have an opposite meaning from the underlined word.

1. Modern medicine and new methods of food production allow adults to live longer and babies to <u>survive,</u> not die soon after birth.

   _____

2. Farming methods are not always modern. These <u>out-of-date</u> methods cause farms to be unsuccessful.

   _____

3. These problems are <u>worsening</u>, not getting better.

   _____

> A definition or explanation follows the connecting words *that is* and *in other words*.
>
> *Example:*   These people believe that life would be better in the <u>suburbs</u>—that is, the areas just outside the city. (<u>Suburbs</u> are the areas just outside the city.)

C. Write definitions of the underlined words on the lines.

1. Millions of people are moving away from <u>rural</u> areas. In other words, in much of the world there is an exodus from the countryside to the cities.

   _____

2. The <u>crisis</u> is worsening daily; that is, this time of terrible difficulty is just beginning.

   _____

Sometimes details about a vocabulary item give clues to its meaning.

D. Write the answers to the questions about the underlined word or words in each item.

1. If they have cars, they would like to avoid the traffic that they get into when they <u>commute</u> daily from their homes to their offices and back.

    a. What part of speech is <u>commute</u> in this sentence (noun, verb, adjective)?

        _____

    b. What do people who <u>commute</u> want to avoid? _____ What do they

        have? _____

    c. How often do they <u>commute</u>? _____

    d. Where do they go when they <u>commute</u>? _____

    e. What does <u>commute</u> mean? _____

2. The <u>statistics</u> are not pleasant. In 1987, the world population reached five billion. One billion of these people lived in cities in developing nations. People who study population growth <u>predict</u> that by the year 2025 the population will be over eight billion, and they say that cities in developing countries will be home to almost four billion of these people.

    a. What part of speech is <u>statistics</u>? _____

    b. What is similar about all of the information in these sentences? (In what

        form are the pieces of information?) _____

    c. What are <u>statistics</u>? _____

    d. What kind of verb is <u>predict</u>? (Does it express action, condition, or speech?)

        _____

    e. What do people make predictions about? _____

    f. What does <u>predict</u> mean? _____

Understanding Reading Structure

A. In the reading selection at the beginning of the chapter, there are letters next to the five paragraphs. Match each paragraph and its letter with a topic; write the letters on the lines.

1. _____ Predictions about world population growth by the year 2025

2. _____ People who are moving to urban areas

3. _____ Introduction: People who want to escape from the problems of cities

4. _____ Conclusion: Conditions in crowded cities

5. _____ Reasons for the increase in population in many urban areas

B. A reading may express one main idea, which sums up (summarizes) the topics of all the paragraphs in the selection. Circle the number of the main idea of the reading.

1. People everywhere want to move to cities.
2. There are many people who can't find work in big cities.
3. The world population is growing fast because of modern medicine and new methods of food production.
4. Overpopulation is causing the beginning of a crisis, especially in cities in developing nations.

C. Turn back to the beginning of the chapter and answer the questions in the "Preparing to Read" section.

Discussing the Reading

1. Do you come from a big city, a suburb, or a rural area?
2. What do you think are some reasons that there are so many homeless people in many U.S. cities?
3. What solutions do you suggest to urban problems?
4. Do you think that overpopulation will be as bad as people predict? How can we avoid this crisis?

PART TWO

SICK BUILDING SYNDROME

Skimming for Main Ideas

As you learned in Chapter 1, a paragraph usually tells about one topic. Often one sentence, which tells the topic and the main idea of the paragraph, is the *topic sentence.*

Read these paragraphs quickly. Do not use a dictionary and don't worry about the details. Then underline the topic sentence of each paragraph.

Sick Building Syndrome

A   When Oakland High School in California moved into a new building, the students and teachers noticed a strong smell. Then almost half of the students began to have headaches and sore throats and to be very tired. These three symptoms disappeared on weekends. The cause was a mystery. Experts came to investigate and find the cause of the sickness. Finally, they discovered that the air in the building was not safe to breathe. They were surprised to find that the cause was the shelves in the school library! These shelves were made of particleboard—that is, an inexpensive kind of board that is made of very small pieces of wood held together with a chemical. This is just one example of a modern problem that is most common in cities—*indoor* air pollution.

B   People have worried about smog for many years, and the government has spent billions of dollars to try to clean up the air of big cities. But now we find that there is no escape from unhealthful air. Recent studies have shown that air *inside* many homes, office buildings, and schools is full of pollutants: chemicals, bacteria, smoke, and gases. These pollutants are causing a group of unpleasant and dangerous symptoms that experts call "sick building syndrome." A "sick building" might be a small house in a rural area or an enormous office building in an urban center.

C   A recent study reached a surprising conclusion: Indoor air pollution is almost always two to five times worse than outside pollution. This is true even in buildings that are close to factories that produce chemicals. The solution to this problem would seem very clear: Open your windows and stay out of modern office buildings with windows that don't open.

D Unfortunately, the solution might not be so simple. Better ventilation—a system for moving fresh air—can cut indoor air pollution to a safe level, but *lack* of ventilation is seldom the main cause of the problem. Experts have found that buildings create their own pollution. Imagine a typical home. The people who live there burn oil, wood, or gas for cooking and heating. They might smoke cigarettes, pipes, or cigars. They use chemicals for cleaning. They use hundreds of products made of plastic or particleboard; these products—such as the shelves in Oakland High School—give off chemicals that we can't see but that we *do* breathe in. And in many areas, the ground under the building might send a dangerous gas called *radon* into the home. The people in the house are breathing in a "chemical soup," and medical experts don't yet know how dangerous this is for the human body.

Now read the selection again. Use your dictionary only when absolutely necessary, and try to guess the meanings of new words from the context.

Discussing the Reading

1. Is there a problem with smog in your city? When is it worst? What are the causes?
2. Have you ever experienced sick building syndrome? How did you feel?
3. How many possible pollutants can you find in your home and classroom?

PART THREE

BUILDING VOCABULARY AND STUDY SKILLS

Parts of Speech

To guess the meaning of a new word from the context, you may find it helpful to know its "part of speech"; that is, is the word a noun, a verb, an adjective, or a preposition? Many words can be more than one part of speech.

Examples: He tried to <u>answer</u> the question. (<u>Answer</u> is a verb; it is part of the infinitive <u>to answer</u>.)

It's difficult to find an <u>answer</u> to the problem. (<u>Answer</u> is a noun.)

In some cases, different parts of speech (usually a noun and a verb) have the same spelling but different pronunciations.

Examples: We can <u>contrast</u> the problems of rural and urban areas. (<u>Contrast</u> is a verb; the emphasis—the syllable stress—is on the second syllable, -<u>trast</u>.)

In Latin America, by <u>contrast</u>, there won't be much more of an exodus to urban areas. (<u>Contrast</u> is a noun; it is the object of the preposition <u>by</u>. The emphasis is on the first syllable, <u>con</u>-.)

A. Study and pronounce the words in this chart.

Noun	Verb	Noun	Verb
answer	answer	dream	dream
cause	cause	house	house†
change	change	increase	increase*
contrast	contrast*	study	study
crowd	crowd	worry	worry

*The noun has the accent on the first syllable; the verb has the accent on the last syllable.
†The singular noun ends in a voiceless sound (/s/); the verb ends in a voiced sound (/z/).

B. Complete each sentence with words from the chart in Exercise A. Use the same
word for both blanks of each item, and write the part of speech —(n) for *noun* or
(v) for *verb*—in the parentheses after each blank.

1. What *cause*s (v) air pollution? One *cause* (n) is traffic.

2. Some people avoid subways because of the big _____s (   ) of people
    who _____ (   ) onto the trains of the mass-transit system twice a
    day.

3. Can we solve the problem of overcrowding? No one can _____ (   )
    this question. We don't have the _____ (   ).

4. In some cities, people without _____s (   ) may have to sleep in the
    streets. It is difficult to _____ (   ) all the people who need
    apartments.

5. The cost of housing doesn't go down; it _____s (   ) every year. Often
    old people with little money have to move because of the _____ (   ).

6. A recent _____ (   ) has shown that indoor air pollution is a growing
    problem. Experts are _____ing (   ) the situation and trying to find
    solutions.

7. People who live in big cities often _____ (   ) about crime.
    _____ (   ) can cause illness.

8. The _____ (   ) of some people is to move to a quiet rural area. Other
    people _____ (   ) of moving to a city.

> Many words are related to one another; they have the same stem (base word) but different endings.
>
> *Example:*   After they lived in the <u>suburbs</u> for a year or so, they began to see that there are disadvantages as well as advantages to <u>suburban</u> life. (Suburbs is a plural noun; it is the object of the preposition <u>in</u>. Suburban is an adjective; it describes the noun <u>life</u>.)

C. Study and pronounce the words in this chart.

Noun	Verb	Adjective	Adverb
creation	create	creative	creatively
crowd	crowd	crowded	
difference	differ	different	differently
difficulty		difficult	
life	live	livable	
pollution, pollutant	pollute	polluted	
prediction	predict	predictable	predictably
safety	save	safe	safely
solution	solve	solvable	
suburb		suburban	
	worsen	worse	

D. Complete each sentence with the missing words from the chart above. Use forms of the base word (the words to the left of each section) and write the part of speech in the parentheses after each blank— (*n*) for *noun*, (*v*) for *verb*, (*adj*) for *adjective*, and (*adv*) for *adverb*.

1. solve: They are trying to find a *solution* (*n*) to the problem of over-crowding, but this is a difficult problem to *solve* (*v*).

2. pollute: Most people know about air _____ (   ) in big cities, but they're just beginning to learn about the many _____ s (   ) that we have *inside* buildings.

3. crowd: There are _____ s (   ) of people everywhere; the mass transit system is especially _____ (   ).

4. <u>safe</u>: The city is not _____ (   ) because of crime. People can't leave

their homes _____ (   ) at night, and the police don't provide for

their _____ (   ).

5. <u>live</u>, <u>suburb</u>: Many people prefer to _____ (   ) in the

_____^s (   ); they say that _____ (   )

_____ (   ) is more pleasant than city living.

6. <u>predict</u>, <u>worse</u>: Some people _____ (   ) that urban life will get

_____ (   ); according to their _____^s (   ), conditions will

_____ (   ) every year.

7. <u>differ</u>: The causes of indoor air pollution _____ (   ) from area to

area. One reason for the _____ (   ) is that people heat their homes

_____ (   ). People in some areas burn wood for heat; in other areas

they use something _____ (   ).

Using the Dictionary (Parts of Speech)

You know that you don't need to look up every new word in a dictionary because you can often guess the meanings from the context. Sometimes, however, you may want to use a dictionary for other purposes—for instance, to find out the part of speech of a word or to learn related words.

A dictionary will tell you the parts of speech a word can be, usually with these abbreviations: *n. = noun, v. = verb, adj. = adjective, adv. = adverb, prep. = preposition, conj. = conjunction.* The abbreviation appears before the meanings of the word with that part of speech.

Example: This dictionary entry shows that the word <u>reason</u> can be a noun (with four meanings) or a verb (with one meaning). A related adjective is <u>reasonable</u>.

rea·son[1] /riy'zən/ *n*   **1** purpose, cause (for a belief or act): *The reason for the error was clear.*   **2** an excuse: *I didn't have any reason for being late.*   **3** the ability to think clearly: *She is normally a person of good reason.*   **4** good judgment: *He has lost all reason!*
reason[2] *v*   to persuade or think in a sensible way: *I tried to reason with him, but he won't listen to me.*
rea'son·a·ble *adj*   having reason or sense: *She is normally a very reasonable person, but today she's upset.*

If possible, everyone in the class uses the same kind of dictionary for the following exercises. Work quickly. The first student with the correct answers is the winner.

A. Find these words in your dictionary. Write the part of speech on the lines before each word—(*n*) for *noun*, (*v*) for *verb*, (*adj*) for *adjective*, and (*adv*) for *adverb*. Some words, in different contexts, can be more than one part of speech.

1. _*adj*_ terrible	6. _____ water	11. _____ air
2. _*n,v*_ discipline	7. _____ expert	12. _____ produce
3. _____ value	8. _____ commute	13. _____ enormous
4. _____ original	9. _____ farm	14. _____ mystery
5. _____ pleasant	10. _____ smog	15. _____ individual

B. Complete the chart. Write the appropriate related words under each heading. (**X** means that no word of that part of speech exists.)

Nouns	Verbs	Adjectives	Adverbs
surprise	surprise	_surprising_ _surprised_	_surprisingly_
exactness	_____	_____	exactly
_____	educate	_____	_____
_____		_____	
_____	believe	_____	_____
_____		formal	_____
origin	_____	_____	_____
_____	prepare	_____	X
consideration	_____	_____	_____
_____	survive	survivable	X
_____			

PART FOUR

SCANNING FOR INFORMATION

You scan city maps to quickly find the information that you need—usually street names. Sometimes maps give other information as well. Study the following vocabulary.

boat launching = a place where you can put your boat into the water

zoo = a place in a city for wild animals, such as lions, bears, and elephants

groceries = things in a food store

produce = fresh fruit and vegetables

museum = a building where people can see art, important historical items, and so on

exhibit = a show; something to see (usually in a museum)

planetarium = a building where people study the stars

breathtaking = very beautiful

trail = a small road for people to walk on

A. Scan the list of "outstanding attractions." Write the answers to the questions that follow it.

Outstanding attractions

VANCOUVER

(A) Stanley Park—A 404 hectare playground 10 minutes from downtown includes zoo, with polar bears and penguins. A miniature railroad and children's zoo open during summer months. An aquarium with killer whales and sea otters. 🚌 Take an 11 STANLEY PARK BUS which may be boarded along the north side of Pender. Returns over the same route to downtown but as 17 OAK BUS.

(A1) The Vancouver Art Gallery—owns the largest collection of works by westcoast artist Emily Carr, and also has a continuing programme of contemporary exhibitions. Located at 1145 W. Georgia St. until early autumn of 1983, thereafter at 800 W. Georgia St. — a magnificent building that was formerly the Court House. For information call 682-5621.

(B) MacMillan Planetarium—Shows feature the nature of the universe. Closed Mon. For information call 736-4431. **Vancouver Museum**—Exhibits of local history, anthropology and natural science with gift shop and restaurant. **Maritime Museum**—Collection of B.C. and naval memorabilia. Home of the **R.C.M.P. St. Roch**, the only vessel to sail the N.W. Passage in both directions. 🚌 Board 22 MACDONALD BUS on west side of Burrard, alight at Cypress. Walk 4 blocks north. Return to downtown over same route via the 22 KNIGHT BUS.

(C) Robsonstrasse—Section of downtown Robson Street offers European atmosphere in boutiques, restaurants and speciality stores. Within walking distance of downtown.

(D) Chinatown—North America's second largest Chinese community. The commercial centre stretches along three blocks of Pender between Gore and Carrall Streets. Numerous restaurants, curio shops and oriental stores. 🚌 Take a 19 KINGSWAY or 22 KNIGHT bus going east on Pender. Return on a 15 CAMBIE or 22 MACDONALD.

(E) Gastown—Where Vancouver began now has antique shops, restaurants, smart stores and lively nightclubs, all with an old-time charm. Open daily. 🚌 Take a 50 FALSE CREEK bus on the Granville Mall which will loop into Gastown via Cordova, Columbia to Powell, and return to the Granville Mall via Powell, Water and Cordova.

Outstanding attractions

VANCOUVER

(F) Granville Island Public Market—Located at the south side of False Creek under Granville Street Bridge, Vancouver's Granville Island Public Market offers fresh produce, fresh fish and seafood, meats and other groceries and plants. Several places for snacks or meals, with lots of parking. Open 9 a.m. to 6 p.m. every day, except Mondays ▬▬ Board 20 GRANVILLE BUS on west side of Granville Mall. Alight at Granville and Broadway and transfer to 51 GRANVILLE ISLAND BUS. Return to downtown via reverse of outbound trip.

(G) Queen Elizabeth Park—A flower lover's delight, in two former stone quarries. Houses the Bloedel Conservatory, a triodetic dome filled with tropical plants. Highest point within the city limits. Bring your camera. ▬▬ Board 15 CAMBIE BUS on west side of Burrard Street, the 15 CAMBIE routes via Burrard Robson, Cambie. Passengers alight at 33rd Avenue for Queen Elizabeth Park. Return to downtown as 19 KINGSWAY BUS.

(H) Van Dusen Gardens—One of the most comprehensive collections of ornamental plants can be found at this attraction. Man made lakes and many large stone sculptures add interest, here too is MacMillan Bloedel Place with exhibits on the forest industry ▬▬ Take the #17 OAK BUS on Granville Mall heading North. Disembark on Oak St. at 37th Ave. Return to downtown via the 11 STANLEY PARK.

(I) Hastings Mill Store—The first store and post office built in Vancouver is now a small local museum. Open 10-4 daily from June to mid-September and from 1-4 weekends the rest of the year. ▬▬ Board 4 FOURTH BUS on west side of Granville Mall at any stop south of Pender Street. This bus takes you to Alma; disembark. Walk four blocks north to Pt. Grey Road. Return to downtown by the 24 NANAIMO bus.

attraction = the ability to attract

(J) University of B.C.—Well known for its many beautiful gardens scattered over its 396 hectare campus. Visitors are welcome and Visitinfo booths dispense campus maps and specific information on Nitobe Japanese Memorial Gardens, the Rose Garden, Museum of Anthropology and Fine Arts Gallery. The **Museum of Anthropology**— on N.W. Marine Drive at U.B.C., a new building on the water side of Marine Drive housing world famous collection of B.C. Coastal Indian Art and other Artifacts from many cultures. ▬▬ Board a 10 TENTH-U.B.C. BUS anywhere along the Granville Mall southbound. This BUS terminates within the campus area. Return to downtown by the 34 HASTINGS EXPRESS.

(K) Pacific National Exhibition Grounds—Site of Western Canada's largest fair — Many professional sporting events take place here. Coliseum is the home of the Vancouver Canucks Hockey team. The Track has horse racing four times weekly from April to October. B.C. Pavilion has a large three-dimensional map of the province and the B.C. Sports Hall of Fame. Also Playland Amusement Park with the giant Roller-coaster ▬▬ Board a 14 HASTINGS or 16 RENFREW BUS on Granville Mall northbound, alight on Hastings Street at Renfrew. Return to Downtown as 18 ARBUTUS or 16 RENFREW.

(K1) The Arts, Sciences & Technology Centre—600 Granville St. Vancouver's new "hands-on" museum. Located downtown, Vancouver's transit system provides easy access to this interesting and educational collection of participatory exhibits which demonstrate a fascinating blend of art, science and technology. Many exciting special events take place regularly. Come and discover, explore, and experiment. For more information call 687-8414.

BURNABY

(L) Simon Fraser University. Architecturally outstanding university atop Burnaby Mountain. Student guided tours daily July and August and Saturday and Sunday the rest of the year. ▬▬ Board a 14 HASTINGS BUS on Granville Mall northbound. Transfer at Kootenay Loop to 35 WESTRIDGE SFU BUS for Simon Fraser University. Return to downtown via reverse of outbound trip.

Centennial Park—On Burnaby Mountain below Simon Fraser campus are picnic sites and a restaurant, with a view of the city and Indian Arm.

(M) Heritage Village—Burnaby's recreation of a typical village of the turn of the century, containing an apothecary shop, general store, blacksmith, school house, Garage, log cabin, church and soda parlour. **Burnaby Art Gallery**—Adjacent to Heritage Village at 6344 Gilpin Street. Emphasis on contemporary prints. In the garden, sculptures and 200 varieties of Rhododendrons. ▬▬ Board 820/120 CANADA WAY BUS on Melville Street directly behind the Royal Centre or at designated stops along Hastings Street eastbound. Closest bus stop is Burnaby Municipal Hall. Return to downtown via reverse of outbound trip.

NEW WESTMINSTER

(N) Irving House—A stately old home built in 1882 and preserved, adjacent to Royal City Museum at 302 Royal Avenue. See also the Japanese Friendship Gardens and Queens Park. ▬▬ Board 820/120 CANADA WAY as outlined in **M** above and alight in New Westminster at Columbia and 8th Street. Transfer to eastbound 96 SIXTH STREET BUS and request to alight on Agnes at Merrivale (one block behind Irving House). Return to downtown via reverse of outbound trip.

NORTH SHORE

(O) Capilano Suspension Bridge—One of the world's longest suspension bridges — 137 metres across Capilano Canyon, 70 metres above the river. Illuminated at night during the summer. ▬▬ By SEA-BUS, to Lonsdale Quay. Transfer to 246 HIGHLANDS BUS. Alight at Ridgewood and walk north approximately 1½ blocks. To return downtown, reverse movement.

(P) Capilano Salmon Hatchery— in Capilano Canyon Park. Guided tours available. **Cleveland Dam**—A fine hiking and picnic area with a view of the twin peaks called the Lions. ▬▬ By SEA-BUS, to Lonsdale Quay. Transfer to 246 HIGHLAND BUS to Edgemont at Ridgewood and transfer to 232 QUEENS BUS.

(Q) Grouse Mountain—Take the superskyride to the top of Grouse Mountain for a breathtaking view of Vancouver day or night. 1100 metres above Vancouver. Once at the top visitors can enjoy a walk through the nature trail around Blue Grouse Lake; a ride up the Peak Chair to a 1250 metre viewpoint or relax in our Chalet's Lounge, Restaurant or Cafeteria. For reservations and information call 984-0661. Be sure and visit our Gift Shops at the Chalet. ▬▬ By SEA-BUS, to Lonsdale Quay. Transfer to 246 HIGHLANDS BUS to Edgemont at Ridgewood and transfer to a 232 QUEENS BUS.

(R) Cates Park—On the road to Deep Cove, a 23 hectare wooded waterside park and boat launching site. Swimming and scuba diving. ▬▬ Board 210 MOUNTAIN H'WAY BUS northbound on Burrard north of Smithe, or eastbound on Hastings, to Phibbs Exchange. Transfer to 212 DOLLARTON BUS to Cates Park. Return to downtown via reverse of outbound trip.

(S) The Park & Tilford Gardens—A unique eight garden complex at 1200 Cotton Road. Visitors welcomed year round. Illuminated at night in summer. Permanent displays and special seasonal displays. Free parking. ▬▬ Board 210 MOUNTAIN H'WAY BUS northbound on Burrard north of Smithe, or eastbound on Hastings, to Phibbs Exchange. Transfer to 239 CROSSTOWN BUS ("Park Royal") to Gardens. By SEA-BUS, to Lonsdale Quay. Transfer at Quay to 239 CROSSTOWN BUS ("Phibbs Exchange or Capilano College") to Gardens. Return to downtown via reverse of outbound trip. 987-9321.

1. What city are these attractions in? _Vancouver_

2. Fill in the blanks in this chart.

PLACE	WHAT IS IT? or WHAT DOES IT OFFER?
(A) _Stanley Park_	_a playground with a zoo_
(D) _China town_	_second largest chinatown with numerous resturant curio shops and oriental stores._
(F) _Granville Island public market_	_fresh produce with lots of parking_
(I) _Hasting Mill Store_	_The first store and post office built in a small local museum._
(K1) _The art, sciences & technology centre_	_museum_
(Q) _Grouse Mountain_	_park and scenic view_

3. Now answer these questions about the places on your chart.

   a. How many minutes is Stanley Park from downtown? _10 minutes_

   b. When is the children's zoo in Stanley Park open? _during summer month_

   c. How large is Vancouver's Chinatown? _second largest in North America_

   d. What can you buy at the Granville Island Public Market?
   Fresh produce, fresh fish and seafood, meat and other groceries and plants several places for snacks or meal

   e. What hours is the market open? _open 9:00 a.m. to 6:00 p.m_

   f. What day is it closed? _monday_

   g. Why is the Hastings Mill Store an attraction? _Because the first store and post office built in vancouver is now a small local museum._

   h. What is the telephone number of the Arts, Sciences, and Technology Centre?
   The telephone number is 687-8414

   i. Can you ride to the top of Grouse Mountain in the daytime, at night, or both?
   yes once at top visitors can enjoy a walk the nature trail Blue Grose Lake a ride up the peak chair to a 1250 meter viewpoint or relax at the (R. C. L)

   j. Do you need to bring food when you go to Grouse Mountain, or can you eat there?
   No. you can't but, you can eat there

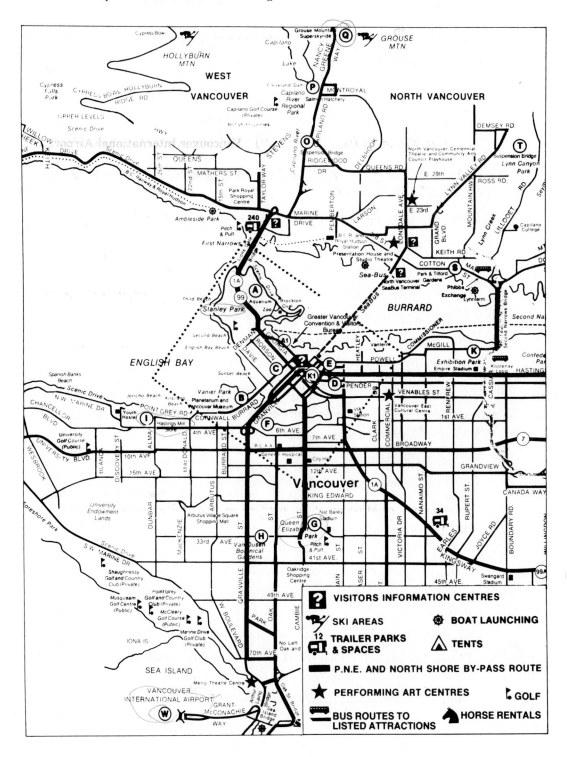

B. Now scan the map on page 36 and complete the exercises.

1. Draw a circle around each of these places on the map.

   (A) Stanley Park   (I) Hastings Mill Store

   (B) MacMillan Planetarium   (Q) Grouse Mountain

   (G) Queen Elizabeth Park   (W) Vancouver International Airport

2. Scan the explanation of symbols at the bottom of the map. Then write the meanings of these symbols.

   ? _visitors information centers_   ⊕ _Boat launching_

   ⚘ _ski Areas_   ⛳ _Golf_

3. Answer these questions.

   a. Is there a visitors' information center at Vancouver International Airport?

      _No_

   b. What are two places where you can ski? _Grouse mountain_
      Holly Burn mountain

   c. What is the name of one boat launching? _Ambleside park, sea bus, phibbs Exchange Lynnmm._

C. Now work in pairs. Ask and answer questions, like those above, about the list of attractions and the map.

Going Beyond the Text

Bring to class maps of cities that show attractions for visitors. Discuss new vocabulary. Then summarize the information on your map for the class; tell about the interesting things in that city.

3

BUSINESS AND MONEY

PART ONE

THE PSYCHOLOGY OF MONEY

Getting Started

Look at the pictures and discuss them.

1. What kinds of people do you see in the four pictures? What are they doing? Why?
2. In your opinion, how and why does each person spend money? What can you say about each person's money habits?

Preparing to Read

As you read the following selection, think about the answers to these questions.

1. What can money habits show about people?
2. What can money be a symbol of?
3. What are "compulsive spenders" and "bargain hunters?" Why do they spend money?
4. How is psychology important in sales methods?
5. Give an example of a "personality problem" in relation to money, and give a possible solution.

The Psychology of Money

[A]   Are you a compulsive spender, or do you hold on to your money as long as possible? Are you a bargain hunter? Would you rather use charge accounts than pay cash? Your answers to these questions will reflect your personality. According to psychologists, our individual money habits not only show our beliefs and values, but can also stem from past problems.

[B]   Experts in psychology believe that for many people, money is an important symbol of strength and influence. Husbands who complain about their wives' spending habits may be afraid that they are losing power in their marriage. Wives, on the other hand, may waste huge amounts of money because they are angry at their husbands. In addition, many people consider money a symbol of love. They spend it on their family and friends to express love, or they buy themselves expensive presents because they need love.

[C]   People can be addicted to different things—e.g., alcohol, drugs, certain foods, or even television. People who have such an addiction are compulsive; i.e., they have a very powerful psychological need that they feel they *must* satisfy. According to psychologists, many people are compulsive spenders; they feel that they must spend money. This compulsion, like most others, is irrational—impossible to explain reasonably. For compulsive spenders who buy on credit, charge accounts are even more exciting than money. In other words, compulsive spenders feel that with credit, they can do anything. Their pleasure in spending enormous amounts is actually greater than the pleasure that they get from the things they buy.

[D]   There is even a special psychology of bargain hunting. To save money, of course, most people look for sales, low prices, and discounts. Compulsive bargain hunters, however, often buy things that they don't need just because they are cheap. They want to believe that they are helping their budgets, but they are really playing an exciting game: When they can buy something for less than other people, they feel that they are winning. Most people, experts claim, have two reasons for their behavior: a good reason for the things that they do and the real reason.

[E]   It is not only scientists, of course, who understand the psychology of spending habits, but also businesspeople. Stores, companies, and advertisers use psychology to increase business: They consider people's needs for love, power, or influence, their basic values, their beliefs and opinions, and so on in their advertising and sales methods.

[F]   Psychologists often use a method called "behavior therapy" to help individuals solve their personality problems. In the same way, they can help people who feel that they have problems with money: They give them "assignments." If a person buys something in every store that he enters, for instance, a therapist might teach him self-discipline in this way: On the first day of his therapy, he must go into a store, stay five minutes, and then leave. On the second day, he should stay for ten minutes and try something on. On the third day, he stays for fifteen minutes, asks the salesclerk a question, but does not buy anything. Soon he will learn that nothing bad will happen to him if he doesn't buy anything, and he can solve the problem of his compulsive buying.

Getting the Main Ideas

Write T on the lines before the statements that are *true,* according to the reading. Write F before the statements that are *false.*

1. *T*   According to psychologists, a person's money habits might reflect his or her personality.

2. *T*   For some people, money may be a symbol of love, strength, or influence.

3. *F*   All people spend money for exactly the same reason: that they need to buy things.

4. *T*   People who look for the lowest possible prices will never have money problems because they will keep to their budgets.

5. *T*   Businesspeople and advertisers can use the psychology of money to increase sales.

6. *F*   People can never change their money habits because these habits come from their past beliefs and values.

Guessing Meaning from Context

Sometimes other words in a phrase give clues to the meaning of a new vocabulary item.

Example: Some people <u>save</u> money. (Save expresses an action that people can do with money.)

A. Write the missing words in the phrases. Choose from these words:

needs   accounts   hunting   money   ✓amounts   problems

1. huge   *amounts*
2. bargain   *hunting*
3. charge   *accounts*
4. waste   *money*
5. satisfy   *needs*
6. personality   *problems*

B. Match these words with their meanings. The phrases above will help you. Write the letters on the lines.

1. _e_   huge
2. _a_   bargain
3. _c_   charge
4. _f_   waste
5. _b_   satisfy
6. _d_   personality

a. something that you can buy cheaply
b. take care of; be enough for
c. postpone or delay payment until a bill comes
d. the nature or character of a person
e. very big; enormous
f. use wrongly; use too much of

Sometimes certain abbreviations (shortened forms of words) help you understand a new word or phrase. Here are two:

  i.e. = that is = in other words
  e.g. = for example

C. Circle the words that give clues to the meanings of the underlined word(s). Then circle the letter of the correct meaning of the underlined word(s).

1. People can be addicted to different things—e.g., alcohol, drugs, certain foods, or even television. People who have such an addiction are compulsive.

    addicted:
    a. satisfied with
    b. alcoholic
    c. unable to have
    d. unable to stop having

    addiction:
    a. strong need
    b. food with alcohol
    c. satisfaction
    d. comfort

2. People who have such an addiction are compulsive; i.e., they have a very powerful psychological need that they feel they *must* satisfy.

    a. satisfied
    b. having a power to cause someone to do something
    c. having a strong need
    d. having a psychologist

3. This compulsion, like most others, is irrational—i.e., impossible to explain reasonably.

    a. compulsive
    b. not reasonable
    c. a strong psychological need
    d. something you can explain

D. Now read the selection at the beginning of the chapter again carefully. Try to guess the meanings of new words from the context. Use your dictionary only when absolutely necessary.

Check your answers in the "Getting the Main Ideas" section, which follows the reading. Correct your errors.

Understanding Reading Structure

A. Match the paragraphs in the reading selection with their topics. Write the letters of the paragraphs on the lines.

1. *B*　　Money as a symbol of other things
2. *A*　　Money habits as an expression of personality
3. *E*　　The use of the psychology of money in business
4. *F*　　Therapy for spending problems
5. *D*　　Psychological reasons for bargain hunting
6. *C.*　　Addiction to spending money

B. Circle the number of the *one* main idea of the reading selection.

1. People who buy on credit are more exciting than people who keep to their budgets.
2. People who are compulsive spenders probably didn't get much love when they were children.
3. Spending habits, which reflect personality, are a form of behavior that people can change.
4. Behavior therapy will help scientists, advertisers, and businesspeople.

C. Turn back to the beginning of the chapter and answer the questions in the "Preparing to Read" section.

Discussing the Reading

1. Do you believe that there is a "psychology of money?" Why or why not?
2. Describe your spending habits. What, in your opinion, do they show about your personality?
3. Do you believe that behavior therapy for people with money problems is a good idea? Why or why not? Describe some typical problems that people might have. Suggest some solutions.

PART TWO

BUSINESS IN THE FUTURE

Read these paragraphs quickly. Do not use a dictionary and don't worry about the details. Then underline the topic sentence of each paragraph, the sentence that tells the main idea.

Business in the Future

A   Imagine the typical work situations of the fairly recent past. A traditional woman's workplace was the home. Her occupation was a combination of housekeeper, cook, driver, babysitter, teacher, and gardener. A man's workplace was probably in a factory or an office. Factory workers, like other blue-collar workers, probably used machinery, but some amount of the work was manual. Office workers, like other white-collar workers, didn't work with machines or their hands. Instead, they dealt with ideas, numbers, and people. Most of them had secretaries who typed, filed papers, and answered phones.

B   Technology has already caused changes in these traditional work situations, but we will see more changes in the future. The increasing use of robots—machines that do the jobs of human beings—will mean fewer jobs for blue-collar workers. In the United States, for example, 33% of all workers now have manufacturing jobs; however, these jobs in factories will decrease to 11% at the beginning of the twenty-first century. Blue-collar workers in the future will not need much education or skill, but their pay will be low.

C   The use of computers, already very important today, will continue to create enormous changes for white-collar workers. In offices, as in factories, there will be a need for fewer people, but those people will need more skills. Secretaries, for instance, will need to be able to use word processing and other computer packages. In addition, many office workers will be free to work in several locations—e.g., the office and the home. This will be possible because of computer networks—groups of connected computers. These computer networks will cause even more changes in family life: Today most men and over half of all women leave the house each day to go to work, but in the future both men and women may choose to stay home with a computer and still be able to receive a paycheck.

D   And how will people spend this paycheck? Up until now, consumers have been buying most of the things that they need or want in stores. They've driven or taken public transportation to supermarkets, shopping centers, department stores, and specialty shops, where they've looked for sales, bargains, and discounts. They've examined products and made their choices. Then, with the help of salesclerks, they've paid cash, written checks, or used credit cards to buy the merchandise. Then they've taken the items home. Until now, most consumers have been shopping in this way; however, experts predict that shopping habits may greatly change in the future.

E   Already, some people are shopping less and less in stores and more and more with computers or videoscreens. Some consumers now use their computers to order certain merchandise, such as airline tickets, computer products, and videotapes, by telephone. These items arrive soon in the mail at their homes or workplaces. An even more modern method of shopping, however, is through *videocatalogues* in hotels, supermarkets, and other public places. Videocatalogues are computers with screens that show pictures of products to buy. Shoppers simply touch the screens to get information, focus on merchandise, make choices, and order products. After the shoppers pass their credit cards through the machines, their orders go to a warehouse, which sends them the items.

Discussing the Reading

1. Has technology caused changes in traditional work situations in your country? If so, how?
2. Do you use a computer? If so, when did you first learn to use one? What changes did it make in your life?
3. How do people in your country usually pay for merchandise? Is the use of credit cards very common?
4. Do you know about other new marketing methods (besides videocatalogues)? Describe them.

PART THREE

BUILDING VOCABULARY AND STUDY SKILLS

Related Words

Which word in each group does not belong? Cross it out. Explain the reasons for your answers.

1.	psychologist	scientist	~~company~~	therapist
2.	stores	shops	markets	checks
3.	computers	telephones	video	specialty
4.	cash	credit	center	money
5.	comfort	bargain	discount	sale
6.	shopping	businessman	salesclerk	advertiser
7.	merchandise	products	systems	items
8.	complete	power	influence	strength
9.	values	accounts	beliefs	opinions
10.	spend	claim	waste	save

Parts of Speech

To guess the meaning of a new word from the context, you might find it helpful to know its "part of speech"; that is, is the word a noun, a verb, an adjective, an adverb, etc.? Sometimes you can tell the part of speech from the suffix (the word ending). Here are some common suffixes, listed by the parts of speech that they usually indicate.

Nouns	Adjectives
-er/-or	-ive
-ist	-able/-ible
-sion/-tion	-(u)al
-ment	-ic(al)
-ee	-ful
-(i)ty	-ant/-ent
-ance/-ence	-ous
-ure	-ar(y)

A. Are the following words nouns or adjectives? The suffixes will tell you. On the lines, write *n* or *adj*. (In a few cases, both answers may be correct.)

1. *adj* compulsive
2. *n* spender
3. *adj* possible
4. *n* hunter
5. *n* psychologist
6. *n* personality
7. *adj* individual
8. *adj or n* important
9. *n* influence
10. *adj* basic
11. *n* assignment
12. *adj* instance
13. *n* transportation
14. *n* specialty
15. *n* computer
16. *adj* automatic
17. *adj* elementary
18. *n* addition
19. *n* expensive
20. *n* different
21. *n* television
22. *adj* addiction
23. *adj* pleasure
24. *adj* enormous
25. *adj* scientist
26. *adj* information
27. *adj (n)* protective
28. *adj* special
29. *adj* consumer
30. *adj (n)* public
31. *adj (n)* beautiful
32. *adj (n)* cultural
33. *n* culture

B. Complete each sentence with words related to the underlined words. Then look back at the list of suffixes to check your answers.

1. Every <u>person</u> has his or her own *personality* in relation to money. A person's ___*basic*___ opinions and values form the <u>basis</u> of his or her habits.

2. Bargain ___*hunter*___s are always <u>hunting</u> for discounts and low prices. For some <u>addictive</u> personalities, shopping for bargains is a kind of *addiction* .

3. <u>Specialty</u> shops often sell ___*special*___ items from different countries of the world. Shopping in these <u>pleasant</u> stores can be a *pleasure* .

4. A "money-back guarantee" *protective* *consumer*s. People who buy merchandise from mail-order houses should have this <u>protection</u>; if they send products back before they <u>consume</u> them, the company will return their money.

5. Through <u>computerized</u> methods of shopping, you can order items in an <u>instant</u>. For *instance* , you can touch a videoscreen that sends information to a *computer* .

6. Advertising is a kind of *information* that has a strong *influence* on consumers; it should not only <u>influence</u> people to buy products, but also <u>inform</u> them of basic facts.

Increasing Reading Speed: Reading in Phrases

Students usually need to read quickly because they have to read a lot of material. Interestingly, fast readers usually understand reading material better than slow readers.

Slow readers often read one word at a time, like this:

| According | to | psychologists, | our | individual |

| money | habits | show | our | beliefs | and | values. |

Faster readers don't usually read individual words. Instead, they take in several words at a time, like this:

| Experts in psychology | | believe that for many people, |

| money is an important symbol | | of strength and influence. |

If you try to read more and more words together, you can improve your reading speed.

A. Read these sentences in phrases, as shown:

1. | Husbands who complain | | about their wives' spending habits |
   | may be afraid | | that they are losing power | | in their marriage. |

2. | Many people | | are compulsive | | in their addictions— |
   | i.e., they must satisfy | | their needs | | to feel comfortable. |

3. | Psychologists often use | | a method called "behavior therapy" |
   | to help individuals | | solve their personality problems. |

Certain words often belong together in phrases. For example, a noun phrase can include adjectives and other words before or after the noun. A verb phrase may include noun objects, adjectives, or adverbs. A prepositional phrase includes an object after a preposition, and an infinitive phrase may include an object after the verb.

Examples:

Noun Phrases	Verb Phrases	Prepositional Phrases	Infinitive Phrases
money habits	spend money	for their	to save money
a symbol of	ask the clerk	behavior	to feel
love	a question	on the next day	comfortable

B. Which words belong together in reading? Read the following sentences in phrases and separate the phrases with lines. (There are several correct possibilities.)

1. /Do you want to avoid the traffic jams, noise, and pollution/of downtown shopping areas? With a mail-order catalogue,/you can choose merchandise/from the comfort of your home./First,/you should carefully study the pictures/of products and the facts (color, size, price, etc.) about them in the book./After you make your choices,/you can write the necessary information/on the/order form and send it with a check/to the mail-order house./

2. /Most people,/even compulsive spenders,/keep their money in banks—in checking and savings accounts. To put money into accounts, you write out forms called deposit slips./On/these slips of paper,/you/put down the amount of money you are depositing—the currency/(cash in paper bills) and the checks. /You add up the amounts,/subtract the money that you want to receive in cash,/ and write the total deposit./You endorse (write your name on the back of) all your checks/and/bring everything to the teller's window/at the bank.

3. /Nowadays,/to save time,/many people bank by mail/or use/the instant-teller machines outside their banks./They put checks and deposit slips/into bank envelopes,/which they seal and mail or put into the machines./They can also make payments/(for their houses, cars, loans, etc.) in these ways./People who have special cards and numbers can withdraw certain amounts of cash/from the instant tellers./The bank statements that they receive/at the end of the month/will/include the amounts that they have deposited/or/withdrawn by mail or machine./

PART FOUR

SCANNING FOR INFORMATION

A. The following vocabulary items often appear on bank forms. Match them with their meanings. If necessary, look back at the paragraphs above for context clues.

1. __c__ deposit
2. __f__ withdraw
3. __g__ currency
4. __h__ enclose
5. __a__ slip
6. __e__ endorse
7. __b__ seal
8. __d__ teller
9. __i__ cash

a. a piece of paper; a form
b. close
c. put money into (a bank account)
d. a person who works at a bank window
e. sign (write your name on)
f. take money out (of a bank account)
g. paper bills
h. put in
i. paper money and coins

B. Scan the banking forms below and on pages 51 and 52, and write the answers to the questions.

BANK OF AMERICA   Checking Deposit

| | | | | | — | | | | | | LIST CHECKS BY BANK NO | DOLLARS | CENTS |

ACCOUNT NUMBER

Pablo Ramos
NAME (PLEASE PRINT)

ADDRESS

CITY   STATE   ZIP CODE

DATE

PLEASE SIGN IN TELLER'S PRESENCE FOR CASH RECEIVED.

	DOLLARS	CENTS
CURRENCY	$50	00
COIN		
CHECKS 16–66	25	00
92–101/1210	107	62
TOTAL OF CHECKS LISTED ON REVERSE		
SUBTOTAL	182	62
◄ LESS: CASH RECEIVED		
TOTAL DEPOSIT	$182	62

R-3 1-83 BANK OF AMERICA NT&SA

⑆510000354⑆

a.

BANK OF AMERICA   Savings Deposit

| | | | | | — | | | | | |

ACCOUNT NUMBER

Mohammed El-Gamal
NAME (PLEASE PRINT)

ADDRESS

CITY   STATE   ZIP CODE

NEW PASSBOOK BALANCE

PLEASE SIGN IN TELLER'S PRESENCE FOR CASH RECEIVED

	DOLLARS	CENTS
DATE		
LIST CHECKS BY BANK NO	DOLLARS	CENTS
CURRENCY		
COIN		
CHECKS 62–20 ₁	255	00
16–66 ₂	100	00
16–4 ₃	40	00
₄		
SUBTOTAL	395	00
◄ LESS CASH RECEIVED	− 95	00
TOTAL DEPOSIT	$300	00

S-151-2 (BANK OF AMERICA NT&SA

⑆5010⑈0000⑆

b.

```
┌─────────────────────────────────────────────────────────────────────────┐
│  BA BANK OF AMERICA                          Savings Withdrawal          │
│  ┌──┬──┬──┬──┐ ┌──┬──┬──┬──┐         NOT NEGOTIABLE                      │
│  │  │  │  │  │─│  │  │  │  │                                              │
│  └──┴──┴──┴──┘ └──┴──┴──┴──┘                                             │
│  ACCOUNT NUMBER                              DATE                         │
│  RECEIVED FROM BANK OF AMERICA              $ 75.00                       │
│   Seventy-five and no/100s ─────────────────────────── DOLLARS           │
│                          X                                               │
│                          PLEASE SIGN IN TELLERS PRESENCE FOR CASH RECEIVED│
│  FOR BANK USE ONLY ▼     Hon-May Fong                                     │
│  ACTIVITY CHARGE         NAME (PLEASE PRINT)                             │
│  NEW P.B. BALANCE        ADDRESS                                         │
│  ENTERED BY                                                              │
│  CONTRA                  CITY            STATE          ZIP CODE          │
│  S-155 1-83 BANK OF AMERICA NT&SA                                        │
│     ⑈50 10⑈0000⑈                                                         │
└─────────────────────────────────────────────────────────────────────────┘
```

c.

1. Match the forms with these descriptions. Write the letters of the forms on the lines.

   __b__   a deposit slip for a savings account

   __a__   a deposit slip for a checking account

   __d__   an envelope to deposit money after banking hours

   __c__   a form to take money out of a savings account

2. How much money is Pablo Ramos depositing in his checking account? __$182.63__ How much of the deposit is in cash? __$50.00__ How many checks is he depositing? __2__ Is he taking any money from the bank with him? __No.__

3. How much money is Mohammed El-Gamal depositing in his savings account? __$300.00__ How much of this is in cash? __0__ How many checks is he depositing? __3__ Is he taking any of this money with him? __yes__ If so, how much? __$95.00__

4. How much money is Hon-May Fong withdrawing from her savings account? __$75.00__ When will she sign the form? __From of teller__

d.

 BANK OF AMERICA

Instant Deposit Envelope

Deposits

Make deposits for Checking, Regular Savings, Investors Passbook, Christmas Club, Business Checking, and Business Savings.

- **Fill out and enclose a deposit slip. (For Christmas Club deposits, please use your coupon.) Total checks carefully.**

- **Write "for deposit only" when you endorse each check. Do not enclose cash. The bank will not send you a receipt.**

Deposits will appear on your bank statements.

No Cash Please

Payments

Make loan payments (real estate, home improvement, car, boat, etc.), BankAmericard,® Visa® , Bank of America MasterCard® , and PersonaLine® or CustomLine® Credit payments. This service may also be used to make Instalment Collection and Safe Deposit payments.

- **Fill out and enclose a payment coupon (for each account).**

- **Enclose check made payable to Bank of America. Do not enclose cash.**

Payments will appear on your bank statements.

BANK OF AMERICA NT&SA · MEMBER FDIC

5. Write T (*true*) or F (*false*) on the line before each of the following statements about the banking envelope.

a. __T__   This envelope is for deposits to a checking account.

b. __T__   This envelope is for deposits to a savings account.

c. __F__   This envelope is for withdrawals from a savings account.

d. __T__   This envelope is for payments on a loan.

e. __T__   You need to put a deposit slip and a check (or checks) into this envelope.

f. __F__   You may put currency into this envelope.

g. __T__   You need to write "for deposit only" and sign each check.

h. __T__   The bank will send you a letter about your deposit.

C. Discuss other new vocabulary on the banking forms. Talk about kinds of checking and savings accounts.

Going Beyond the Text

Bring to class other banking forms and brochures about banking services. Discuss new vocabulary. Summarize the information for the class.

4

JOBS AND PROFESSIONS

WORKAHOLISM

Getting Started

Look at the picture and discuss it.

1. What is this man doing? Why is he doing so many things at the same time?
2. Do you think this man is happy with his life? Why or why not?
3. Do you know anyone similar to this man? Tell about that person.

Preparing to Read

As you read the following selection, think about the answers to these questions.

1. What is a workaholic?
2. Where is workaholism especially common?
3. What are some disadvantages of workaholism? Some advantages?
4. Are you a workaholic?

Workaholism

A   Most workers spend eight or nine hours on the job. They work because it's unavoidable. They need to make enough money for necessities: food, rent, clothing, transportation, tuition, and so on. They spend about one-third of their lives at work, but they hate it. They complain and count the minutes until quitting time each day—or the days until their next vacation.

B   By contrast, there are some people who actually enjoy work—in fact, they *love* to work. They spend many extra hours on the job each week and often take work home with them. These workaholics are as addicted to their jobs as other people are to drugs or alcohol.

C   In some urban centers, workaholism is so common that people do not consider it unusual: They accept the lifestyle as normal. Government workers in Washington, D.C., for example, frequently work sixty to seventy hours a week. They don't do this because they *have* to; they do it because they *want* to. Hundreds of workaholics in New York City tried to go to work even in the famous blackout of 1977. There was no electricity—no air conditioning, elevators, or lights—but many people went to their offices anyway. They sat impatiently on the steps outside their office buildings and did paperwork or had business meetings.

D   Workaholism can be a serious problem. Because true workaholics would rather work than do anything else, they probably don't know how to relax; that is, they might not enjoy movies, sports, or other types of entertainment. Most of all, they hate to sit and do nothing. The lives of workaholics are usually stressful, and this tension and worry can cause health problems such as heart attacks or stomach ulcers. In addition, typical workaholics don't pay much attention to their families. They spend little time with their children, and their marriages may end in divorce.

E   Is workaholism always dangerous? Perhaps not. There are, certainly, people who work well under stress. Some studies show that many workaholics have great energy and interest in life. Their work is so pleasurable that they are actually very happy. For most workaholics, work and entertainment are the same thing. Their jobs provide them with a challenge; this keeps them busy and creative. Other people retire from work at age sixty-five, but workaholics usually prefer not to quit. They are still enthusiastic about work—and life—in their eighties and nineties.

F   Why do workaholics enjoy their jobs so much? There are several advantages to work. Of course, it provides people with paychecks, and this is important. But it offers more than financial security. It provides people with self-confidence; they have a feeling of satisfaction when they've produced a challenging piece of work and are able to say, "I made that." Psychologists claim that work gives people an identity; through participation in work, they get a sense of self and individualism. In addition, most jobs provide people with a socially acceptable way to meet others. Perhaps some people are compulsive about their work, but their addiction seems to be a safe—even an advantageous—one.

G   People who are addicted to work are similar to one another in some ways. Here is a list of ten characteristics of workaholics. Which ones apply to you? Check your answers.

YES   NO

☐ ☐   1. Do you get up early even if you go to bed late?

☐ ☐   2. Do you read or work while you eat?

☐ ☐   3. Do you make lists of things to do?

☐ ☐   4. Do you find it unpleasant to "do nothing?"

☐ ☐   5. Do you usually have a lot of energy?

☐ ☐   6. Do you work on weekends and on holidays?

☐ ☐   7. Can you work anytime and anywhere?

☐ ☐   8. Do you prefer not to take vacations?

☐ ☐   9. Do you think you probably won't want to retire?

☐ ☐   10. Do you really enjoy your work?

If you answered "yes" to eight or more questions, you might be a workaholic.

Getting the Main Ideas

Which statements are *true* about workaholics, according to the reading? Check them.

1. _F_   They spend no more than eight to nine hours on the job.

2. _F_   They complain a lot about their jobs and watch the clock.

3. _✓T_   They spend a lot of time working at their jobs and at home.

4. _F_   They work only because they have to.

5. _T_   They would rather work than rest.

6. _T_   They may have health problems from their inability to relax.

7. _T_   They may be happy because their work provides a lot of pleasure.

8. _F_   They retire from their jobs before the age of sixty-five.

9. _T_   They probably have a feeling of satisfaction and a sense of identity.

10. _T_   They probably meet people through their work.

Guessing Meaning from Context

A. Circle the words that give clues to the meanings of the underlined word(s). Then circle the letter of the correct meaning of each underlined word.

1. Most people need to work to make enough money for necessities: food, rent, clothing, and transportation.

    a. things in a city
    b. things that they need
    c. things for work
    d. things that they don't have

2. These workaholics are as addicted to their jobs as other people are to drugs or alcohol.

    a. people who drink too much alcohol
    b. drug addicts
    c. people who work
    d. compulsive workers

3. The lives of workaholics are usually stressful, and this tension and worry can cause health problems such as heart attacks or stomach ulcers.

    stressful:
    a. busy
    b. compulsive and addicted
    c. tense and worried
    d. emphasized

    ulcers:
    a. a break in the skin or area inside the body
    b. food
    c. headaches
    d. difficulty with breathing, especially in certain work situations

4. Hundreds of workaholics in New York City tried to go to work even in the famous blackout of 1977. There was no electricity.

    a. a very dark night
    b. time without electric power
    c. time of dirty streets
    d. increases in crime

5. For most workaholics, their jobs provide a challenge; this keeps them busy and creative.

    a. solution to problems
    b. advantage
    c. prediction of success
    d. call for energetic work

6. Other people <u>retire</u> from work at age sixty-five, but workaholics usually prefer not to quit.

    a. avoid work
    b. leave their jobs
    c. lose power
    d. hold on to their jobs

7. Their jobs keep them busy and creative; they are still <u>enthusiastic</u> about work—and life—in their eighties and nineties.

    a. individualistic
    b. wanting a rest
    c. very interested
    d. impatient

8. Work provides people with <u>self-confidence</u>; they have a feeling of satisfaction when they've finished a challenging piece of work and are able to say, "I made that."

    a. belief in their ability
    b. inability to relax
    c. discipline
    d. ability to memorize

9. Psychologists claim that <u>work</u> gives people <u>an identity</u>; through participation in work, they get a sense of self.

    a. cultural individualism
    b. special creative qualities
    c. values and opinions
    d. ideas about who they are

B. Read the selection at the beginning of the chapter again carefully. Try to guess the meanings of new words from the context. Use your dictionary only when absolutely necessary.

    Check your answers in the "Getting the Main Ideas" section, which follows the reading selection. Correct your errors.

Understanding Reading Structure

A. Match the paragraphs in the selection with their topics. Write the letters of the paragraphs on the line.

1. _F_   The advantages of workaholism

2. _A_   Feelings of "normal" workers about their jobs

3. _B_   A definition of workaholism

4. _G_   A "test" of the characteristics of workaholics

5. _C_   Examples of workaholism in big cities

6. _D_   Problems of workaholism

7. _E_   People for whom workaholism is not dangerous

B. Circle the number of the one main idea of the reading selection.

1. Workaholism can lead to serious problems, but it can also create a happy life.
2. Workaholics are usually successful people, but they don't stay married long.
3. People who enjoy their work usually enjoy movies, sports, and other kinds of entertainment.
4. People who work even under difficult conditions may be very creative.

C. Turn back to the beginning of the chapter and answer the questions in the "Preparing to Read" section.

Discussing the Reading

1. In your opinion, is workaholism an addiction? What are its advantages? Its disadvantages?
2. Should a workaholic try to change his or her lifestyle? Why or why not? If so, how?
3. People such as the painter Pablo Picasso or the musician Pablo Casals enjoyed working even when they were very old. What were some possible reasons for this?
4. Can you think of other people who never wanted to retire?

PART TWO

WORKING PEOPLE SPEAK OUT

Skimming for Main Ideas

Read these paragraphs quickly, without using a dictionary. Then underline the topic sentence, which tells the main idea, of each paragraph.

Working People Speak Out

A   A serious actor is always working—but not always for pay. If an actor wants to succeed, he has to be a workaholic because he works every minute of the day—except when he's sleeping. For instance, any good actor has to spend a lot of time in classes where he studies human emotions, such as sadness, happiness, or anger; in these classes, he concentrates on methods to express these emotions to the audience in the theater. This is very challenging. Even outside classes, an actor is always watching people and studying their unique characteristics. Perhaps 85% of an actor's work is *looking* for work: You have to send out letters, meet people who might be able to offer you work, and so on. In this country, it's hard for an actor to find a job, and most jobs don't last long. You might work for a few months on a movie in Hollywood or a play in New York; then it's time to look for new work. A person in the entertainment business needs a lot of patience and discipline.

—Armin Shimerman, actor

B   When you own a bookstore, you have to like people. You can't avoid them! If your store is going to make money, you have to provide books that interest as many people as possible. Therefore, you need to carry a large variety: cookbooks, novels, "how-to" books (*How to Solve Marriage Problems, How to Pass College Entrance Exams, How to Prevent Crime,* etc.), literature, art books, and so on. People like to talk about their favorite books, so a person who works in a bookstore has to know something about everything. I think some of my customers are interesting: There's one woman who reads six or seven books a week. Her favorite is

Gone with the Wind, and she's read it again and again—at least once a year *for the past sixty years!* On the other hand, some of my customers are really boring; they talk and talk about things I'm not interested in because I'm a "captive audience"—I mean, the customers know *I* won't try to escape. I'm a good listener—and besides, I *can't* leave the store.

—Susana Cox, bookstore owner

C   In police work, you can never predict the next crime or problem. No working day is identical to any other, so there is no "typical" day for a police officer. Some days are relatively slow, and the job is boring; other days are so busy that there is no time to eat. I think I can describe police work in one word: variety. Sometimes it's dangerous. One day, for example, I was working undercover; that is, I was on the job, but I was wearing normal clothes, not my police uniform. I was trying to catch some muggers who were stealing money from people as they walked down the street. Suddenly, seven guys jumped out at me; one of them had a knife, and we got into a fight. Another policeman arrived, and together, we arrested

three of the men; but the other four ran away. Another day, I helped a pregnant woman. She was trying to get to the hospital, but there was a bad traffic jam. I put her in my police car to get her there faster. I thought she was going to have the baby right there in my car. But fortunately, the baby waited to "arrive" until we got to the hospital.

—William de la Torre, police officer

Viewpoint

In your opinion, how do the three speakers in the reading selection feel about their work? Why do you think so?

Discussing the Reading

1. Would you like to have a job as an actor or actress, a bookstore owner, or a police officer? Why or why not?
2. Talk for one minute about your work (or work you want to do in the future).
3. From the work descriptions you have just heard, choose the most interesting job. Explain your choice.
4. In your opinion, what is the best job in the world? Why?

PART THREE

BUILDING VOCABULARY AND STUDY SKILLS

Adjective and Noun Phrases

Some words often appear together in phrases. In some phrases, there is a hyphen (-).

Examples: To get merchandise from a mail-order company, you dial a toll-free telephone number.

The last word of a phrase is usually a noun or an adjective. The first word may be a noun, an adjective, or an adverb.

Examples: city life (= noun + noun)
social sciences (= adjective + noun)
especially interesting (adverb + adjective)

A. Complete each sentence with the missing words. Choose from the following:

financial	air	city
self	specialty	mass
socially	quitting	shopping
business	office	traffic

1. Most workers work only for *financial* security, and they count the hours until _quitting_ time.

2. People who enjoy their work may have a lot of _self_-confidence. They might spend a lot of time at work because it is a _socially_ acceptable way to meet people.

3. During the famous New York blackout, when there was no _air_-conditioning in their _office_ buildings, many people had _business_ meetings outside.

4. Some advantages of big _city_ life are the _shopping_ centers with their interesting _specialty_ shops, and their _mass_ transportation systems. A disadvantage is the _traffic_ jams.

B. Match the pairs of words by writing the letters on the lines.

1.	_d_ high	a.	administration
2.	_a_ business	b.	hunting
3.	_h_ drinking	c.	therapy
4.	_e_ public	d.	school
5.	___ bargain	e.	transportation
6.	___ charge	f.	discipline
7.	_c_ behavior	g.	account
8.	_f_ self-	h.	water

Compound Words

Some words belong together in "compounds" (long words that consist of smaller words).

Examples: I talked to a <u>salesclerk</u> at the <u>supermarket</u>.

A. Draw a line between the two words of each compound. Then match the words with the definitions by writing letters on the lines.

1. _h_   black|board
2. _e_   teenage
3. _j_   overcrowding
4. _a_   classroom
5. _i_   yardwork
6. _b_   downtown
7. _c_   videotape
8. _f_   paperwork
9. _d_   paycheck
10. _g_   undercover

a. room in a school
b. the center of a city
c. a recording with television pictures
d. money for work
e. between the ages of thirteen and nineteen
f. jobs that require reading and writing
g. acting secretly
h. a surface on the wall to write on
i. jobs in the garden
j. too many people in one place

B. How many compound words or phrases can you make from these words, in any order? Work as fast as you can. Write them on the lines, add hyphens if necessary, and then check them in your dictionary. The student with the most correct words or phrases at the end of a time limit is the winner.

high	college	exam	tuition	life	school
net	self	public	science	planning	service
office	work	police	transportation	confidence	city

1. _high school_
2. _net work_
3. _college tuition (life)_
4. _self service (confidence)_
5. _office work._
6. _public transportation_
7. _exam science_
8. _public school_
9. _police office (work)_
10. _transportation service_
11. _life science._
12. _____
13. _____
14. _____
15. _____
16. _____

Increasing Reading Speed: Reading in Phrases

> Fast readers usually read several words (a phrase) at a time.

Which words belong together in the following reading? Read the sentences in phrases and separate the phrases with lines. (There are several correct possibilities.)

If you want/to apply for a job,/you might look through the classified advertisements in the newspaper. These ads give you information about the work and the companies. For example, a company that talks about "excellent benefits" in its ad may offer good health insurance, a pension plan (for retirement), and vacation pay. Some companies may pay workers for the cost of transportation. Advertisements also tell the requirements that employees must meet—necessary experience, skills, and so on—and describe the work that they will do.

Left-to-Right Eye Movements

> Slow readers look at the same words several times. Their eyes move back and forth over each sentence. Fast readers usually move their eyes from left to right one time for each line. They don't look back very often. A fast left-to-right eye movement increases reading speed. The following exercises will help you improve your reading speed.

Your teacher will tell you when to begin each section. Look at the underlined word at the left of each line. Read across the line, from left to right, as fast as you can. Some words in the line are the same as the underlined word. Circle them. At the end of each section, write down your time (the number of seconds it took you to finish). Try to read faster with each section.

<u>banking</u>	banks	banking	bank	banking	banking
<u>loan</u>	loans	lend	alone	loaning	loan
<u>savings</u>	savings	save	savings	saving	saver
<u>benefit</u>	benefits	benefit	benefited	benefit	beneficial
<u>employer</u>	employ	employee	employer	employed	employment

Time: _____

experience	experience	experienced	expertise	experience
opening	opening	opening	opened	opening
excellent	excel	excelled	excellent	excellent
tellers	retell	tellers	teller	telling
account	account	accounts	account	accounting

Time: _____

part-time	part-time	part-time	full-time	part-timer
position	possible	position	positive	position
public	public	private	publicity	publicize
appointment	appoint	appointed	appointment	appointment
insurance	insurance	insure	assurance	insurance

Time: _____

salary	salary	celery	salaries	salaried	sales
typing	typing	typed	type	typing	typing
skills	skilled	skill	skills	skills	skillful
apply	applied	apply	apply	apply	application
ability	ability	able	capable	ability	capability

Time: _____

opportunity	opportunity	opportune	community	opportunity
equal	equal	equal	unequal	equality
computer	computer	computed	computation	computer
equivalent	equal	equivalent	equivalent	equivalent
resume	resumed	resume	resume	presume

Time: _____

minimum	minimal	minimum	memorize	minimum	mini
industry	industrial	industrious	industry	industries	industry
optional	option	options	optional	optional	optional
degree	degree	agree	disagree	degree	disagreed
trainee	trained	train	training	trainee	trainee

Time: _____

<u>aptitude</u>	aptitude	ability	aptitude	attitude	aptitudes
<u>printing</u>	printed	prints	reprint	printing	printing
<u>mechanical</u>	mechanic	mechanical	machine	mechanical	mechanic
<u>secretary</u>	secretarial	secrets	secretary	secretaries	secretary
<u>financial</u>	finances	finance	financial	finally	financial

Time: _____

<u>accountant</u>	accounting	accountant	accounts	accountant
<u>required</u>	required	required	required	requirement
<u>mature</u>	maturity	mature	premature	mature
<u>dictation</u>	dictation	dictation	dictator	dictate
<u>manage</u>	management	manager	managing	manage

Time: _____

PART FOUR

SCANNING FOR INFORMATION

A. Here are some common abbreviations (shortened forms of words) from advertisements. Match them with their meanings. Write the letters on the lines.

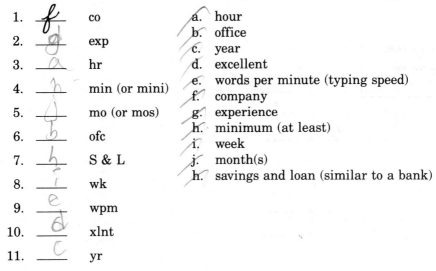

1. _f_   co
2. _g_   exp
3. _a_   hr
4. _h_   min (or mini)
5. _j_   mo (or mos)
6. _b_   ofc
7. _h_   S & L
8. _i_   wk
9. _e_   wpm
10. _d_   xlnt
11. _c_   yr

a. hour
b. office
c. year
d. excellent
e. words per minute (typing speed)
f. company
g. experience
h. minimum (at least)
i. week
j. month(s)
h. savings and loan (similar to a bank)

B. Scan the following classified ads. The numbers next to the groups of statements refer to the numbers next to the ads (there is *not* a group of statements for every ad). Write T on the lines before the *true* statements; write F on the lines before the *false* statements. If the ad does not give enough information, write I (*impossible to know*).

1.

BANKING
LOAN AGENTS
Aggressive S & L is looking for experienced loan agents, S/F.V. South Bay & other prime territories. We are a direct lender offering 17 day processing & 24 hr. approval for FHA, VA & conventional loans. Our commissions, incentive & benefit programs are tops in the industry. For interview call Tom Smith National S & L, 800/647-0747 or 800/425-6000.
Equal Oppty Employer

2.

BANKING
LOAN PROCESSOR
Fast growing S & L has immediate opening for that person with 2 yrs. min. experience with conventional & govt loan processing. We are looking for someone with current experience. We offer xlnt benefits, pleasant working conditions & opportunity for growth. Contact: Judy at First International S & L, 818/647-0600 or 800/224-4200.
Equal Oppty Employer

3.

★ BANKING/TELLERS ★
We have 18 open positions with major banks & S&L's. We need 14 Tellers & 4 New Accounts people. Minimum 1 yr experience, xlnt benefits & future. Call Today!

✔ THE DAVIS AGENCY
26400 Fair Oaks Enc.
464-5000
Eves & wknds by appt.

4.

CLERICAL
COLLECTION ACCOUNT REPRESENTATIVE

We are looking for a few outgoing individuals interested in working part-time. Your work hours would be 2:00 p.m. to 4:00 p.m. Monday-Friday. This position involves public relations, heavy use of phone, as well as some door to door contact (this is done by previously scheduled appointments).

We require light typing and good communication skills, a good driving record and proof of insurance. We offer good salary and mileage reimbursement. Please apply in person or call for more information (647-4000).

College Students
Encouraged to Apply

2. a. __T__   This job is at a savings and loan company.

   b. __F__   It requires three years' experience.

   c. __I__   Men and women can apply.

3. a. _____   This job is for a loan officer.

   b. _____   It requires a college degree.

   c. _____   It offers good benefits.

4. a. _____   This is a full-time job.

   b. _____   It requires some typing.

   c. _____   It may be a good job for college students.

5.

> **COMPUTER OPERATOR**
> Burbank entertainment co seeks detail-oriented individual with 6 mos operating experience & or education. Good communication skills & ability to work any shift a must. Xlnt benefits & working environment. Please call Janet 921-2700. Equal Oppty Employer M-F-H.

6.

> **Computer Operator IBM SYSTEM 23**
> Printing corp is seeking an operator with bookkeeping background - 1 yr experience on IBM SYSTEM 23 or equivalent. Salary commensurate with experience full benefits pkg. (No phone calls please) Send resume: A.L. Johnson & Son., 9612 Beverly Dr. No. Hollywood 91605 Att. Louis Johnson

7.

> **ENGINEER - ELECTRICAL DESIGN**
> Min. of 10 yrs experience in power lighting design for industrial, commercial & hospitals. Min. of 5 yrs experience in U.S.A. Salary based on experience. Xlnt benefits. Non-smoker. Van Nuys 818-621-7020.
>
> **ENGINEER/ELECTRONIC**
> Wilson Industries   265-0211

8.

> ENGINEER
> RF DESIGN ENGINEER
> VHF TX RX
> Degree optional
> Star Industries
> Mike Lyndon, 360-2420

9.

> **ENGINEERING** TRAINEE. Must have good math, neat printing, good mechanical aptitude. Elizabeth, 240-2650.

10.

> **SECRETARY** general ofc. Type 60 - wpm, financial statements, for Encino CPA firm. Accounting firm experience required.   240-0577

11.

> **SECRETARY** Legal Trainee. Dynamic Encino law firm desires bright individual with good office skills. Call Wendy 105-0020.

12.

> **SECRETARY** Part Time Mature non-smoker, typing, dictation required. Property Management Co.-Encino Call Monday 380-9216

13.

> **SECRETARY** Typist. Busy pool construction office needs take-charge person. Construction scheduling, heavy phones. 501-2530

14.

> **TEENAGER** to do 4-5 hrs of yard work per wk. Sherman Oaks area. $5 hr. 091-2611

5. a. _____ This job is with an entertainment company.

    b. _____ It requires one-half year of experience.

    c. _____ The person who gets this job will use a computer.

7. a. _____ This job is good for a person without much experience.

    b. _____ It is good for a person who doesn't smoke.

    c. _____ The person who gets this job will type and answer phones.

9. a. _____ This job is good for a person without much experience.

    b. _____ It requires a college degree.

    c. _____ It offers excellent salary and benefits.

10. a. _____ This job requires a typing speed of at least sixty words per minute.

    b. _____ It requires experience.

    c. _____ It is with a bank.

14. a. _____ This job is part-time.

    b. _____ It is at a computer company.

    c. _____ It is for people over thirty years old.

C. Find the appropriate job for these people. Write the ad number(s) on the line.

1. _____ A man is good at computer work. He wants to meet actors and actresses.

2. _____ A fifty-year-old woman has excellent office skills. She can't work all day. She doesn't smoke.

3. _____ A woman wants to work with money but doesn't want to be a bank teller. She knows about loans.

4. _____ A sixteen-year-old boy wants to earn some extra money. He can't type or use a computer. He likes to be outside.

5. _____ A young man types very fast and takes shorthand. He wants to become a lawyer.

D. Work in pairs. Ask and answer questions like those above about the classified ads.

Going Beyond the Text

Bring to class classified ads for jobs from local newspapers. Discuss new vocabulary and abbreviations. Choose jobs that interest you. Explain them to the class.

5

LIFESTYLES

OUR CHANGING LIFESTYLES: TRENDS AND FADS

Getting Started

Look at the pictures and discuss them.

1. What are the people in these pictures wearing? What are they doing?
2. What else do you see in each picture? What do you know about each of these things?

3. About when (what general time) does each picture take place?
4. How are these scenes similar to (or different from) scenes in your country?

Preparing to Read

As you read the following selection, think about the answers to these questions.

1. What are fads? How are they different from trends?
2. What are some examples of fads?
3. What things go in and out of style?
4. Why do people follow fads?

Our Changing Lifestyles: Trends and Fads

A person who comes to live in the United States for a few years usually notices that lifestyles seem to change very fast. It is more than just clothing and hairstyles that are in style one year and out of date the next; it's a whole way of living. This person might notice that one year people wear sunglasses on top of their heads and that they wear jeans and boots; that they drink white wine and eat sushi at Japanese restaurants; that for exercise they jog several miles a day. However, the next year they notice that everything has changed. Women wear long skirts; people drink expensive water from France and eat pasta at Italian restaurants; everyone seems to be exercising at health clubs.

Almost nothing in modern life escapes the influence of fashion; food, music, exercise, books, slang words, movies, furniture, places to visit, even *names* go in and out of fashion. For a while, it seems that all new parents are naming their babies Heather, Dawn, Eric, or Adam. These names are "in." Then, suddenly, these same names are "out," and Tiffany and Jason are "in." It's almost impossible to write about specific fads because these interests that people enthusiastically follow can change very quickly.

In the United States, even *people* can be "in" or "out." Like people in any country, Americans enjoy following the lives of celebrities: movie stars, sports heroes, famous artists, politicians, and the like. But Americans also pay a lot of attention to people who have no special ability and have done nothing very special. In 1981, for example, an unknown elderly woman appeared in a T.V. commercial in which she looked at a very small hamburger and complained loudly, "Where's the beef?" These three words made her famous. Suddenly she appeared in magazines and newspapers and on TV shows. She was immediately popular. She was "in." In 1987 an exterminator in Dallas, Texas decided that he would be very happy if he could find more customers for his small business; he needed more people to pay him to kill the insects and rats in their houses. He put an unusual advertisement in a Dallas newspaper: He offered to pay $1,000 to the person who could find the biggest cockroach. This strange offer made him suddenly famous. There were stories about him nationwide—from New York to California. He was "in." However, this kind of fame does not last long. Such people are famous for a very short time. They are fads.

What causes such fads to come and go? And why do so many people follow them? Although clothing designers and manufacturers influence fads in fashion because they want to make a profit, this desire for money doesn't explain fads in other areas, such as language. For example, why have teenagers in the past twenty-five years used—at different times— the slang words *groovy, boss, awesome,* or *rad* in conversation instead of simply saying *wonderful?* According to Jack Santino, an expert in popular culture, people who follow fads are not irrational; they simply want to be part of something new and creative, and they feel good when they are part of an "in group." Fads are not unique to the United States. Dr. Santino believes that fads are common in any country that has a strong consumer economy—e.g., Britain, Japan, and Germany. However, in the United States there is an additional reason for fads: Most Americans seem to feel that something is wrong if there isn't frequent change in their lives.

E   Dr. Santino points out that it's sometimes difficult to see the difference between a *fad* and a *trend.* A fad, he says, lasts a very short time and is not very important. A social trend lasts a long time and becomes a true part of modern culture. A trend might be the use of personal computers; a fad might be certain types of computer games. A recent trend is the nationwide interest in good health, but many fads come from this trend: aerobic dancing, special diets, imported water, and the like.

F   A person who participates in fads should remember that they come and go very fast, and they often come back in style after ten to fifteen years of being "out." So it might be a good idea never to throw anything away! Mickey Mouse watches and Nehru jackets may soon be "in" again!

Getting the Main Ideas   *Fad — fashion.*

Write T on the lines before the statements that are *true,* according to the reading. Write F on the lines before the statements that are *false.*

1. _T_ Fashion influences many things in addition to clothing and hairstyles.

2. _T_ Fads come and go very quickly.

3. _F_ All people who are famous have done something very special.

4. _T_ People who follow fads want to be part of something new and creative.

5. _F_ Americans are the only people who follow fads.

6. _F_ Trends are the same as fads.

Guessing Meaning from Context

A. Circle the words that give clues to the meaning of each underlined word. Then circle the letter of the correct meaning of the underlined word.

1. <u>Lifestyles</u> seem to change very fast. A lifestyle is more than just clothing and hairstyles that are in fashion one year and out of date the next; it's a whole way of living.

    a. styles of clothes
    b. living habits
    c. costs of living
    d. networks of friends

2. It's almost impossible to write about specific <u>fads</u> because these interests that people enthusiastically follow change very quickly.

    a. clothing styles
    b. famous people
    c. things that people are very interested in
    d. things that people try to write about

3. In 1987 an <u>exterminator</u> in Dallas, Texas decided that he would be happy if he could find more customers for his small business; he needed more people to pay him to kill the insects and rats in their houses.

    a. customer
    b. person who has a business
    c. person who cleans houses for customers
    d. person who kills small, common, harmful animals

4. There were stories about him <u>nationwide</u>—from New York to California.

    a. everywhere in the country
    b. a big nation
    c. from south to north
    d. in New York

5. Although clothing designers and manufacturers influence fads in fashion because they want to make a <u>profit</u>, this desire for money doesn't explain fads in other areas, such as language.

    a. money that people steal
    b. clothing design
    c. money that people make
    d. new fad

6. Why have teenagers in the past twenty-five years used—at different times— the slang words *groovy, boss, awesome,* or *rad* in conversation instead of simply saying *wonderful?*

   a. informal
   b. long
   c. formal
   d. nouns

7. It's sometimes difficult to see the difference between a fad and a trend. A fad lasts a very short time and is not very important. A social trend lasts a long time and becomes a true part of modern culture.

   a. a fad
   b. a fad that doesn't disappear quickly
   c. a social fad
   d. a modern fad

B. Read the selection at the beginning of the chapter again carefully. Try to guess the meanings of new words from the context. Use your dictionary only when absolutely necessary.

   Check your answers in the "Getting the Main Ideas" section, which follows the reading selection. Correct your errors.

Understanding Reading Structure

Circle the number of the one main idea of the reading selection.

1. Trends and fads are the same thing.
2. Fads are common in the United States because clothing manufacturers make a lot of money if styles change every year.
3. Fads usually last a very short time.
4. People follow many different kinds of fads because they like to be part of something new and creative.

Discussing the Reading

1. What are some fads these days in clothing, language, food, and so on? Are these fads part of any social trend?
2. Who are some celebrities these days? Are there any fashions in clothing that these celebrities are making famous?
3. Do people in your country follow fads? If so, what are some fads from the past ten years?
4. Are there any fads that you follow? If so, why do you do this?

PART TWO

BREAKING STEREOTYPES: AN INSIDE LOOK

Skimming for Main Ideas

Read each paragraph quickly, without using a dictionary. Then circle the number of the sentence that best expresses the main idea.

Breaking Stereotypes: An Inside Look

A   People worldwide believe certain stereotypes about people from other countries. Some stereotypes are positive and some are negative, but all are somewhat dangerous—or at least unkind—because they are too general. Although stereotypical ideas are partly right, they are also partly wrong. A stereotype often begins with the word *all*: "All people from that country are poor." "All people in this city are impolite." People who believe a certain stereotype usually do so because they lack knowledge. Before going to another country or after being in that country for only a short time, people often carry many stereotypes with them; they believe that they "know" about the country. However, after living there for a *long* time, meeting many people and having many different experiences there, they change their opinions about stereotypes. As people learn more about another culture, they begin to see and appreciate the great variety of customs, educational levels, beliefs, and lifestyles.

1. Stereotypes are always wrong.
2. It's good to live in another country for a long time and learn about different lifestyles.
3. People who don't know much about another culture may have over-simplified ideas—stereotypes—about it.
4. There is a variety of lifestyles in every culture.

B   I remember I used to believe a lot of stereotypes about North Americans. Before I came here to travel (and later to live for a few years), I thought that I already knew about American and Canadian culture. For example, I used to think that everyone here spent a lot of time and money on new fads. I thought that most people were rich workaholics who lived in the suburbs and commuted to the cities every day. I was sure that all American families drove their big cars to baseball games every weekend, where they drank beer and ate hot dogs. I was certain that nobody knew anything about my country or world politics. As I visited people in dif-

ferent parts of the States and Canada, however, many of my ideas changed.
I discovered that it's difficult to describe a "typical" North American.

1. People who live in the United States have different lifestyles from
   people who live in Canada.
2. Everyone has a lot of stereotypes about North Americans.
3. Most North Americans follow fads, go to baseball games, have big
   cars, live in the suburbs, and know nothing about other countries.
4. Ideas that people have about another culture can change when they've
   actually spent time with different people from that culture.

C   When I first came here on vacation, I stayed in motels, ate in inexpensive restaurants, and concentrated on going sightseeing to places such
as Disneyland. It was interesting, but I didn't get to know any of the
people here. I saw them in public places, but I didn't know how they lived.
So I contacted a friend of my parents by phone, and she invited me to
stay with her family for a few days. The Harrison family lives in a small
town in Connecticut, which almost seems to be a suburb of New York
City. The wife, Gina (my parents' friend), takes a commuter train to work
in New York, where she teaches languages at a two-year college. Her
husband, Robert ("Bob"), is a police officer who hopes to retire before he
turns fifty. He dreams of moving to a small house on top of a mountain
somewhere in the countryside, where he wants to cut wood, catch fish,
write a novel, and "live a simple life." Gina laughs and says they can't

afford to live a simple life because the two kids will need to go to college in a few years. Their kids seem to follow each new fad that comes along (e.g., pictures of rock music stars all over their bedrooms). They go to school, of course, but they're also interested in so many other activities—school plays, football, guitar lessons, etc.—that they're almost never home. The Harrisons are a busy family with a lot of energy. They don't spend much time together because each family member has his or her own interests. In some ways, the Harrisons fit my stereotypical ideas of a North American family.

1. The Harrisons fit several of the stereotypes of a "typical" American family.
2. Most Americans and Canadians dislike their lifestyles and want to move to the countryside.
3. The members of the Harrison family don't seem to love each other very much because they never spend any time together.
4. It's interesting to go sightseeing to places such as Disneyland, but it's also interesting to see how people actually live.

D   While I was at the Harrisons', Bob contacted a friend of his in San Francisco. He mentioned me in his letter, and I received an invitation to stay with Craig Burton and Lisa McKinney when I traveled west. Craig and Lisa are a couple who live downtown in an old house that they are trying to renovate; they can't pay workers to fix up their house, so they're doing most of the renovation work themselves. Lisa and Craig met each other years ago when they were both traveling around Europe. Typical college students of the time, they were interested in politics and impatient for social change, so together they demonstrated against war and worked to solve social problems. Nevertheless, when they had to get jobs, they gave up most of their political activities, and nowadays they don't travel much, either. They get pleasure and satisfaction from working on their house; they also enjoy yardwork, and when they have free time, they invite friends to weekend barbecues. Their values and goals are different now from twenty years ago; nevertheless, for me, Lisa and Craig present a contrast to the "typical American family."

1. Lisa and Craig got married after they traveled around Europe, and now they are living in an old house.
2. Because they weren't successful in changing society through political action, they got jobs and stopped traveling.
3. A couple without children who live in a downtown area present a contrast to the stereotype of the American family.
4. People don't keep the same values and goals that they had when they were in college.

E   I think that my favorite visit was with the least typical American "family" I met during my travels. There were eight elderly people—from sixty-five to eighty-five years old—living together in a communal home. One warm summer afternoon, as we sat and talked in their backyard, the family told me about the problems of the elderly in North America. Many older people not only have unavoidable health problems but also financial difficulties; besides, they often feel unsafe, useless, and alone. By contrast, the enthusiastic people in *this* group have great energy and interest in life. They can satisfy their needs and get help from others in their communal house. Several of them are good cooks; some enjoy yard work; others provide transportation to the store, the doctor, and so on; still others offer entertainment—they play the piano, sing and dance, tell stories, etc. The most important advantages of their lifestyle, however, are the security, the sense of importance, the self-confidence, and the friendship that these elderly people offer one another. I consider my experience with this family one of the most valuable of my trip.

1. The communal lifestyle may provide many advantages to older people who no longer live in the "typical American family."
2. Elderly people who live alone often get sick and are afraid of crime.
3. If people have the opportunity, they will choose to live in big family groups rather than in couples or alone.
4. A good place to stay when you travel is in a communal house because there are many people to talk to.

Viewpoint

In your opinion, which family did the speaker in the selection in Part Two like the most? The least? Why do you think so?

Discussing the Reading

1. What stereotypes did you have of North Americans before you knew much about their culture? Have your ideas changed?
2. What stereotypes do people from other countries have about *your* culture? How are these ideas incorrect?
3. Which lifestyle from the reading is most similar to your own? How?

PART THREE

BUILDING VOCABULARY AND STUDY SKILLS

Suffixes and Prefixes

> Suffixes (word endings), such as *-er, -sion,* and *-ive,* often indicate the part of speech of a word (see the list on page 46). Here are some more suffixes, listed by the parts of speech that they usually indicate.
>
> | Nouns | Verbs | Adjective | Adverb |
> |-------|-------|-----------|--------|
> | -ess | -ate | -less | -ly |
> | -ship | -ize | | |
> | -ism | -en | | |

A. Write *n* on the lines before the nouns, *v* on the lines before verbs, *adj* before adjectives, and *adv* before adverbs. In some cases, two answers are correct. (If necessary, refer to the list of suffixes on page 46.)

1. *n* attention
2. *n* entertainment
3. *n* organization
4. *adj* international
5. *n v* vacation
6. *n* visitor
7. *n* information
8. *adj* hopeful
9. *n* general
10. *adj* typical
11. *adj* pleasant
12. *n* individualism

13. *adj* communal
14. *adv* exactly
15. *v* worsen
16. *adj* frequently
17. *n* workaholism
18. *n* tourist
19. *adj* religious
20. *v* participate
21. *n* hostess
22. *n* experience
23. *n* traveler
24. *n* member

25. *adj* enjoyable
26. *adj* positive
27. *n* description
28. *v* concentrate
29. *v* renovate *to fix up*
30. *adv* socially
31. *n* friendship
32. *v* memorize
33. *adj* dangerous
34. *adv* impatiently
35. _____ characteristic

The prefix (beginning) of a word sometimes gives a clue to its meaning. Some prefixes create a word with an opposite meaning.

Examples: We've <u>discovered</u> many <u>unusual</u> hotels in our travels. (<u>Discover</u> means to "uncover" information—i.e., to find out something that we didn't know before. <u>Unusual</u> means "not usual"—i.e., out of the ordinary.)

The following prefixes can have the meaning "no" or "not."

un-   in-   im-   dis-

B. Use one of the prefixes above to change each word into its opposite. Use your dictionary, if necessary.

1. *un*pleasant

2. *im*patient

3. *in*expensive

4. *un*characteristic

5. *un*avoidable

6. *un*usual

7. *un*safe

8. *in*frequent

9. *dis*count

10. *dis*advantage

11. *im*possible

12. *un*interesting

Here are some other prefixes with their usual meanings.

con-/com- = with, together
ex-/e- = out of, from
inter- = between, among
mis- = wrong

pre- = first, before
re- = again, back
trans- = across

C. The definitions on the right are based on the meanings of prefixes. Match them with the words on the left by writing the letters on the lines.

1. _g_   reflect
2. _i_   contact
3. _c_   transit
4. _a_   international
5. _j_   preparation
6. _b_   experience
7. _e_   replace
8. _d_   prevent
9. _h_   combination
10. _f_   concentrate

a. among different countries
b. get knowledge from life (not books)
c. moving people or things across places
d. stop something before it happens
e. provide something again
f. put together in one place
g. throw back; give back an image of
h. joining together of people or things
i. get together or talk with
j. getting ready for something before it happens

Some words have only one meaning. You can find the meaning in a dictionary entry, which sometimes includes an example.

D. Read these dictionary entries and answer the questions about them.

sight·see·ing /ˈsaɪtˌsiʸɪŋ/ *n*   visiting places of interest usu. while on a vacation: *We often go sightseeing.* -see also SIGHT[1]   **-sightseer** /ˈsaɪtˌsiʸər/ *n*

ren·o·vate /ˈrɛnəˌveʸt/ *v* **-vated, -vating**   to repair; put back into good condition: *to renovate an old house* **-renovation** /ˌrɛnəˈveʸʃən/ *n*

1.   What part of speech is *sightseeing?* __n__

2.   What is the dictionary definition of the word? _____
     _____ visiting places of interest usu. while on a _____ vacation. _____

3.   What word is related to it? __sightseer__

4.   What part of speech is *renovate?* __v__

5.   What is the dictionary definition of the word? __to repair put back__
     _____ into condition _____
     _____

6.   What word is related to it? __renovation__

Most words, however, have more than one meaning. Often the same word can be more than one part of speech, and each part of speech can have different meanings.

Example: The word <u>style</u> is most commonly a noun. In the first dictionary entry, it has five meanings; the last meaning is part of a hyphenated phrase. <u>Style</u> can also be a verb, with two other forms.

style[1] /staɪl/ *n*   1 a general way of doing something: *the modern style of building|a formal style of writing*   2 fashion, esp. in clothes: *the style of the 30's*   3 a type or sort, esp. of goods: *They sell every style of mirror.|a hair style*   4 high quality of social behavior, appearance, or manners: *She gives dinner parties* **in style** (= in a grand way), *with the best food and wine.*   5 **-style** in the manner of a certain person, place, etc.: *He wears his hair short, military-style.*
style[2] *v* **styled, styling**   to form in a certain pattern, shape, etc.: *The dress is carefully styled.*

E. Refer to the dictionary entries above to answer these questions.

1. What part of speech is the word *style* when it means "fashion, especially in clothes?" _n_ Give an example of this use of the word in a phrase. _style of 30's_

2. How many meanings does the word *style* have as a noun? _5_ As a verb? _1_

3. Write the part of speech of the word *style* in each of these sentences.

   When they travel, they go in *style*. _n_

   The couple preferred a modern *style* of life. _n_

   All the people in the house *styled* their own hair. _v_

4. Write the dictionary definition of the word *style* in each of these sentences.

   When they travel, they go in *style*. _high quality of social behavior, appearance or manners._

   The couple preferred a modern *style* of life. _a general way of doing something the modern style of building a formal style of_

   All the people in the house *styled* their own hair. _v. to form in a certain pattern, shape_

   In my travels, I saw many *styles* of furniture, clothing, etc. _a type or sort esp. of goods._

F. Read the following dictionary entries, paying close attention to the parts of speech, the different meanings, and the examples for each meaning. Then write the part of speech and the meaning of the underlined word in each sentence.

1. There have been travelers' organizations for many years; they are not a <u>novel</u> idea.

   adjective — new

   Are you going to write a <u>novel</u> about all your experiences?

   _____

nov·el[1] /ˈnɑvəl/ *n*   a long written story dealing with invented people and events: *"War and Peace," the great novel by Leo Tolstoy*
novel[2] *adj*   new; not like anything known before; *a novel suggestion, something we hadn't tried before*

2. The communal houses were <u>concentrated</u> in the downtown area of the city.

   verb — to (cause)

   The family made drinks from a <u>concentrate</u>.

   noun — form of something

   Workaholics are always <u>concentrating</u> on their jobs.

   verb — to keep or driect

con·cen·trate[1] /ˈkɑnsənˌtreɪt/ *v* **-trated, -trating**   1 [*on, upon*] to keep or direct (all one's thoughts, efforts, attention, etc.): *You should concentrate on the road when you're driving.|If you don't concentrate more on your work, you'll lose your job!*   2 to (cause to) come together in or around one place: *Industrial development is concentrated in the Northeast.| The crowds concentrated in the center of the town near the stores.*
concentrate[2] *n*   a CONCENTRATED (1) form of something; *orange juice concentrate*

3. It's easier to get a job if you have the right <u>contacts</u>.

   noun — joperson one knows who can help us

   Before you arrive, you have to <u>contact</u> your host by telephone.

   verb — to get in touch with someon

   I've lost <u>contact</u> with the friends I made during my travels.

   noun — conditition of meeting

con·tact[1] /ˈkɑntækt/ *n*   1 the condition of meeting, touching, or receiving information from: *Have you been in contact with your sister recently?|to make contact with the ship by radio|She has lost all contact with reality.*   2 *infml* a social or business connection; person one knows who can help one: *I've got a contact in the tax office. She can help us.*   3 an electrical part that can be moved to touch another part to complete an electrical CIRCUIT
contact[2] *v*   to get in touch with (someone); reach (someone) by telephone, etc.

4. I very much value the friendships I
    made on my travels.

    Verb — to consider to be
    of gre

    That hotel has comfortable rooms for the
    money; it is an excellent value.

    n — worth compared with
    the amount paid

    What is the present value of the house
    where you live?

    n — the worth something in
    money or as comared with

5. The people I stayed with downtown were
    my favorites.

    n — something or someone
    that is loved above all others

    The children fought with each other
    because their parents had favorites.

    n — some who receives too
    much favor

    What is your favorite city for
    sightseeing?

    adj — being a favorite

val·ue[1] /ˈvælyuʷ/ *n*   1 [U] the degree of usefulness of something: *You'll find this map of great value/of little value in helping you to get around the city.* |*The government sets a higher value on defense* (= considers it more important) *than on education.*   2 [C;U] the worth of something in money or as compared with other goods for which it might be changed: *Because of continual price increases, the value of the dollar has fallen in recent years.*|*I bought this old painting for $50, but its real value must be about $500.*|*The thieves took some clothes and a few books, but nothing of great value.*   3 [U] worth compared with the amount paid: *We offer the best value in the city: only three dollars for lunch with coffee and dessert.*|*You always get value for your money at that store.* (= the goods are always worth the price charged) —see also VALUES; WORTHLESS (USAGE) —**valueless** *adj*

value[2] *v* **-ued, -uing** [T]   1 to calculate the value, price, or worth of (something): *He valued the house and its contents at $75,000.*   2 to consider to be of great worth: *I've always valued your friendship very highly.*

fa·vor·ite[1] *AmE* ‖ **favourite** *BrE* /ˈfeʸvərɪt/ *n*   1 something or someone that is loved above all others: *These books are my favorites.*   2 *derog* someone who receives too much FAVOR[1] (3): *A teacher shouldn't have/make favorites in the class.*   3 (in horseracing) the horse in each race that is expected to win: *The favorite came in second.* —compare OUTSIDER (2) —see FAVORABLE (USAGE)

favorite[2] *AME* ‖ **favourite** *BrE adj*   being a favorite: *What's your favorite television program?* —compare FAVORABLE; see FAVORABLE (USAGE)

PART FOUR

SCANNING FOR INFORMATION

A. Read the following explanation and study the vocabulary.

Most cities offer a lot of activities for people with different lifestyles. Also, there are many activities and classes for people who are trying to change their lifestyles. The advertisements in this section are from an urban newspaper.

turn of the century = a time around the year 1900

inn = a small hotel

word processing = use of a computer to write letters, papers, etc.

career = job; profession

burnout = a person's condition when he or she is very tired of his or her job or way of life and wants a change of lifestyle

meditation = deep, peaceful thinking

voter turnout = the number of people who vote in an election

pamphlet (or brochure) = a small book that explains or describes something

stress = worry or nervousness that is the result of problems

B. Scan the newspaper ads for information. Then match the following telephone numbers with the correct services. Write the letters on the lines.

1. __d__   ZCLA Zen Mountain Center   a. 555-0020
2. __c__   Bret Lyon's Acting Workshop   b. 823-1966
                                           c. 390-4306
3. __a__   Westside Counseling Center   d. 387-2351
                                           e. 555-9802
4. __e__   Rent-a-Word

5. __b__   The Venice Beach House

1.

BED AND BREAKFAST BY THE SEA

Our unique and elegant turn-of-the-century Inn offers the perfect beach hideaway.

Escape on a romantic sojourn: antique suites, blazing fires, and fresh flowers throughout.

Enjoy a champagne breakfast in bed or in the parlor overlooking the gardens.

The Venice Beach House

No. 15, 30th Avenue, Venice 90291
Reservations (213) 823-1966

2.

RENT-A-WORD
Word Processing

Computer Rental Time
$4 per hr. eves. and Suns.
$7 per hr. Mon.-Sat., 9–5
free training
typing service available

11 Elm St.

Los Angeles, CA 90004

555-9802

3.

CAREERS FOR PEOPLE

Job "burnout"?
Looking for new directions?
Professional testing
and consulting to help
you achieve your career goals.
Evening appointments available.

**Joseph Simms, Ph.D.
(213) 395-4169**

5.

1984 Summer Retreat

Zen Meditation

may 29 - august 26

An intensive program of Zen meditation, work, and study in the beautiful San Jacinto Mountains of Southern California. Attend all or part.

ZCLA Zen Mountain Center
905 So Normandie Ave.
Los Angeles, California 90006

(213) 387-2351

4.

- living with change
- anger control
- seminars on personal relationships
- stress relief

555-0020
insurance-approved
free pamphlets

Westside Counseling Center

6.

Self-Expression: VOICE • ACTING

Read about the workshop
in the April PLAYBOY.

New class May 5-6
Bret Lyon, Dr. Fine Arts. Yale
Free Brochure, 390-4306

7.

★ **Volunteers** ★

Tired of party politics?

Voter Registration Program, a non-partisan, tax-deductible citizens' effort to increase the voter turnout, needs you to answer calls on the VOTER HOTLINE.

Call today:
1-800-84-VOTER

C. Which advertisements might the following people call for information? Write the number(s) of the advertisements on the lines. In some cases, more than one answer is possible.

A middle-aged woman has been working as an urban planner for over twenty years. She's a workaholic who hasn't taken a vacation in almost ten years. In the past five years she's begun to hate her job. Where might she go to:

1. _1,5_   relax for a few days in a quiet, beautiful place?

2. _3,4_   get some advice about a change of career?

A police officer has recently quit his job and become a novelist. He loves to write, but he has two problems: He doesn't type well and he hasn't made any money since he quit the police force. Which advertisements might he call about if he wants:

3. _2_   a secretary to type his novel?

4. _3_   someone to tell him about his financial future?

A high-school student is having some serious problems. He doesn't have many friends because he gets angry very easily, and he doesn't express himself well. What can he try that might help him to:

5. _4_   control his anger?

6. _6_   express his ideas and feelings?

D. Answer the following questions about the ads.

1. At the Venice Beach House, where do they serve breakfast? _____
   In bed or in the parlor

2. How much do you have to pay to use the terminal at Rent-a-Word on a Sunday or an evening? _$4_ How much does it cost on a Wednesday morning? _$7_
   What is the fee for training? _free_

3. How does the Westside Counseling Center help people? _Living with change_
   anger control, stress relief, seminars on personal
   relationship.

4. When is the summer retreat in the San Jacinto Mountains open? _May 29, Aug 26_
   Is it possible to attend for only one week? _1 week_

5. What is the Voter Registration Program trying to do? _to increase the_
   voter turnout

6. What kinds of classes does Dr. Bret Lyon offer? _Self - Expression_
_____ _voice - Acting_

E. Discuss other new vocabulary in the newspaper ads. Which ads interest you? Why?

Going Beyond the Text

Bring to class the "calendar" sections from local newspapers and the ads for things to do. Discuss new vocabulary. Summarize the information. Choose things to do and explain your choices.

6

TRAVEL AND TRANSPORTATION

PART ONE

THE ROMANCE OF TRAIN TRAVEL

Getting Started

Look at the picture and discuss it.

1. Where and when is this scene happening?
2. What is going on in the picture?
3. What feelings does the picture give you?
4. What do you think is going to happen next?

Preparing to Read

As you read the following selection, think about the answers to these questions.

1. Why do many people consider train travel romantic?
2. What is the "Orient Express"? What is its history?
3. What do people do on the "Mystery Express"?
4. What special trips can travelers take in India?

The Romance of Train Travel

A   If there is one main characteristic of the modern world that makes our lives different from our grandparents', it is probably speed. We are always on the move, and we don't have much patience with slow systems of transportation. We want to *get* there, and we want to do it *fast!* Car-makers, airline owners, and the planners of mass transit systems all share a common goal. They are all trying to provide us with faster and faster ways to reach our destinations.

B   Nevertheless, many of us actually want to slow down. Although we complain when our plane isn't on schedule or when we have to wait in a traffic jam, we also complain about always being in a hurry. Every once in a while, we hear the sound of a train whistle—clear and high in the night air—and we feel sad. There is a strong sense of nostalgia for other places and other times, when life was slower and, perhaps, better.

C   Why does a train whistle bring on a feeling of nostalgia? Perhaps it's because many of us remember a favorite novel or movie that took place on a train, and the story told of danger and excitement. There's a sense of romance about a train that simply doesn't exist on a modern jet plane. Several railroad companies are taking advantage of the nostalgia for train travel. They are offering unique tours for travelers who aren't in a hurry and who enjoy the romance of the past.

D   For almost a hundred years, the famous Orient Express carried roy-alty (kings and queens from many countries), the rich (such as the Roths-childs and the Vanderbilts), spies like Mata Hari and Sydney Reilly, and dangerous international criminals. It was the scene of mystery, crime, and often history. But after World War II, when air travel became popular, it never got back its old sense of romance, and it finally went out of business in 1977. Soon after that, however, an American businessman began to buy the old Orient Express cars and fix them up. He restored the train to its former condition, and, since 1982, the Venice Simplon Orient-Express (V.S.O.E.) has run twice a week from London to Venice and back. Although the twenty-four-hour trip doesn't offer the danger and excitement—the adventure—of the past, it offers luxury: rich dark wood, fresh flowers, champagne, very special food, and live entertainment in a bar car with a piano.

E   Another famous excursion by train is the Trans-Siberian Special, which makes just three trips each summer from Mongolia to Moscow. As passengers board the train at the beginning of their trip, they toast one another with Russian vodka at a welcoming party. For the next week they cross the Soviet Union with occasional stops for sightseeing in big cities and small villages. In addition, there is a bonus on this trip; this extra advantage is a daily lecture on board the train in which an expert on Soviet life explains Russian history and culture to the passengers.

F   If you are looking for fun and adventure, you might want to try the "Mystery Express," which runs from New York to Montreal, Canada. This trip interests people who have always wanted to play a role in an Agatha Christie play or a Sherlock Holmes detective novel. A typical journey on the Mystery Express offers the opportunity to solve a challenging murder mystery right there on the train. In the middle of the night, for instance, there might be a gunshot; soon, the passengers learn that there has been a "murder" on board. For the rest of the trip, everyone on board participates in solving this mystery by exchanging information and opinions about the crime. By the time the train has pulled into Montreal, the traveling "detectives" will have figured it out and caught the "criminal." Of course, no *real* crime takes place. The "murderer"—as well as several other passengers—are actually actors. The trip is a safe, entertaining, and very creative weekend game.

G   If you're looking for variety and beauty on a train journey, you might want to try the trains of India. The Indian government offers several special tours. One, a fifty-mile trip on the famous "Toy Train," takes seven hours one way. The train travels through rich, luxurious forests with flowers, trees, and more than six hundred varieties of birds. Before it reaches its destination, it makes several stops so that passengers can take photographs or have picnics if they want to.

H   Another tour, "Palace on Wheels," is for travelers with more time and money. Each of the luxurious cars on this train used to belong to a maharajah, or Indian prince. For seven days, passengers go sightseeing to palaces and cities where musicians, camels, and women with flowers meet them.

I   Perhaps the most unusual Indian train is "The Great Indian Rover," for travelers who are interested in religion. On this six-day tour from Calcutta, passengers travel to famous places such as Lumbini (in Nepal), where Buddha was born, and Bodhgaya, where Prince Gautama sat under the bodhi tree and became Buddha.

Getting the Main Ideas

A. Write T on the lines before the statements that are *true,* according to the reading. Write F on the lines before the statements that are *false.*

1. _F_   Most people want to travel on trains because they are fast.

2. _T_   Many exciting stories (in books and in movies) happened on trains.

3. _T_   There are various kinds of special trips that travelers can take by train.

B. Write __O__ in the blanks before the statements about the "Orient Express," __M__ before the statements about the "Mystery Express," __I__ before the statements about train trips in India, and __TS__ before statements about the Trans-Siberian Special.

1. __M__   Travelers try to solve a mystery on the train.

2. __I__   The train travels through beautiful forests and cities, where people stop to go sightseeing.

3. __M__   There are actors on the train who play a game with the travelers during the trip.

4. __O__   The train used to carry kings and queens, rich families, and dangerous international criminals.

5. __O__   This European train no longer offers danger and excitement, but luxury.

6. __I__   People who are interested in Buddhism can visit famous religious places on this trip.

7. __TS__   An expert explains history and culture to passengers on this train.

Guessing Meaning from Context

Many words with one basic meaning have other, secondary meanings that are less common.

Example: Rich people travel on a luxurious train with rich dark wood and fresh flowers. (The basic meaning of rich is "having a lot of money." Before wood, rich means "of high quality.")

A. The underlined words that follow express secondary meanings. For each item, circle the words that give clues to the meaning of the underlined word. Then circle the letter of the appropriate meaning for this context.

1. Since 1982, the Orient Express has run twice a week from London to Venice and back.

   a.   moved its legs at a speed faster than walking
   b.   traveled
   c.   worked
   d.   managed; taken care of

2. It offers live entertainment in a bar car with a piano.

    live:
    a. not dead
    b. have life
    c. carrying electricity
    d. in person; not on T.V. or radio

    car:
    a. part of a train
    b. automobile
    c. form of transportation
    d. motor

3. As passengers board the train at the beginning of their trip, they toast each other with Russian vodka at a welcoming party.

    board:
    a. piece of wood
    b. get off
    c. get on
    d. carry suitcases

    toast:
    a. piece of cooked bread
    b. drink alcohol
    c. cook bread
    d. drink in honor of someone

4. The train travels through rich, luxurious forests with flowers, trees, and more than six hundred varieties of birds.

    rich:
    a. having a lot of money
    b. of high quality
    c. thick and deep
    d. not poor

    luxurious:
    a. very expensive
    b. very comfortable
    c. having places for kings and queens
    d. full of plants and animals

When a word is part of a phrase, it may have a different meaning from the same word by itself.

Example: We had such a busy schedule on our trip that we were always running behind schedule. (A schedule is a time plan of things to do; behind schedule means "late; after the planned time.")

B.   For each item, circle the words that give clues to the meaning of the underlined phrase. Then circle the letter of the appropriate meaning.

1.   We are always on the move, and we don't have much patience with slow systems of transportation.

   a.   taking a train
   b.   going somewhere
   c.   changing from one house to another
   d.   making decisions

2.   Although we complain when our plane isn't on schedule, we also complain about always being in a hurry.

   a.   early
   b.   on time (at the planned time)
   c.   things to do
   d.   on a list

3.   Several railroad companies are taking advantage of people's nostalgia for train travel; they are offering unique tours for travelers who enjoy the romance of the past.

   a.   making use of
   b.   being good for
   c.   doing bad things to
   d.   not telling the truth about

4.   The "Mystery Express" interests people who have always wanted to play a role in an Agatha Christie play or a Sherlock Holmes detective novel.

   play a role:
   a.   watch
   b.   write; create
   c.   read
   d.   take part; act

   detective novel:
   a.   a book about a person who solves mysteries
   b.   a story about an actor
   c.   a person who writes novels
   d.   a train traveler

5. By the time the train has <u>pulled into</u> Montreal, the traveling detectives [*gumshoes*] will have <u>figured out</u> the mystery and caught the criminal.

pulled into:
a. not pushed
b. moved quickly
c. arrived at *(circled)*
d. been on schedule

figured out:
a. understood by thinking *(circled)*
b. used numbers
c. expected
d. written down the solution to

C. Find words in the reading selection with the following meanings and write the words on the lines. The letters in parentheses indicate the paragraphs in which the words appear.

1. rate of movement (A): _speed_
2. goal (last stop) of a trip (A): _destinations_
3. a tube that makes a high, musical sound (B): _whistle_
4. feeling of wanting something from the past (B): _nostalgia_
5. the quality of love or adventure (C): _Romance_
6. people whose job it is to find out secret information (D): _spy_
7. a trip for sightseeing (E): _excursion_
8. towns (E): _villages_
9. extra advantage (E): _bonus_
10. find an answer to (F): _____
11. sound of a murder weapon (F): _gunshot_
12. people who travel on a train, bus, plane, etc. (F): _passengers_
13. a long trip (G): _journey_
14. planned trips that include several places (G): _tours_

D. Read the selection again carefully. Try to guess the meanings of new words from the context. Use your dictionary only when absolutely necessary.
    Check your answers in the "Getting the Main Ideas" section, which follows the reading selection. Correct your errors.

Understanding Reading Structure

Many reading selections follow an *outline*. The outline is the plan of the material; it shows the relationship of the topics and ideas. The general parts of a main topic appear below it, and each part may include details.

Example:

The Romance of Train Travel

I.   Introduction
   A. Speed of the modern world (*a*)
   B. Nostalgia for slower times (*b*)
II. The nostalgia of train travel (*c*)
III. Unique train trips
   A. The Orient Express (*d*)
     1. History
     2. The present
   B. The Trans-Siberian Special (*e*)
   C. The Mystery Express (*f*)
   D. Tours in India
     1. The Toy Train (*g*)
     2. The Palace on Wheels (*h*)
     3. The Great Indian Rover (*i*)

A. The parentheses in the sample outline above indicate paragraphs of the reading selection. Write the letters of the paragraphs inside the appropriate parentheses.

B. Answer these questions about the outline.

1. What is the topic of the whole outline? *The Romance of Train Travel*

2. What two topics form the introduction? *Speed of the modern world Nostalgia for slower times*

3. What topic comes before the descriptions of unique train trips? *The nostalgia of train travel*

4. Which topic includes the history of a train? *The Orient express*

5. How many different tours are there in India? *3*

C. Now circle the number of the *one* main idea of the reading selection.

1. Train travel is no longer popular because it is too slow for the modern world.
2. People feel nostalgic when they hear a train whistle.
3. Journeys on the Mystery Express are more exciting than trips on the Orient Express.
4. Passengers can enjoy luxury, solve mysteries, see beautiful sights, or visit religious places on special train trips.

Making Inferences

> A reading selection often gives information from which a reader can infer (figure out) other information.
>
> *Example:*   Many of us actually want to slow down. When we hear the sound of a train whistle, we feel a strong sense of nostalgia for other times. (These sentences do not say, but they imply, or suggest, that a train whistle reminds us of the past, when trains moved more slowly than modern transportation.)

A. Complete each sentence by circling the letters of *all* the information that the reading states or implies.

1. Trains may make people feel nostalgic because _____ .

   a. they move more slowly than jet planes
   b. they are always on schedule
   c. they remind us of romantic stories of adventure
   d. they are less expensive than cars

2. The Orient Express _____ .

   a. was well-known because exciting things happened on it
   b. carried many important and famous people
   c. did not run for five years
   d. is a European train

3. The Mystery Express _____ .

   a. runs in Europe and Asia
   b. offers more than just a form of transportation
   c. provides entertainment to its passengers in the form of a mystery game
   d. costs more than other train trips because of the actors on board

4.   The Indian "Toy Train" _____ .

    a.   provides a beautiful variety of things to see
    b.   offers a journey of several weeks
    c.   is not in a hurry
    d.   is smaller than other trains because it is for children

5.   The Indian government _____ .

    a.   offers various tours for passengers with different interests
    b.   uses trains that used to belong to Indian royalty
    c.   provides entertainment and religious experiences for passengers on board
        the trains
    d.   is only for people who follow the teachings of Buddha and believe in
        Buddhism

B.   Turn back to the beginning of the chapter and answer the questions in the "Preparing to Read" section.

Discussing the Reading

1.   Have you ever traveled on a train? Describe your most interesting experiences.
2.   Would you like to take any of the trips described in the reading? Which one(s)? Why?
3.   Which kind of travel do you prefer (plane, train, bus, car, ship, etc.)? Why?
4.   Do you ever read mystery stories or see mystery movies? If so, what are your favorites?

PART TWO

MYSTERY ON THE NORTH AMERICAN EXPRESS

Skimming for Main Ideas

Read the parts of this selection quickly, without using a dictionary. After each part, circle the number of the sentence that best expresses the main idea.

Mystery on the North American Express

A   Edward Grimsley, the famous detective, was sitting in the luxurious bar car of the North American Express. He was enjoying a glass of champagne and exchanging stories with other passengers about their favorite journeys. Grimsley always had a good time when he traveled by train; it gave him the opportunity to take it easy for a few days and not think about his work as a private eye. As the train sped across Canada, the few people still in the bar car talked late into the night about travel, politics, entertainment, and even religion.

1. Edward Grimsley liked luxury.
2. A famous detective was traveling on a train.
3. Train travel is a relaxing way to spend time.
4. The North American Express is not a real train line.

B   It was almost 1:00 A.M. when Grimsley, who was feeling very tired, stood up and said, "Well, I guess I'll turn in. Good night, all." He went back to his sleeping compartment, pulled down the bed, and soon fell into a deep sleep.

Early in the morning—much earlier than he wanted to wake up—there was a loud knock on the door of his compartment. Although he was still half asleep, he opened the door and saw a man in a conductor's uniform.

"Sorry to bother you, Mr. Grimsley," the conductor said.

"What?" said Grimsley, not really wide awake yet. "You want to see my ticket? Now? Isn't it a little early?"

"Oh, no, no, no," said the conductor. "Not your ticket. We need your help. You see, there's been a crime on the train. Could you please help us find the criminal?"

Although he was not at all happy about working on a crime during his vacation, Grimsley didn't lose his temper. "I'll meet you in ten minutes," he said sleepily. Then he jumped into his clothes and went to the bar car to meet the conductor, Bill Thornton.

1. Edward Grimsley was a deep sleeper; he got upset when the conductor woke him up.
2. There had been a murder on the train.
3. Grimsley did not want to work during his vacation.
4. The detective agreed to help solve a mystery on the train.

C   Thornton was sitting with a beautiful, well-dressed woman. She looked upset. Her hands were shaking, and her eyes were red. Grimsley thought that she might burst into tears again.

"This is Christina Royal," Thornton said as Grimsley took a seat. "I'm afraid that she's at the end of her rope. Late last night, someone stole a very expensive necklace from her compartment while she was sleeping."

"How did the thief get in?" asked Grimsley.

Christina Royal shook her head. "I haven't the slightest idea," she answered. "My door was locked." She looked sadly at Grimsley. "Oh, please find the person who took my necklace. It belonged to my grandmother and to her mother and before that to the wife of a maharajah!"

"Don't worry—we'll get to the bottom of this," Grimsley said. "I'll need to ask some questions, and I'll have to see a list of the passengers on board."

"Right here," Thornton said, as he gave Grimsley the passenger list.

"Hmmm," Grimsley said as he looked over the list. "I see that Willie Brown is on board. He's a well-known thief who just got out of prison last month."

Thornton jumped up. "That's him! He's the thief! Let's go to his compartment and get the necklace! Then when we pull into Toronto, we'll turn him over to the police."

1. A thief stole a very expensive necklace from a passenger's compartment.
2. Christina Royal was very upset about the crime because the necklace had belonged to a maharajah.
3. Grimsley is going to study the list of passengers to solve the mystery.
4. Thornton is going to get back the necklace for Christina Royal.

D

"Hold your horses," Grimsley said, with one hand on Thornton's shoulder. "What?"

"Sit down and be patient," Grimsley said. "Don't be in such a hurry. We don't want to point the finger at the wrong person."

"Of course not," said Thornton. "You're right. Sorry! I've never caught a criminal before. Sure, I've read a lot of underlined whodunits, and I've seen a lot of mysteries in the movies, but there's never been a real crime on any train that I've worked on—not even back in 1980, when I worked for a few months on the Orient Express, where you might expect a crime!" Thornton grinned from ear to ear. "But I love a good mystery," he said happily. "Now we've got a real one, and I guess I'm a little too enthusiastic. I'm sorry I jumped the gun. I'll try to be more patient."

"Good," said the detective, "because I now know who the thief is—and it's not Willie Brown."

1. Edward Grimsley is a careful detective who thinks a lot about a crime before he solves the mystery.
2. Bill Thornton has read and seen a lot of mystery stories.
3. Thornton has never solved a crime on a train.
4. While Grimsley was talking to Thornton, he figured out the solution to the mystery.

Understanding Idioms

> An idiom is a phrase that means something different from the individual words in it. Idioms are common in informal English. The reading selection contained many of them.
>
> *Example:*   It was very early in the morning. Although Grimsley was not really <u>wide awake</u> yet, he <u>jumped into his clothes</u>, left his sleeping compartment, and went to the bar car to meet the conductor.

A. To figure out the meaning of the underlined idioms in the example above, answer the following questions.

1. What time of day was it? *It was very early in the morning*

2. How do people usually feel at that time? *was not really wide awake yet*

3. What does <u>wide awake</u> mean? *awake all the way*

4. What was Grimsley probably wearing at that time? *He probably wearing jeans. or*

5. What did he have to do before he left his sleeping compartment? *he jumped into his clothes*

6. What does <u>jumped into his clothes</u> mean? *be ready to go out*

B. For each of the following items, find an idiom in the reading that has a similar meaning and write it on the line.

SECTION A

1. enjoyed himself: *had a good time*
2. relax: *to take it easy for few days and not think about his work*
3. detective: *private eye*

SECTION B

1. go to bed: *turn in*
2. sleepy: *Half sleep*
3. not at all sleepy: *wide awake*
4. get angry: *Lose his temp (Raise voice)*
5. got dressed: *jumped into clothes*

jumped the Gun
to be nasty

SECTION C

1. begin to cry: _eyes were red. (burst into tears)_
2. sat down: _took seat_
3. feeling hopeless, not seeing a solution: _at the ends of her rope_
4. don't know at all: _slightest idea_
5. find the cause: _get to the bottom of this month_

SECTION D

1. don't rush into a decision quickly: _Hold your horse_
2. accuse of doing something wrong: _to point the finger at the wrong person_
3. mysteries: _whodunit_
4. smiled broadly: _grinned from ear to ear_
5. started to do something before he should: _I jumped the Gun_

Making Inferences

A reading selection often gives information from which a reader can infer (figure out) other information.

Read each section carefully. On the short lines, put a check next to each statement that you can infer from the information in that section. Do not check the other statements, even if you think they are true. On the line after each statement that you check, write the phrases from which you inferred the information.

1. Edward Grimsley, the famous detective, was sitting in the luxurious bar car of the North American Express. He was enjoying a glass of champagne and exchanging stories with other passengers about their favorite journeys. Grimsley always had a good time when he traveled by train. As the train sped across Canada, the few people still in the bar car talked late into the night about travel, politics, entertainment, and even religion.

   a. __✓__ Edward Grimsley liked champagne. _was enjoying a glass of champagne_

   b. _____ Grimsley liked to stay up late to talk about things other than mysteries. _talked late into the night about travel, politics, entertainment, and even religion_

c. _____   Grimsley traveled only by train because he was afraid of planes.

He always had a good time when he traveled by train

d. _____   Grimsley has solved mysteries in the past. *Famous detective*

politics, entertainment, and even religion

2. Early in the morning, there was a loud knock on the door of Grimsley's compartment. He opened the door and saw a man in a conductor's uniform.

"Sorry to bother you, Mr. Grimsley," the conductor said.

"What?" said Grimsley, not really wide awake yet. "You want to see my ticket? Now? Isn't it a little early?"

"Oh, no, no, no," said Bill Thornton. "Not your ticket. We need your help. You see, there's been a crime on the train. Could you please help us find the criminal?"

a. _____   Bill Thornton was the train conductor. _____

_____

b. _____   It was Thornton's job to solve mysteries on the train. _____

_____

c. _____   Conductors collect tickets from passengers. _____

_____

d. _____   A criminal has murdered a passenger. *there's been a crime*
on the train

3. Thornton was sitting with a beautiful, well-dressed woman. She looked upset.

"This is Christina Royal," Thornton said as Grimsley took a seat. "I'm afraid that she's at the end of her rope. Late last night, someone stole a very expensive necklace from her compartment while she was sleeping."

"How did the thief get in?" asked Grimsley.

Christina Royal shook her head. "I haven't the slightest idea," she answered. "My door was locked." She looked sadly at Grimsley. "Oh, please find the person who took my necklace. It belonged to my grandmother and to her mother and before that to the wife of a maharajah!"

a. _____   The train conductor was in love with Christina Royal. _____

_____

b. _____   Christina was upset because her necklace was gone. _____

_____

c. _____   The thief may have a key to Christina's compartment. _____

_____

Hate · ceiling = become very angry

Fork over = Hand over or give

d. _____ Christina's grandmother is going to be very angry at her. _____

_____

4. "Don't worry—we'll get to the bottom of this," Grimsley said. "I'll need to ask some questions, and I'll have to see a list of the passengers on board."

"Right here," Thornton said, as he gave Grimsley the passenger list.

"Hmmm," Grimsley said as he looked over the list. "I see that Willie Brown is on board. He's a well-known thief who just got out of prison last month."

Thornton jumped up. "That's him! He's the thief! Let's go to his compartment and get the necklace! Then when we pull into Toronto, we'll turn him over to the police."

a. _____ Willie Brown is a train passenger who has stolen things before.

_____

b. _____ Thornton appears to believe Willie Brown stole Christina's necklace.

_____

c. _____ Grimsley believes that Willie Brown is the thief. _____

_____

d. _____ Thornton wants to turn Willie Brown over to the police. _____

_____

5. "Sit down and be patient," Grimsley said. "Don't be in such a hurry. We don't want to point the finger at the wrong person."

"Of course not," said Thornton. "You're right. Sorry! I've never caught a criminal before. Sure, I've read a lot of whodunits, and I've seen a lot of mysteries in the movies, but there's never been a real crime on any train that I've worked on—not even back in 1980, when I worked for a few months on the Orient Express, where you might expect a crime!" Thornton grinned from ear to ear. "But I love a good mystery," he said happily. I'm sorry I jumped the gun. I'll try to be more patient."

"Good," said the detective, "because I now know who the thief is—and it's not Willie Brown."

a. _____ Thornton is an impatient person. _____

_____

b. _____ Thornton mentions he worked on the Orient Express train line in 1980.

_____

c. _____ Thornton has been telling the truth. _____

_____

d. _____ The thief is not Willie Brown. _____

_____

Discussing the Reading

Reread the paragraph on page 94. Use the information in it to solve the mystery. (The answer is on page 119.) Talk about your answers to these questions.

1. Who was the thief?
2. How do you know?

PART THREE

BUILDING VOCABULARY AND STUDY SKILLS

Expressions and Idioms

A. Complete each sentence with the missing words. Choose from these expressions.

play a role	half asleep	in a hurry
behind schedule	burst into tears	turn in
at the end of his rope	private eye	lose his temper
take photographs	take advantage of	

ahead of schedule

1. People who are always ___*in a hurry*___ complain when their plane is ___*behind schedule*___.

2. Tourists like to travel slowly so that they can ___*take advantage of*___ the beautiful places on their tours; they often stop with their cameras to ___*take photographs*___ .

3. The detective knew that the woman he was talking to was lying: she wasn't a rich princess at all, but she knew how to ___*play a role*___ . Even her crying was an act; she didn't really need to ___*burst into tears*___ at all.

4. "That was a great book," said the passenger as he put down his mystery novel. "Some day I'd like to become a ___*private eye*___ and solve crimes myself."

5. "I'm too sleepy to talk anymore," Grimsley said. "In fact, I'm ___*half asleep*___ already, so I'm going to go to my compartment and ___*turn in*___ ."

6. The man was so upset about the crime that he didn't know what to do; he was ___*at the end of his rope*___ ; he was also angry, so he began to ___*lose his temper*___ as he talked.

Many dictionaries provide the meanings of expressions and idioms, as well as individual words. These phrases appear in the same entries as the most important word in the phrases.

Example: This entry includes two expressions with the word train: by train means "in a train"; train of thought means "a chain of thoughts."

> **train**[1] /treʸn/ *n*   1 a line of connected railroad cars drawn by an engine: *to travel* **by train**   2 a long line of moving people, vehicles, or animals   3 a part of the back of a long dress that spreads over the ground   4 a chain of related events, thoughts, etc.: *The telephone rang and interrupted my* **train of thought.**

B. Read the meanings of the expressions and idioms in the following dictionary entries. Then complete the sentences that follow with the correct forms of the appropriate phrases.

[I]· Intransitive = No direct object
[T]· Transitive =

> **board**[1] /bɔrd, boʷrd/ *n*   1 [C] a long thin flat piece of cut wood; PLANK[1] (1)   2 [C] a flat piece of hard material used for a particular purpose: *She put the list on the* BULLETIN BOARD. |*He wrote the date on the* BLACK-BOARD. a nail sticking out of the FLOORBOARD   3 [U] (the cost of) meals: *I pay $100 a week for room and board.*   4 [C *often cap.*] a committee or association, as of company directors, government officials, etc., with special responsibility: *He has joined/been elected to the board of a new company.|Mary is a workers' representative on the Board. | The Board is meeting the union today in the* **boardroom.**   5 **above board** (usu. of an action in business) completely open and honest   6 **across the board** including all groups or members, as in an industry: *a wage increase of $20 a week across the board*   7 **on board** in or on (a ship or public vehicle): *They got on board the train.|She enjoys life on board ship.* —compare ABOARD

> **jump**[1] /dʒʌmp/ *v*   1 [I] to push oneself into the air by the force of one's legs; spring: *The horse jumped over the fence.|She jumped out of the window.|*(fig.) *He keeps jumping from one subject of conversation to another.*   2 [T] to spring over: *The dog jumped the stream.*   3 [I] to make a quick sudden anxious movement: *The noise of the gun made him jump.*   4 [I] (esp. of prices and quantities) to rise suddenly and sharply: *The price of oil jumped sharply in 1973.*   5 **jump the gun** to start something (like a race) too soon   6 **jump down someone's throat** *infml* to begin to disagree with someone before they have finished talking.
> **jump at** sthg.   *v prep* [T]   to be eager to accept: *She jumped at the chance to go abroad.*

1. It was time for the train to leave, so all the passengers got
   on board .

2. Everyone who worked at the company got higher paychecks; it was an increase in salary _across the board_.

3. The detective didn't believe the businessman's claims; he didn't think his company was _above board_ .

4. I love mysteries, so I would _jump at_ the chance to help solve one.

5. When you buy expensive merchandise, you should always make careful choices; you shouldn't _jump the gun_ and decide too quickly.

6. Please let me speak and don't get angry; you don't have to _jump down my throat_

C. Read these sentences. Look up the meanings of the underlined idioms in your dictionary. Then match the idioms in the left-hand column with their meanings on the right by writing the letters on the lines.

I think I'd be good at it; I hit the nail on the head in this one.

They like to take their time.

She was crying only crocodile tears.

"I'm dead tired."

Finally he hit the roof.

They like to get the show on the road as quickly as possible.

1. _a_	take one's time	a. not hurry; move in a relaxed way
2. _d_	hit the nail on the head	b. very sleepy
3. _f_	crocodile tears	c. start an activity
4. _c_	get the show on the road	d. figure out something; get it exactly right
5. _b_	dead tired	e. get very angry
6. _e_	hit the roof	f. fake (not real) tears

Increasing Reading Speed

The following exercises may help you to improve your left-to-right eye movements and to increase your reading speed.

Your teacher will tell you when to begin each section. Look at the underlined phrase to the left of each line. Read across the line, from left to right. Circle the phrases that are the same as the underlined phrase. At the end of each section, write down your time (the number of seconds it took you to finish). Try to read faster with each section.

play a role	play a game	eat a roll	play a role
	read a role	play a role	roll a ball
on schedule	behind schedule	on schedule	on schedule
	a train schedule	on schedule	to schedule
half asleep	in a deep sleep	very sleepy	half asleep
	half asleep	sleeping deeply	half asleep
in a hurry	in a hurry	hurry up	in a hurry
	no hurry	in a hurry	in a hurry
turn in	turn up	turn out	turn in
	turn in	turn on	turn over

Time: _____

private eye	private eye	private life	in private
	private eye	private car	private school
by train	train track	by train	train of thought
	by train	in the rain	train line
take your time	on time	take your time	behind the times
	take your time	time after time	take your time
hit the roof	hit the roof	hit the roof	hit the roof
	hit the ball	get a hit	hit the roof
on the road	on the way	on the road	hit the road
	on the road	the roadway	in the road

Time: _____

mail order	mail order	mail a letter	order mail
	mail order	mail order	mail order
charge account	charge it	charge account	charge an order
	charge account	bring a charge	charge account
drug addiction	addicted to drugs	drug addicts	drug addiction
	drug addiction	drug addiction	drug addiction
lifestyles	style of life	in high style	lifestyle
	lifestyles	lead a life	lifestyles
see the sights	see the sights	sightseeing	eyesight
	keep sight	see the sights	sight something

Time: _____

tour rates	tour rates	touring cars	tour rating
	taking tours	tour rates	touring rate
scenic drive	drive to scenery	scenic drive	dull scenery
	scenic route	scenic drive	scenic drive
water cascade	waterfall	water cascade	water cascade
	cascading water	water cascade	water cascade
volcanic rock	volcano rock	volcanic steam	volcanic rock
	volcano rock	volcanic action	volcanic rock
festive dinner	festive time	festive dinner	fancy dinner
	fun dining	festive dinner	fun festival

Time: _____

international flavor	international place	international tour
	go international	international flavor
en route	en route	in route
	a route	
national park	national park	nation of parks
	national parking	national park service
head toward	head back	heading for
	head toward	head toward
	head toward	head toward
elegant hotels	elegant hotels	elegance in hotels
	elegantly dressed	elegant hotels

Time: _____

rolling hills	roll up the hill	rolling hills
	eating rolls	rolling highways
Continental Divide	continent of Europe	Continental Divide
	divide continents	continental tour
hearty breakfast	heart attack	heartfelt thanks
	hurtful breaks	hearty breakfast
end the journey	end the journey	the journey's end
	the end of a journey	end the journey
overnight stay	stay overnight	overnight hotel
	overnight stay	stay over for the night

Time: _____

PART FOUR

SCANNING FOR INFORMATION

A. Read the following explanation and study the vocabulary.

When we're planning a vacation, we usually read travel brochures to help us make decisions. Pages 116–118 are taken from a pamphlet about train tours of North America.

motorcoach = bus

board = get on (a train, bus, ship, or plane)

view = see

lodge = a hotel (usually in the mountains)

calves

tour = go from place to place

ferry = boat

head toward = go to; go in the direction of

glacier = a large "river" of ice

ABBREVIATIONS

NY = New York

Chi = Chicago

Dep = depart (leave)

Ret = return

B. Scan the brochure on the following pages and answer these questions.

You can find the answers to the following questions on the map.

1. According to the map, in which two cities may passengers join this tour?

   _____ *N. Y.   Chicango* _____

2. How (by what means of transportation) will they get from New York to Salt Lake City? *Train* From Bozeman to Seattle? *fly* From Seattle to Victoria? *ferry* From Jasper National Park to Lake Louise? *Bus*

3. How many national parks will passengers visit on this tour? *5* How many countries will they see? *2*

You can find the answers to the following questions in the schedule.

4. How many days will people who join the tour in Chicago travel? *20 days*

MAJESTIC AMERICANA [R]
20 Days from Chicago— $3098 to $3498
23 Days from New York— $3648 to $4358

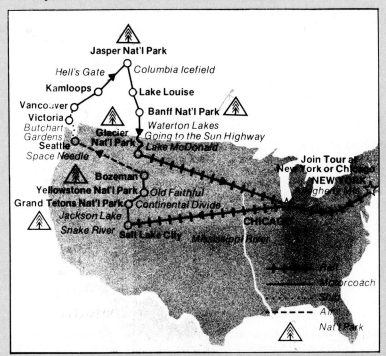

Best of the Northwest & Canadian Rockies: Lake Louise, Jasper, Banff Glacier, Grand Teton & Yellowstone Nat'l Parks

Day 1 Tue—NEW YORK: Our Four Winds adventure will begin when we board the *Broadway Ltd.* at Penn Station. Enjoy dinner while we cruise to Chicago!   **Broadway Ltd.** *D*

Day 2 Wed—CHICAGO/THE "LOOP"/LAKEFRONT DRIVE: We arrive in Chicago. We'll see the "Loop," then travel Lake Shore Drive. Later, board the *California Zephyr* with our Chicago tour members.   **California Zephyr** *B-L-D*

Day 3 Thu—RAIL CRUISING/SALT LAKE CITY: Take advantage of our train's observation car as we travel through the Rocky Mountains to Utah.   **Little America** *B-L-D*

Day 4 Fri—SALT LAKE CITY: Look forward to a morning tour of Salt Lake City, including the Great Salt Lake. Later, we'll go to the historic Temple Square for an organ recital. Get ready for tonight's welcome dinner.   **Little America** *B-D*

Day 5 Sat—GRAND TETONS: Enjoy a scenic drive to the Grand Teton Mountains through beautiful country.   **Inn at Jackson Hole** *B-L*

Day 6 Sun—SNAKE RIVER FLOAT TRIP/ YELLOWSTONE: Today view the Grand Teton valley up close when Four Winds takes you on a gentle Snake River raft cruise. We'll lunch at Jackson Lake Lodge before continuing on to Yellowstone.   **Old Faithful Inn** *B-L-D*

Day 7 Mon—YELLOWSTONE NAT'L PARK/ FOUNTAIN PAINTPOTS: This afternoon we'll tour the dazzling Fountain Paintpots of molten clay, opal and quartz. **Lake Yellowstone Hotel** *B-L-D*

Day 8 Tue — MUD VOLCANO/MAMMOTH HOT SPRINGS/SEATTLE: In Canyon Village we view a mud volcano then visit Mammoth Hot Springs—a dazzling hot water cascade. We'll fly to Seattle this evening.   **Park Hilton** *B-L*

Day 9 Wed—SEATTLE TOUR/SPACE NEEDLE: This afternoon we tour the "City of Seven Hills." Tonight Four Winds hosts a festive dinner at the 600-foot high Space Needle.   **Park Hilton** *B-D*

Day 10 Thu—PUGET CRUISE/VICTORIA: Today we take a lovely morning ferry across Puget Sound to enchanting Victoria. You'll have the afternoon free.   **The Empress** *B-D*

Day 11 Fri—BUTCHART GARDENS/VAN- COUVER: This morning we savor the international flavor of Butchart Gardens. Later we'll ferry to Vancouver.   **Hyatt Regency** *B*

Day 12 Sat—VANCOUVER: Today we tour delightful Vancouver.   **Hyatt Regency** *B*

Day 13 Sun—FRASER CANYON/HELL'S GATE/KAMLOOPS: After breakfast, we ride to Kamloops. We'll see Fraser Canyon and take an aerial tram at Hell's Gate.   **Hospitality Inn** *B-L*

HOW YOU WILL TRAVEL

The **MAJESTIC AMERICANA** travels via deluxe motorcoach and in sleeper accommodations on North America's great name trains. All tours utilize a combination of Std. Pullman and Superliner sleeping cars. Tour rates are the same for both. Here's how you will travel:

From/To	Train	Equipment
NY/Chi/NY	*Broadway Limited*	Std. Pullman
Chi/Salt Lk.	*California Zephyr*	Superliner
Glacier/Chi	*Empire Builder*	Superliner

Meals: B—Breakfast; L—Lunch; D—Dinner. 51 meals included out of 65; 22B; 13L; 16D.

Departs Tue./Returns Wed.—23 Days

Tour #	Dep:NY	Join:Chi	Ret:Chi	Ret:NY
RE-341	Jun 19	Jun 20	Jul 9	Jul 11
RE-342	Jul 10	Jul 11	Jul 30	Aug 1
RE-343	Jul 17	Jul 18	Aug 6	Aug 8
RE-344	Jul 24	Jul 25	Aug 13	Aug 15
RE-345	Aug 7	Aug 8	Aug 27	Aug 29
RE-346	Aug 21	Aug 22	Sep 10	Sep 12
RE-347	Sep 4	Sep 5	Sep 24	Sep 26

Day 14 Mon—KAMLOOPS/YELLOWHEAD PASS/JASPER NAT'L PARK: Head for Jasper Nat'l Park this morning via scenic Yellowhead Pass. En route we'll see the legendary Thompson River.   **Jasper Park Lodge** *B-L-D*

Day 15 Tue—JASPER NAT'L PARK: Today we tour the best of Jasper—Canada's largest national park.   **Jasper Park Lodge** *B-D*

Day 16 Wed—COLUMBIA ICEFIELDS/"SNO- COACH" RIDE/LAKE LOUISE/BANFF: We head toward the Columbia Icefields—where Four Winds has arranged a safe but exhilarating snocoach ride across six-mile Athabasca Glacier. Later we'll stop at Lake Louise—mineral deposits have given it a unique green color. Spend the next two nights at one of Canada's most elegant hotels. **Banff Springs Hotel** *B-L-D*

Day 17 Thu—BANFF NAT'L PARK: You have the whole day at leisure to enjoy Banff Nat'l Park's varied beauty. You can visit the Natural History Museum.   **Banff Springs Hotel** *B-D*

Day 18 Fri—GLACIER NAT'L PARK: Enjoy Montana's rolling hills and lush valleys as we motor to Glacier Nat'l Park. We'll lunch at Fort Macleod.   **Many Glacier Hotel** *B-L-D*

Day 19 Sat—GOING-TO-THE-SUN HIGHWAY: We cross the Continental Divide as we travel through Glacier Nat'l Park via the Going-to-the-Sun Highway. Tonight Four Winds hosts a gala farewell dinner.   **Glacier Park Lodge** *B-L-D*

Day 20 Sun—HOMEWARD BOUND: After a hearty breakfast we begin our return trip on the *Empire Builder.* As the train heads east, share your "Majestic Americana" adventures with your Four Winds friends.   **Empire Builder** *B-L-D*

Day 21 Mon—CHICAGO: Those passengers who joined us in Chicago will end their journey here. New York-bound travelers will continue tomorrow after an overnight stay in the Windy City.   **Palmer House** *B-L*

Day 22 Tue—CHICAGO: You'll have the day to rest, shop, or see Chicago's sights before we board our New York-bound train this afternoon.   **Broadway Ltd.** *B-D*

Day 23 Wed—Our rail adventure ends in New York this evening.   *B*

---

5. What are the names of the three trains that passengers will take during this tour? *Broad-way Limited, california Zephyr, Empire Builder,*

6. What do these letters mean?

    B = *Breakfast*

    L = *Lunch*

    D = *Dinner.*

7. How many meals are included in the price of the tour? *51*

8. Which train goes from New York to Chicago? *Broadway Limited*

9. On Day 2 of the tour, which train will passengers travel on? *California Zephyr*

10. Which mountains will the tour travel through on Day 3? *Rocky mountain*

11. At the end of Day 6, in what hotel will travelers spend the night? *old faithful inn*

12. On Day 10, how will people get to Victoria? *ferry (Boat)*

13. Where will people stay in Vancouver? *Hyatt regency*

14. What will travelers tour on Day 15? *Jasper Nat'l park*
    Where will they stay that night? *Jasper park Lodge.*

15. On Day 16, the passengers will ride across Athabasca Glacier. How large is this ice field? *snocoach of miles*

16. What kind of museum can people visit in Banff National Park? *natural history museum*

17. What will travelers do in Chicago on Day 22? _rest, shop, or see chicago's sights_

18. What is the number of the tour that leaves New York on July 24? _RE 344_

    When does it return to New York? _Ret   Aug. 15._

C. Work in pairs. Ask and answer questions like those above about the travel brochure.

Going Beyond the Text

Bring to class brochures, maps, and other information about tours and travel. (These items are available at travel agencies.) Discuss new vocabulary and summarize the tours. Choose your favorite tour and explain your choice to the class.

Solution to the Mystery

The thief was the conductor, Bill Thornton. He knew that there was a famous thief on board, so he had the passenger list ready for Edward Grimsley. He wanted everyone to think that Willie Brown had taken the necklace. In talking to Thornton, however, Grimsley heard him tell a lie: Thornton said he had worked on the Orient Express in 1980, but Grimsley knew that the train line hadn't been in business that year. (See page 94.) Also, Christina Royal's compartment had been locked during the night, and conductors have keys.

7

NORTH AMERICA: THE LAND AND THE PEOPLE

NORTH AMERICAN INDIANS

Getting Started

Look at the map of North America to the right and discuss it.

1. What does this map show? Describe the geography.
2. What kind of people are in the pictures? What are the things shown, and how did people probably use them?
3. When did these scenes take place?

Preparing to Read

As you read the following selection, think about the answers to these questions.

1. Who were the first people to live in North America, and how did they get here?
2. Describe how the various Indian groups were living when the first Europeans arrived in North America.
3. What has happened to American Indians since the Europeans came?
4. What is the life of the Indians like now?

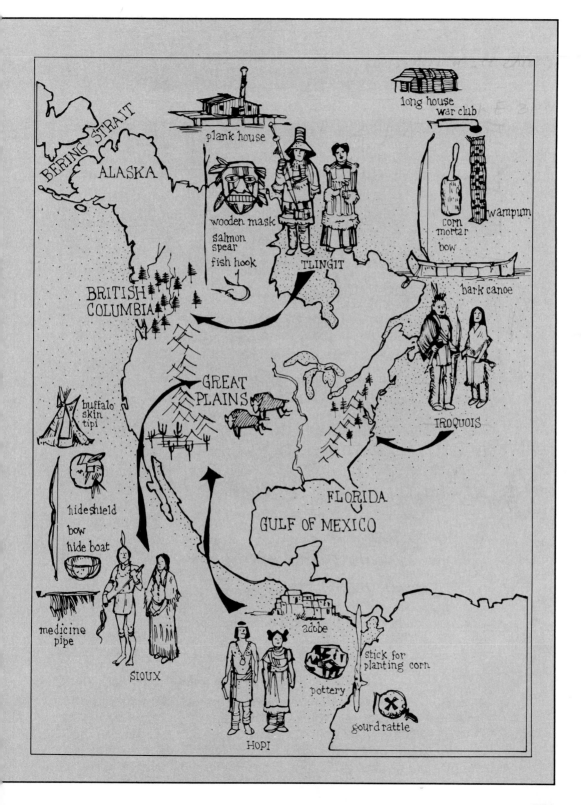

BERING STRAIT

ALASKA

BRITISH COLUMBIA

plank house

wooden mask

salmon spear

fish hook

TLINGIT

long house

war club

corn mortar

bow

wampum

bark canoe

IROQUOIS

GREAT PLAINS

buffalo skin tipi

hide shield

bow

hide boat

medicine pipe

SIOUX

FLORIDA

GULF OF MEXICO

adobe

pottery

stick for planting corn

gourd rattle

HOPI

121

North American Indians

A   The first people to live in North America were the American Indians, or Native Americans. According to the religious and folk stories of many Indian groups, their earliest ancestors arrived in North America from the inside of the earth. Modern scientists, however, believe that the first Native Americans came from Asia 15,000 to 20,000 years ago across the Bering Strait from Siberia to Alaska. They were nomads; that is, they did not live in one place, but instead were always on the move as they looked for food. In other words, the first American Indians were hunters who followed the animals—their food source—during times of migration from place to place. Together, the nomadic people and animals slowly migrated toward the south.

B   These early inhabitants spread out all over the North American continent (now Canada, the United States, and Mexico). There was a great variety of languages, religious beliefs, and customs among the many tribes, or groups, of Indians. By the time the first Europeans arrived, the Indians were living in several different "culture areas." The members of various tribes in each center of culture had frequent contact with one another and shared similar characteristics, but they didn't have much in common with tribes in other culture areas. For example, the Pima and Papago tribes of the southwestern desert had similar customs and habits, but their lifestyle was completely different from that of the Sioux, who lived on the plains, the Apaches, in the Southwest, and the Kwakiutl and Tlingit, on the Northwest Coast, or the Natchez and Tonkawas, on the Gulf Coast and in Florida.

C   The lifestyle of the people who lived in each culture area reflected the geography of that area. The inhabitants of the Northwest Coast (now British Columbia, Canada) lived by hunting and fishing, but they didn't lead a nomadic life. They didn't need to follow animals from place to place because they could take advantage of the resources where they were living. The oceans and rivers produced salmon, halibut, and many other fish. The forests were rich in animal life; they offered deer, elk, and bear, as well as smaller animals. In the forests, the inhabitants could also find berries to eat and wood for boats, furniture, and houses. Geography influenced other areas of life, too. Hunting was seasonal work, best in the summer; therefore, the tribe members were very busy at certain times of the year, but in other seasons, they had the opportunity to spend time in creative activities such as woodworking—an art form for which the Northwest Coast Indians became well known.

D   Unlike the inhabitants of the Northwest Coast, the Indians of the eastern plains had an agricultural society; they lived in farming communities and raised crops of corn, beans, squash, and tobacco. The members of these tribes lived differently from those in the Northwest: Because there were so few trees on the flatlands, their houses were of earth instead of wood. While the food was growing, the people stayed in their communities. After the harvest, when they had brought in the crops, the Indians rode west—on horses they had gotten from Spanish farmers—to hunt buffalo. During the months when they were looking for buffalo, the hunters' lifestyle was similar to that of the nomadic tribes on the western plains. To these Plains Indians—both eastern and western—the buffalo was very important. It provided many necessities: meat, skin for tipis (houses that people could carry), clothing, and materials for spoons, bags, and beds. The buffalo hunt was also central to many artistic, social, and religious activities.

E   When Europeans arrived on the North American continent several hundred years ago, the Native Americans' old way of life began to change. The differences between Europeans' and Indians' values soon led to difficulties. As the whites moved west, they took over more and more of the land for themselves. Native Americans lost not only their land but also their lives—to widespread wars and to sicknesses that were nonexistent in North America before the Europeans came. But they had lost something even more important: their sense of identity. When the Plains Indians, for instance, lost their hunting grounds, and when the buffalo became almost extinct, the most important characteristic of their society—the buffalo hunt—was gone.

F   Today, some Native Americans are holding on to their traditional ways of living. For instance, in Alaska and Canada, some Indians depend almost completely on hunting and fishing, just as their ancestors did. This way of life preserves the customs that hold the society together. For example, in late summer people in the Yukon fish for salmon. Each person in the family plays a role in this activity; the men catch the fish, the women and girls cut, dry, and smoke the fish, and the older people give advice. The native peoples hunt different animals in different seasons. The hunt is essential; people neither have nor want supermarkets in their villages. Although they have accepted some modern technology (such as snowmobiles, to help them cross the many miles of snow, and motors on their fishing boats), these people live as they have done for thousands of years.

G   However, most Native Americans today live either in urban areas or on reservations—land that the government set aside for them—and have not been able to keep to traditional ways. Although some groups are relatively wealthy, most are very poor and have had to receive help from the government. In recent years, many tribes have begun to regain their sense of identity and their cultural heritage. They are having "wars" once again—this time in court, where they have succeeded in several legal battles. They are fighting to win back their land and their fishing and hunting rights—the basis of their ancestors' way of life.

Getting the Main Ideas

Write T on the lines before the statements that are *true*, according to the reading.
Write F before the statements that are *false*.

1. _F_   The first people to live in North America came from Europe.

2. _T_   Indian stories about the first Americans are different from the theories of scientists.

3. _F_   The first people in North America built cities where they stayed for hundreds of years.

4. _F_   The various groups of people formed one society; everyone had the same customs, lifestyles, and habits.

5. _T_   The geography of the area where each group lived influenced the culture of that group.

6. _T_   The arrival of Europeans changed the lives of the people in North America.

7. _F_   Nowadays, most American Indians are identical in values, beliefs, and lifestyles to people who have come to North America from other countries.

Guessing Meaning from Context

> The following exercises present a summary of ways in which the context of a reading can give clues to the meanings of new vocabulary items.
>   There can be a definition of the item in the text—usually after the verb *be*—between commas, dashes (—), or parentheses ( ); or after connecting expressions such as *in other words, that is (i.e.),* and so on.

A. On the lines, write the words and expressions from the reading selection that fit these definitions. The letters in parentheses refer to the paragraphs of the reading where the items appear.

1. the first people to live in North America (A): *American Indians (Native Americans)*

2. people who are always on the move (A): *They looked for food*

3. the area that is now Canada, the United States, and Mexico (B): _____

4. groups of Indians (B): _____

5. an art form with wood (C): _____

6. land that the government has set aside for Indians (G): _____

_____

Sometimes synonyms (words with similar meanings) or explanations of new vocabulary items give further information.

B. Circle the words that explain the missing items. Then fill in each blank with a word from the appropriate paragraph of the reading (shown in parentheses).

1. The ⟨earliest people⟩ to live in North American were the **ancestors** of Indian groups today. (A)

2. Indians who killed animals for food were _____. (A)

3. During times of _____ , the Indians were always on the move. (A)

4. Geography influenced the lives of the people who lived in each area: The _____ of the Northwest Coast lived by hunting and fishing. (C)

5. The Indians who lived in farming communities had an _____ society. (D)

6. Because there were so few trees on the flatlands, the tribes of the eastern _____ made their houses out of earth instead of wood. (D)

7. After they had brought in the crops at _____ time, the Indians rode west to hunt buffalo. (D)

8. The Plains Indians hunted _____ for the necessities of life: meat, skin for houses and clothing, etc. (D)

9. Some tribes have held on to the _____ customs of their ancestors, while others have forgotten the ⟨old ways.⟩ (F)

10. Many modern Indians are having "wars" once again; they are fighting legal *legal battle* in *court* . (G)

11. They have accepted some ⟨modern technology⟩ such as *snow mobil* to help them cross the many miles of snow. (F)

There can be words in a text that express the opposite of a new vocabulary item—usually in a negative clause or after words that show contrast (e.g., *but, yet, however, on the other hand, by contrast, although,* etc.).

C. On the lines, write words or expressions from the appropriate paragraphs of the reading (in parentheses) that express the opposites of these words.

1. people who live in one place (A): *nomads*

2. share (characteristics, interests, etc.) (B): *not much in common*

3. widespread (E): *non existent*

4. poor (G): *wealth*

Examples can offer clues to meaning—sometimes after connecting words (*for example, for instance, such as,* etc.) or with certain punctuation (commas, dashes, parentheses, a colon).

D. On the lines, write examples from the appropriate paragraphs of the reading (in parentheses) for these categories.

1. names of geographical places (A): *Asia; Bering Strait*

2. names of geographical places (B): *North American continent*

3. fish (C): *Salmon*

4. forest animals (C): *deer, and elk, bear.*

5. food (D): *corn, beans, squash.*

E. On each line, write the category that the items are examples of. The letter in parentheses refers to the paragraph where the category appears.

1. Pima, Apaches, Natchez (B): *Indian tribes*

2. oceans, rivers, forests (C): *Geography*

3. summer (C): *season*

4. corn, squash (D): _____

5. meat, clothing (D): _____

Words related to new vocabulary items will probably give clues to the meanings of the items.

F. For each word, write the related word from the appropriate paragraph of the reading (shown in parentheses). Then match each definition below with one of the words by writing its letter in the blank on the right.

1. nomad (A): *nomadic* (adjective) *b*
2. migration (A): _____ (verb) *D*
3. season (C): _____ (adjective) *C*
4. farming (D): _____ (noun) *A*
5. art (D): _____ (adjective) *I*
6. tradition (F): _____ (adjective) *E*

   a. a person who works in agriculture
   b. moving from place to place
   c. happening in a certain time of year
   d. travel regularly from one part of the earth to another
   e. following the customs and ways of one's ancestors
   f. creative

Other meanings of a vocabulary item, or the words in the phrase that it appears in, may give clues to its new meaning.

G. On each line, write a word from the reading that fits both definitions.

1. the world in which we live; the ground where crops grow: *earth*
2. show the way; live (a life): *Lead*
3. a light color; a person with light skin: *white*
4. short fights in a war; disagreements: *battles*
5. correct; a legal advantage that people can claim: *right*

H. Reread the selection carefully. Try to guess the meanings of new words from the context. Use your dictionary only when absolutely necessary.

Check your answers in the "Getting the Main Ideas" section, which follows the reading. Correct your errors.

Understanding Reading Structure

The following outline shows one possible organization of the information in the reading selection.

A. Put these topics in the correct outline order. Write each on the appropriate line. The letters in parentheses indicate paragraphs of the reading.

> The Natives of Alaska and Canada Today
> The Culture Areas of American Indians
> American Indians Today
> The Influence of Geography on Culture
> The Inhabitants of the Northwest Coast
> The Effect of the Europeans on the Indians
> ✔ The First People in North America
> The Inhabitants of the Eastern Plains

North American Indians

I. *The First People in North America* _____ (A)

II. *The culture Areass of American Indians* _____ (B)

III. *The Influnce of Geography on culture* _____ (C)

   A. *The Inhabitants of the northwest coast* _____ (C)

   B. *The Inhabitants of the Eastern plains* _____ (D)

IV. *The Effect of the Europeans on the Indians* _____ (E)

V. *The Natives of alaska and canada Today* _____ (F)

VI. *The culture areas of American Indias American* _____ (G)
Indrans Today

> In many paragraphs, there is a separation of details into subtopics (smaller divisions of information within the main paragraph topic).

B. Refer to the outline above. In the parentheses after the subtopics, write the letters of the paragraphs these subtopics would appear in. Then turn back to the reading selection to check your answers.

  1. The Various Tribes and Their Areas (*B*)
  2. Their Farming (*D*)
  3. The Advantages of Nature ( )
  4. Their Creative Activities ( )
  5. The Buffalo Hunt ( )
  6. The Loss of Land and Life ( )
  7. The Indian Stories of Their Beginnings ( )

8. Their Loss of Identity (   )
9. The Theories of Scientists (   )
10. Their Present Life on Reservations (   )
11. The Nomadic Lifestyle of the Inhabitants (   )
12. Legal Fights for Land and Rights (   )
13. The Use of Some Modern Technology in a Traditional Lifestyle (   )

Making Inferences

A. Complete each sentence by circling the letters of *all* the information that the reading states or implies.

1. The first people to live in North America _____ .

   a. were very religious
   b. were the ancestors of today's American Indians
   c. divided into groups that created a variety of cultures
   d. lived on the coasts, in the desert, and on the plains

2. The Indians of the Northwest Coast _____ .

   a. ate fruit as well as meat and fish
   b. built houses, furniture, and boats
   c. moved to other areas in the winter to find food
   d. could get wood for various purposes

3. The Indians who lived on the flatlands of America _____ .

   a. had no food but buffalo, which they hunted in the forests
   b. built houses from the materials they could find in their area
   c. had a worse culture than the Indians of the coast
   d. stayed in one place during some seasons, but moved around during others

4. When people from Europe came to North America, _____ .

   a. they changed their customs to get along with the Indians
   b. they had wars with some of the Indian tribes
   c. they brought sicknesses with them that the Indians had not known before
   d. they killed buffalo to use their skins for clothing and housing

5. Today there are American Indians who _____ .

   a. keep to the customs and beliefs of their ancestors and live on reservations
   b. like city life
   c. fight battles against Europeans on the plains because they are so poor
   d. want the right to own, and to hunt and fish on, the land that used to belong to their tribes

B. Turn back to the beginning of the chapter and answer the questions in the "Preparing to Read" section.

Discussing the Reading

1. Do you know any American Indians? If so, tell about them.
2. Have you ever visited an Indian reservation? If so, tell about your experiences there.
3. Do you think that the American Indians have a better life now than they did before the Europeans came to North America? Why or why not?
4. Who were the first inhabitants of your country? Tell something about their history and culture.

PART TWO

REGIONAL CUSTOMS

Skimming for Main Ideas

Read each paragraph quickly, without using a dictionary. After each, circle the number of the sentence that best expresses the main idea.

Regional Customs

A   Although the modern lifestyles of people in all areas of the United States and Canada are relatively similar, certain customs exist in only one region or another. By and large, these regional customs, which are popular forms of entertainment, have to do with the geography as well as the history of each region. Perhaps they also give the natives, along with sightseers from other areas, a sense of nostalgia for the past.

1. The modern inhabitants of some areas of North America have held on to the regional customs of their ancestors.
2. Sightseers may travel to areas other than their own to enjoy old regional customs.
3. Geography has influenced modern people as well as the American Indians.
4. It is a good idea to remember the customs of the past.

B   In late winter or early spring, when the sap begins to run in the maple trees of New England (the northeastern region of the United States), a favorite activity among country folk is a maple sugaring-off party. Sap is the clear liquid inside maple trees—and the source of the sweet, golden syrup that North Americans pour over their pancakes at breakfast time. At a sugaring off, the hosts and hostesses heat up the syrup in big pots on the stove. Meanwhile, guests help by setting a long table with spoons, forks, knives, and coffee cups, and by filling huge bowls with fresh, clean

snow. They also make sure that there are enough cake doughnuts and sour pickles. When the maple syrup is ready, someone pours it into small bowls at each table setting, and all the guests take seats in front of the bowls of snow. Then they pour spoonfuls of hot maple syrup onto the snow, where it hardens and cools immediately; they take the syrup from the snow, put it onto their doughnuts, and eat the combination. Every bite of doughnut requires a new spoonful of syrup, and it goes without saying that the doughnut tastes very, very sweet. After just one, many participants are ready to quit. But at that moment, the hosts or hostesses offer them *sour pickles!* Soon they feel like eating more doughnuts with maple syrup.

1. Natives of the New England region of the United States like very, very sweet things to eat.
2. The sour taste of pickles provides a contrast to the sweet taste of doughnuts with maple syrup.
3. A seasonal custom of the northeastern region of the United States is a maple sugaring-off party.
4. When hot, sweet syrup hits cold snow, it gets hard.

C

A unique seasonal activity on the southern California coast is the grunion hunt. Grunion are small fish that come up onto the beach to lay their eggs on certain summer nights. Newspapers usually predict the time of their arrival, and the adventure of a grunion hunt begins several hours in advance. People sit impatiently around a fire on the beach and tell stories or barbecue hot dogs and roast marshmallows. Then, all of a sudden, the participants who are waiting down near the ocean shout, "Grunion!" On a good night, the beach is soon so crowded with the fish that it turns silver. Enthusiastically, all the people head toward the water to try to catch the grunion with their hands, the only legal method of doing so (according to California law). Because the fish are very slippery to the touch, however, people soon discover that following this rule isn't easy. After a successful grunion hunt, participants cook their "harvest" in butter and have a wonderful meal.

1. Because grunion are hard to catch with the hands, people don't like the California law for hunting them.
2. If people read newspapers, they will probably be able to participate in grunion hunts.
3. A meal of grunion with butter tastes especially good on the beach at night.
4. The grunion hunt is an exciting Southern California custom that takes place in the summer.

D Every so often, when the weather begins to turn cool in the fall, inhabitants of the city who grew up in the country feel nostalgic for a special autumn custom: a hayride. After the fall harvest, farmers in the American Midwest often provide a wagon full of hay (the dry grass that farm animals eat) and horses to pull the wagon. Participants in the hayride dress warmly and sit in the hay as the horses pull the wagon on country roads and through forests. All along the way and then around the fire later on, people sing folk songs. But the best part of hayrides, according to the people who have had a lot of experience with them, is the ride home in the clear night air. As the wagon heads back, people keep warm by sitting very close to someone special.

1. People in the Midwest roast hot dogs and marshmallows around fires just like people at beach parties in the West.
2. The hayride is a custom from the past that reflects the seasons of the midwestern region of the United States.
3. The hayride is mainly for city people who want to enjoy a country custom.
4. Because it gets cool in the fall in the Midwest, people wear clothes different from those that people who live in the South wear.

Understanding Idioms

For each item, find an idiom or expression in the reading that has a similar meaning and write it on the line.

PARAGRAPH A

1. or a different one: *or another*

2. generally: _____

3. are related to: _____

4. and also: (two possibilities) _____

PARAGRAPH B

1. putting plates, bowls, spoons, etc. on a table: _____

2. sit down: _____

3. it is obvious (clear): _____

4. want to: _____

PARAGRAPH C

1. produce eggs: _____

2. before in time: _____

3. unexpectedly; suddenly: _____

4. go toward: _____

5. when you feel (something): _____

PARAGRAPH D

1. become colder: _____

2. some time after that: _____

3. return: _____

Making Inferences

Read each section carefully. On the short lines, put a check by the statements that you can infer (figure out) from other information. Do not check the other statements, even if you think they are true. On the line after each statement that you check, write the phrases in the section from which you inferred the information.

1. In late winter or early spring, when the sap begins to run in the maple trees of New England (the northeastern region of the United States), a favorite activity among country folk is a maple sugaring-off party. Sap is the clear liquid inside maple trees—and the source of the sweet, golden syrup that North Americans pour over their pancakes at breakfast time.

   a. ✔ A sugaring-off party is a seasonal activity in the northern part of the United States. *in late winter or early spring / the northeastern region of the United States*

   b. ___ There is sap inside all kinds of trees. _____

   c. ___ Syrup tastes good. _____

2. At a sugaring-off, the participants pour spoonfuls of hot maple syrup onto snow, where it hardens and cools immediately; they take the syrup from the snow, put it onto their doughnuts, and eat the combination. Every bite of doughnut requires a new spoonful of syrup, and it goes without saying that the doughnut tastes very, very sweet. After just one, many participants are ready to quit. But at that moment, the hosts or hostesses offer them *sour pickles!* Soon they feel like eating more doughnuts with maple syrup.

   a. ___ Hot syrup is in liquid form; it becomes hard when it gets cold. _____

   b. ___ Doughnuts and maple syrup are sweet. _____

   c. ___ Participants will feel very sick after a sugaring-off party. _____

   d. ___ If you eat something sour, you may feel like eating something sweet next. _____

3.   A unique seasonal activity on the southern California coast is the grunion hunt. Grunion are small fish that come up onto the beach to lay their eggs on certain summer nights. Newspapers usually predict the time of their arrival, and the adventure of a grunion hunt begins several hours in advance. People sit impatiently around a fire on the beach and tell stories or barbecue hot dogs and roast marshmallows. Then, all of a sudden, the participants who are waiting down near the ocean shout, "Grunion!"

a. _____ People hunt grunion only in Southern California in the summer.

_____

b. _____ The newspaper always tells the exact time that the grunion will

come up onto the beach. _____

c. _____ Grunion taste especially good with marshmallows. _____

_____

d. _____ In a grunion hunt, some people wait down near the water for the

first fish to arrive on the beach. _____

_____

4.   On a good night, the beach is soon so crowded with the fish that it turns silver. Enthusiastically, all the people head toward the water to try to catch the grunion with their hands, the only legal method of doing so (according to California law). Because the fish are very slippery to the touch, however, they soon discover that following this rule isn't easy. After a successful grunion hunt, participants cook their "harvest" in butter and have a wonderful meal.

a. _____ The color of grunion is silver. _____

_____

b. _____ It is against the law to catch grunion with nets. _____

_____

c. _____ It is difficult to hold onto grunion. _____

_____

d. _____ You can't buy grunion in the supermarket. _____

_____

5. Every so often, when the weather begins to turn cool in the fall, inhabitants of the city who grew up in the country feel nostalgic for a special autumn custom: a hayride. After the fall harvest, farmers in the American Midwest often provide a wagon full of hay (the dry grass that farm animals eat) and horses to pull the wagon. Participants in the hayride dress warmly and sit in the hay as the horses pull the wagon on country roads and through forests. All along the way and then around the fire later on, people sing folk songs. But the best part of hayrides, according to the people who have had a lot of experience with them, is the ride home in the clear night air. As the wagon heads back, people keep warm by sitting very close to someone special.

    a. _____   Hayrides are an activity from the past. _____
        _____

    b. _____   It's so comfortable to sit in hay that some participants fall asleep.
        _____

    c. _____   People sing folk songs only in the American Midwest. _____
        _____

    d. __✓__   A hayride can be a romantic activity. _____
        _____

Viewpoint

In your opinion, does the author of the selection like the entertainment of regional customs? _____ Why or why not? _____
_____

Discussing the Reading

1. Which of the regional customs in the reading seems the most fun to you? Why?
2. Do you know about any other regional customs or activities of the United States or Canada? Describe them.
3. Describe regional customs or activities from your country.
4. In your opinion, what is the purpose of regional customs? Why do people hold on to them?

PART THREE

BUILDING VOCABULARY AND STUDY SKILLS

Categories   *careful*

On the lines, write the categories for the numbered groups of words. Choose from the following categories:

animals   activities   areas of study
instruments for eating   ✓fruits and vegetables   sweet foods
geographical features   groups of people   a kind of person
seasons

1. ___*fruits and vegetables*___ : berries, beans, squash, corn
2. ___*animals*___ : deer, elk, bear, buffalo
3. ___*geographical features*___ : desert, plains, coast, ocean
4. ___*groups of people*___ : community, society, tribe
5. ___*activities*___ : hunting, sightseeing, hayrides, barbecues
6. ___*sweet foods*___ : doughnuts, syrup, sugar, marshmallows
7. ___*season*___ : summer, winter, spring, autumn
8. ___*a kind of person*___ : inhabitant, participant, native, guest
9. ___*instruments for eating*___ : bowl, fork, cup, plate
10. ___*areas of study*___ : geography, history, art, agriculture

Prefixes and Suffixes

Here is a summary of word prefixes and suffixes and their approximate meanings.

Prefixes	Meanings
com-/con-	together; with
im-/in-/un-/dis-	not
inter-	between; among
mis-	wrong
pre-	before; first
re-	again; back

Suffixes	Parts of Speech	Meanings
-al	adjective	having the quality of
-ar	adjective	relating to nationality
-(i)an	noun	
-ed	adjective	passive participle
-en	verb	to make; to become
-ence/-ance	noun	state; quality
-ent/-ant	adjective	having the quality of
-er	adjective	comparative form
-er/-or/-ist	noun	a person who
-ess	noun	a person (female)
-est	adjective	superlative form
-ful	adjective	full of
-ible/-able	adjective	having the quality of; able to be
-ic	adjective	having the quality of; affected by
-ing	noun, adjective	active participle
-ion	noun	state; condition
-ive	adjective	having the quality of; relating to
-ly	adverb	manner (how)
-ment/-ness/-ship	noun	state; condition; quality
-(i)ous	adjective	full of
-ure	noun	state; result
-y	adjective	having the quality of; full of

In the parentheses after each word, write the part of speech (*n.* = noun; *v.* = verb; *adj.* = adj.; *adv.* = adverb). Then complete the sentences that follow with the appropriate words.

1. advantage (*n.*), advantageous (*adj*), disadvantage (*n.*)
    Nature provided certain _*advantage*_ s to some American Indian tribes. An area of rich forests was _*advantageous*_ to life. Groups that lived in cold areas were at a _*disadvantage*_.

2. member (*n*), membership (*n*), remember (*v*)
    *member* s of modern Indian tribes often _*remember*_ the language and customs of their ancestors. _*membership*_ in their group is important to them.

3. illegally (*adv*), legal (*adj*), legality (*n*)
    Nowadays Indians sometimes fight in court for their _*legal*_ rights. They claim that the Europeans took away their ancestors' lands _*illegally*_. The courts decide on the _*legality*_ of their claims.

4. farm (*v*), farm (*v*), farming (*n*), farmer (*n*)
    Some Indians stayed in one place to _*farm*_ the land. These _*farmers*_ s raised different kinds of crops on their _*farm*_ s. _*farming*_ was their way of life.

5. ancestor (*n*), ancestry (*n*), ancestral (*adj*)
    Some Indians try to keep to the customs of their _*ancestor*_ s. They know all about their _*ancestry*_ and consider their _*ancestral*_ lands special.

6. similar (*adj*), dissimilar (*adj*), similarity (*n*), similarly (*adv*)
    Groups that lived in different areas were _*dissimilar*_ in their cultures, but tribes that lived in the same cultural area had _*similar*_ customs and lifestyles. Because of the _*similarity*_ of geography, they lived _*similarly*_.

7. succeed (*v*), success (*n*), successfully (*adv*), unsuccessful (*adj*)
    It is difficult to hold on to a grunion _*successfully*_. If grunion hunters are _*unsuccessful*_ in their attempts, they try again. When they _*succeed*_, they put the fish in buckets. Then they have a barbecue to celebrate their _*success*_.

8. hard (*adj*), harden (*v*), harder (*adj*), hardest (*adj*)

    Maple syrup ___*harden*___s when it gets cool. It becomes even

    ___*harder*___ when it touches cold snow. It is ___*hard*___ to eat many of

    the very sweet doughnuts with syrup at a sugaring-off party. The

    ___*hardest*___ thing of all, however, is to get up from the table after the party.

9. serve (*v*), reserve (*v*), reserved (*adj*), reservation (*n*)

    After the hayride, the group is going to go to a restaurant where they

    ___*serve*___ hot food. If the restaurant takes ___*reservation*___s,

    they'll ___*reserve*___ their tables in advance. The group will sit together

    at the ___*reserved*___ tables.

Word Roots

Here are some word roots (also called "stems") that can combine with prefixes
and suffixes to make words.

psych   sent   ist   fine   nat   dict

A. The words in each horizontal row are missing the same word root. Choose from
those above, make necessary spelling changes, and complete the words. Use your
dictionary, if necessary.

Noun	Verb	Adjective	Adverb
de *fin* ition	de *fine*	de *fin* ite	de *fin* itely
pre *sent* ation	pre *sent*	pre *sent* able	pre *sent* ly
_____ure	_____uralize	_____ural	_____urally
ex_____ence	ex_____	ex_____ent	
_____ology		_____ological	_____ologically
pre_____ion	pre_____	pre_____able	pre_____ably

B. Write sentences that show the meanings of some of the words in the chart above.
Leave blanks for the words. Then exchange papers with a classmate. Write the
appropriate words in the blanks. Exchange papers, make corrections, and discuss
the vocabulary.

Learning New Vocabulary

While you are reading, you need to understand vocabulary, but you do not need to learn it actively. Sometimes, however, you may want to remember new vocabulary for use in conversation and writing. These steps may prove useful:

1. Divide a sheet of paper into three columns. Write new words or expressions in the left-hand column. Write the pronunciation under each word or expression. In the middle column, write the definitions. In the right-hand column, write sentences that illustrate the meanings of the items.
2. Look up and write related words, with their definitions and examples, on the same piece of paper.
3. Pronounce the words to yourself. Try to fix their spelling in your mind as you learn them. Repeat the examples to yourself and make up other examples.
4. Cover the words and examples and try to remember them when you read the definitions.
5. Review your list regularly.
6. If desired, put only items that begin with the same letter on each sheet of paper, or write items on separate index cards.

WORD	DEFINITION	EXAMPLE
nostalgia nos·tal´·jə	(N.) homesickness; longing for the past	A train whistle gives me a feeling of <u>nostalgia</u>.
nostalgic	(ADJ.) feeling homesick or longing for the past	The romantic couple had a <u>nostalgic</u> look in their eyes.
nostalgically	(ADV.)	
necessity ne·sess´·ə·ti	(N.) need; condition that makes something necessary	He was forced by economic <u>necessity</u> to steal.
necessitate he·sess´·ə·tāt	(V.) make necessary	The cool weather <u>necessitated</u> wearing heavy coats.
necessarily	(ADV.)	

A. List vocabulary items from this book. Use your dictionary to find related words. Discuss the meanings of the prefixes, the suffixes, and the words themselves. Use the words in sentences. Then list and learn the words you have discussed as described above.

B. Repeat Exercise A above with words you have read or heard in other situations.

PART FOUR

SCANNING FOR INFORMATION

A. Read the explanation and study the vocabulary list.

> Many cities have a monthly magazine that includes a list of activities in and around the city. The following list is from a magazine about Toronto, Canada.

mayor = the political leader of a city

celebrate = to have a special activity for a certain day or situation

costume = clothing that is characteristic of a time or place

calligraphy = special decorative writing

TBA = to be arranged (i.e., nobody knows the information yet)

seniors = "senior citizens"; elderly people (usually over 65)

auto = automobile

model = something (such as a car or train) that is very small but that looks like the normal-sized object

imported = brought in from another country

appreciation = enjoyment

B. Scan the list of events on pages 144–146 to find the answers to these questions.

1. Turn to page 146 and find the end of the list. In what three places do most of these activities take place? _____

   _____

2. Which streetcar can you take to get to the Exhibition Place? _____

3. Which bus goes to the International Centre? _____

4. Which bus can you take to the Harbourfront? _____

5. Whom can you meet on New Years' Day? _____

   Where? _____

   What time? _____

SPECIAL EVENTS

To Jan. 8: Silk Roads · China Ships. Royal Ontario Museum, 100 Queen's Park. See Museums section for this special exhibition of luxury items traded over a span of 2,000 years. Information: 978-3692. Map 48. Teleguide 3139.

To Apr. 1: Mapping Toronto's First Century: 1787-1884. Canadiana Building, 14 Queen's Park Cres. W. See Museums section for this special exhibition of 60 early Toronto maps depicting the city's growth. Information: 978-3692. Map 44. Teleguide 31396.

Jan. 1-2: Mayors' New Year's Day Levees. Celebrate a New Year's tradition by meeting the mayors and members of council of the City of Toronto (City Hall Rotunda, 2pm, *Jan.* 2); the City of North York (North York City Hall, 5100 Yonge St., 2pm-4pm, *Jan.* 1 – music and free refreshments); the City of Scarborough (Scarborough Civic Centre, 150 Borough Dr., 2pm-4pm, *Jan.* 1 – music).

Jan. 5-8: 7th Annual Toronto International World of Motorcycles. International Centre, 6900 Airport Rd., Mississauga. North America's world-class and largest motorcycle show. Public première of all the new 1984 models. Thurs.-Fri. noon-10pm, Sat. 10am-10pm, Sun. 10am-6pm. $5 adults, $3 children 6-12 and seniors, children 5 and under free. Information: 690-0566.**

Jan. 13-22: Toronto International Boat Show. Coliseum, Exhibition Place. Largest boat show ever assembled with over 1,200 boats worth close to $30 million. Québec '84 – display of boating exposition to be held in Québec City next summer. Antique and classic boat exhibit, boardsailing theatre, Ontario Sailing Association demonstrations. Opens 5pm-10pm *Jan.* 13, then 11am-10pm Sat., noon-6pm Sun., noon-10pm weekdays. $5 adults, $3 juniors (5-15) and seniors, children under 5 free. Information: 593-7333, 593-7551.*

Jan. 14-15: Chinese New Year. Harbourfront, 235 Queen's Quay W. The Chinese New Year is celebrated with costume and fashion shows, a Cantonese opera and displays of painting and calligraphy. Sat. 9am-midnight, Sun. 9am-6pm. Most events are free. Information: 364-5665.***

Jan. 17-18: Toronto Furniture Market. International Centre, 6900 Airport Rd., Mississauga. See the latest in Canadian-produced furniture, lighting, bedding and accessories. Both days 6pm -10pm. $2 adults, children under 12 free. Information: 677-8883.**

Jan. 19-22: Money Marketplace. Queen Elizabeth Bldg., Exhibition Place. Investment opportunities, see the Toronto Stock Exchange, buy and sell shares, free seminars on taxation, RRSPs, stocks and bonds and more. Change your financial future by attending this show. Thurs.-Fri. noon-9pm, Sat. 10am-9pm, Sun. noon-6pm. $5. Information: 273-9203, Mr. K. Gordon.*

Jan. 22: The Perfect Touch Bridal Show. Civic Garden Centre, Edwards Gardens, 777 Lawrence Ave. E. (at Leslie St.). Consult the experts when planning your wedding. Noon-9pm. Information: 294-4054. Map 7.

Jan. 27-29: Cycle Canada '84. Automotive Bldg., Exhibition Place. See the latest in motorcycles at this 8th annual show. Antique and custom bike display, action cycle movies, stunt riders, motorcycle fashions and more. Fri. noon-10pm, Sat. 10am-10pm, Sun. 10am-6pm. Call for prices. Information: 977-6318.*

Jan. 27-29: The National Bridal Show. Queen Elizabeth Bldg., Exhibition Place. Over 150 exhibitors to help you plan your wedding. Fashion shows, seminars, door prizes and a honeymoon vacation draw. Fri. 5pm-10pm, Sat. 10am-10pm, Sun. 10am-6pm. $5 adults, children under 12 free. Information: 886-3201.*

Jan. 28-29, Feb. 4-5: Molson Winterfest '84. Harbourfront, 235 Queen's Quay W. Annual winter festival includes ice canoe races, skating, a fiddling contest, ice sculpture contest, hayrides, barbecues and more. Times TBA. Free. Information: 364-5665.***

Feb. 2-5: Camping on Wheels. Automotive Bldg., Exhibition Place. 13th annual showcase of Canadian-made RV products, featuring everything from truck caps to luxury travel trailers and motor homes. Thurs. 5pm-10pm, Fri. noon-10pm, Sat. 10:30am-10pm, Sun. noon-7pm. $4 adults, $3 children and seniors. Information: 593-7333.*

Feb. 3-5: Ultralight Aircraft Exposition. Queen Elizabeth Bldg., Exhibition Place. Exhibits from 75 U.S. and Canadian manufacturers and dealers of these 150-250 lb. motorized single person craft in the largest indoor display of its kind. Fri. 2pm-10pm, Sat. noon-10pm, Sun. noon-6pm. $4 adults, children under 12 free if accompanied by adult. Information: (204) 944-1464, Roland Boily.*

Feb. 10-12: North York Winter Carnival. North York City Hall, 5100 Yonge St. Enjoy a weekend of fun-filled events including pancake breakfasts, bingo, hayrides, Monte Carlo games, barbecue lunches, bartender/waitress races, shuffleboard tournament and much more. Opening 8pm Fri., Sat. 9am–midnight, Sun. 9am–5pm. Free admission. Information: 224-6085. Map 37. Teleguide 3358.

Feb. 10-12: Speed-Sport '84. Automotive Bldg., Exhibition Place. Canada's largest custom car, hot rod and van show. Now celebrating its 25th year, the show has 75,000 visitors annually. Fri. 5pm–11pm, Sat. noon–11pm, Sun. noon–10pm. $5 adults, $2 seniors and children 12 and under. Information: 438-3373.*

Feb. 10-19: Toronto Auto Show. International Centre, 6900 Airport Rd., Mississauga. Premier automotive showcase in Canada with automobiles from 12 countries. Weekdays noon–10:30pm, Sat. 10am–10:30pm, Sun. 10am–8pm. $5 adults, $2.50 seniors, $1.50 children. Information: 493-6863.**

Feb. 22-26: Garden Festival. Automotive and Queen Elizabeth Bldgs., Exhibition Place. Two great shows for the price of one. The Flower and Garden Show (Automotive Bldg.) will feature balcony and townhouse gardens, computer gardening, Florida rooms, new products and much more. The Pool and Spa Show (Queen E. Bldg.) will feature water babies, pools, spas, hot tubs, saunas, outdoor furniture and lighting, playground equipment and more. Wed.–Fri. 1pm–10pm, Sat.–Sun. 10am–10pm. $4 adults, $3 seniors, $2 students (11-18), children 10 and under free. Shuttle bus service between bldgs.*

Feb. 24-26: Sports Expo Ontario. International Centre, 6900 Airport Rd., Mississauga. Bring your sneakers and get involved in this participatory event. Sports courts, golfatron, celebrity athletes, fashion shows, demonstrations, representation from 30 sports associations and more. Fri. noon–10pm, Sat. 10am–10pm, Sun. 10am–6pm. $5 adults, $2 seniors and children 12 and under, children 5 and under free. Information: 444-3980.**

Feb. 29 – Mar. 4: Motorhome & Trailer Show. International Centre, 6900 Airport Rd., Mississauga. One of the largest RV shows in North America. Vans, campers, RV accessories, micro light aircraft, windsurfers and airboats. Wed.–Fri. noon–10:30pm, Sat. 10:30am–10:30pm, Sun. noon–6:30pm. $4 adults, $1 children (and seniors on weekdays only).**

Mar. 2-4: The "Beautiful You" Show. Queen Elizabeth Bldg., Exhibition Place. "Looking good" is this year's theme, with products and services for the skin, hair and body. Spas, electrolysis, estheticians, colour co-ordinating and wardrobe planning, lectures, demonstrations. Fri. 5pm–10pm, Sat. 10am–10pm, Sun. 10am–6pm. $5 adults, special rates for students and seniors, children under 12 free. Information: 886-3201.*

Mar. 5: Sesqui-Eve Gala. Sheraton Centre and Nathan Phillips Square. Come celebrate Toronto's 150th birthday at a party in the Sheraton Centre; the highlight of the evening will be the countdown to midnight at Nathan Phillips Square. Call for details, 947-1984. Subway to Queen station and walk west to Bay St. Map 58.

Mar. 6-11: Quarterama. Horse Palace, Exhibition Place. Horse show featuring 115 events, over 3,000 entries from all over North America and $¼ million in prize money. Tues. 9am–10pm, Wed. – Sat. 7am–10pm, Sun. 9am–7pm. $5 adults, $3.50 youths, seniors and children under 12 free. Information: 632-7889.*

Mar. 9-11: Motion Custom Car Show. International Centre, 6900 Airport Rd., Mississauga. Hot rods, custom cars, street machines, custom vehicles. Feature attraction is Bigfoot, a giant 4x4 pick-up that walks over cars. Fri. 6pm–10pm, Sat. 10am–10pm, Sun. 10am–6pm. Call for prices. Information: 893-1242.**

Mar. 10-11: Toronto Model Railroad Show. Queen Elizabeth Bldg., Exhibition Place. Thirty operating scale model railways, demonstrations on how to build trains, stations and scenery. New and used trains at reduced prices. 11am–6pm both days. $4 adults and seniors, $2 children 6-13, children 5 and under free. Information: 488-9446.*

Mar. 16-18: The Wedding Show. International Centre, 6900 Airport Rd., Mississauga. Over 150 exhibitors to help you plan your wedding. Daily fashion shows, door prize for two to Bahamas, seminars and more. Fri. 4pm–10pm, Sat. 10am–10pm, Sun. 10am–6pm. $5 adults, children under 12 free. Information: 245-0359, John West.**

Mar. 16-25: Canadian National Sportsmen's Show. Coliseum, Exhibition Place. Fishing '84 is this year's theme. Seminars by U.S. and Canadian fishing experts, demonstrations of latest advancements in fishing industry in an aquascope. Also, exhibits on hunting, boating, camping, jogging backpacking. Indoor trout fishing and retriever trials. Weekdays 11am–10pm, Sat. 10am–10pm, Sun. 10am–7pm. $5 adults, $3 juniors (5-15) and seniors, children under 5 free. Information: 593-7333.*

Mar. 17-18: Supercycle Swap Meet & Auction. International Centre, 6900 Airport Rd., Mississauga. Hundreds of new and used bikes, accessories, flea market, awards, well-known drivers, movies and a beer garden. Sat. 10am–10pm, Sun. 10am–6pm. $4 adults, $2 seniors, children under 12 free. Information: 686-1451.**

Mar. 18-25: City Hall Flower Show. A spectacular spring floral display in the rotunda of City Hall, 100 Queen St. W. Free. Information: 947-7341. Map 58.

Mar. 23-25: Toronto Wine & Cheese Show. International Centre, 6900 Airport Rd., Mississauga. Canadian and imported wines, cheeses, breads and bakery products. Seminars on wine and cheese appreciation. Fri.–Sat. noon–10pm, Sun. noon–6pm. Call for prices. Information: 229-2060.**

Mar. 26-28: Canadian Environmental Exposition. Automotive Bldg., Exhibition Place. Plumbing, heating, refrigeration, air-conditioning and ventilating industries are showcased. Mon. 10am–6pm, Tues. 10am–8pm, Wed. 10am–6pm. Free admission. Information: 425-1427.*

Mar. 29 – Apr. 1: Canadian Spring Boat Show. International Centre, 6900 Airport Rd., Mississauga. Pool demonstrations of canoeing, kayaking, boardsailing and sailing. Wooden boat building, racing powerboats, watersports displays and films, radio-controlled boat races. Canada's largest indoor used boat sale. Thurs. 4pm–10pm, Fri. noon–10pm, Sat. 10:30am–10pm, Sun. 11am–7pm. $5 adults, $3 children 6-12 and seniors, children 5 and under free. Information: 298-9913.**

*Exhibition Place: Route 511 streetcar from Bathurst subway station. Map 1.
**International Centre: Martingrove 46 bus from Kipling subway station to Dixon Rd. and Martingrove. Transfer to Malton 58C bus (extra 65¢) west to International Centre. Free parking also available at the Centre. Map 2.
***Harbourfront: Spadina 77B bus from Union or Spadina subway station to 235 Queen's Quay W., west of York St. Map 8. Teleguide 3044.

6. What can you celebrate on January 14–15? _____

   Where does the celebration take place? _____

   Which bus can you take to get there? _____

   What can you see at this celebration? _____

   What are the hours on Saturday? _____

7. What occurs on January 19–22? _____

   Where? _____

   How can you get there? _____

   How much does it cost to enter? _____

   What might you change at this event? _____

8. At the Molson Winterfest (January 28–29, February 4–5), there is one activity

   that usually takes place in the autumn rather than the winter. What is it? ____

9. What are the dates of the Toronto Auto Show? _____

    What are the hours on weekdays? _____

    How much does it cost most adults to enter? _____

    How much does it cost elderly people? _____

10. What is the date of the Sesqui-Eve Gala? _____

    What will people celebrate on this night? _____

    What number can you call for information? _____

Going Beyond the Text

Bring to class city and regional magazines with lists of activities. Discuss new vocabulary. Summarize the most interesting information. Which places would you like to visit? When? Why?

8

TASTES AND PREFERENCES

WHAT CAN WE LEARN FROM ART?

Getting Started

Look at the pictures on the next three pages and discuss them.

1. What kinds of pictures are these? Where might you see them?
2. Describe each picture. If you can, talk about the people and the activities.
3. Compare the pictures. What are the similarities? What are the differences?
4. Which picture do you like the best? Why?

José Clemente Orozco, *Hispano América*, 1932–1934

Preparing to Read

As you read the selection on pages 152–154, think about the answers to these questions.

1. What can we learn from art history?
2. How can art express emotions and feelings?
3. What kind of art do Islamic artists create? Why?
4. What is the purpose of traditional art?
5. Art depends on culture. Can you think of examples to prove this statement?
6. How can the art of one culture influence the art of another?

Francisco Goya, *The Third of May, 1808,* 1814

Islamic bowl with
decoration of
arabesques and
Kufic writing

© ELIOT ELISOFON/ELIOT ELISOFON ARCHIVES, SMITHSONIAN INSTITUTION

Chiwara dancers with headdresses, Bambara people of Mali

COURTESY MUSEO DEL PRADO/ARS NY

Pablo Picasso, *Guernica*, 1937

What Can We Learn from Art?

A   A study of art history might be a good way to learn more about a culture than is possible to learn in general history classes. Most typical history courses concentrate on politics, economics, and war. But art history focuses on much more than this because art reflects not only the political values of a people, but also religious beliefs, emotions, and psychology. In addition, information about the daily activities of our ancestors—or of people very different from our own—can be provided by art. In short, art expresses the essential qualities of a time and a place, and a study of it clearly offers us a deeper understanding than can be found in most history books.

B   In history books, objective information about the political life of a country is presented; that is, facts about politics are given, but opinions are not expressed. Art, on the other hand, is subjective: It reflects emotions and opinions. The great Spanish painter Francisco Goya was perhaps the first truly "political" artist. In his well-known painting *The Third of May, 1808,* he depicted soldiers shooting a group of simple people. This depiction of faceless soldiers and their victims has become a symbol of the enormous power—and the misuse of this power—that a government can have over its people. Over a hundred years later, symbolic images were used in Pablo Picasso's *Guernica* to express the horror of war. Meanwhile, on another continent, the powerful paintings of Diego Rivera, José Clemente Orozco, and David Alfaro Siqueiros—as well as the works of Alfredo Ramos Martinez—depicted these Mexican artists' deep anger and sadness about social problems. In summary, a personal and emotional view of history can be presented through art.

C   In the same way, art can reflect a culture's religious beliefs. For hundreds of years in Europe, religious art was almost the *only* type of art that existed. Churches and other religious buildings were filled with paintings that depicted people and stories from the Bible, the Jewish and Christian holy book. Although most people couldn't read, they could still understand biblical stories in the pictures on church walls. By contrast, one of the main characteristics of art in the Middle East was (and still is) its absence of human and animal images. This reflects the Islamic belief (from the Koran, the book of Islam) that statues are unholy. By Islamic law, artists are not allowed to copy human or animal figures except on small items for daily use (for example, rugs and bowls). Thus, on palaces, mosques, and other buildings, Islamic artists have created unique decoration of great beauty with images of flowers and geometric forms (for example, circles, squares, and triangles). They have also shown great creativity and discipline in their use of Arabic writing as an art form.

D   Art also reflects the religious beliefs of traditional cultures in Africa and the Pacific Islands. In fact, religion is the *purpose* for this art and is, therefore, absolutely essential to it. However, unlike Christian art—which influences people to have religious feelings—the goal of traditional art in Africa and the Pacific is to influence spiritual powers—gods—to enter people's lives. Each tribe or village has special ceremonies with songs and dances to make sure that crops, animals, and tribal members are healthy and increase in number. The dancers in these ceremonies wear unique masks, headdresses, and costumes that they believe are necessary to influence the gods. These masks and headdresses are a very important part of the art.

E   In traditional tribal cultures, art objects—masks, headdresses, statues, etc.—are not created simply for beauty. They are also essential to both religion and daily life. It is impossible to separate art and religion from everyday activities: hunting, war, travel, farming, childbirth, and so on. In the Solomon Islands of Melanesia, for example, the artistic characteristics of common everyday objects are considered to be essential to the successful use of the items. A small figure on a hunter's or soldier's spear is believed to help the spear reach its target (that is, the hunted animal or the enemy in war); a small statue on the front of a boat is supposed to help the boat reach its destination. Another example of the function of traditional art is the use of headdresses in ceremonies of the Bambara people of Mali, in Africa. These headdresses are certainly decorative, but beauty is not the reason they are made. Their purpose is to help the crops grow: They were worn by the Bambara at planting time in dances to celebrate the birth of agriculture. Likewise, among the Bakongo people, there is a rich variety of functional wooden figures: Small statues of ancestors foretell the future, and images of a mother and child give protection to a woman as she gives birth to a baby. To sum up, art in many cultures is believed to serve essential, practical functions.

F   As we've seen, art depends on culture. Similarly, the way that people view art also depends on their cultural background. For most Europeans and Americans, art serves mainly as decoration. It is something on a museum wall or in a glass case. It makes homes more attractive. People look at it and admire it: "Oh, what a beautiful painting!" they might say. "I love the lines and colors." In addition to decoration, ideas are often expressed in this art. "This is a wonderful statue," an admirer might say. "It makes such a strong anti-war statement." However, in much of the rest of the world, art is not considered to be separate from everyday existence. It has a function. A person in a tribal society might look at a mask and say, "Oh, this is a good mask. It will keep my house safe." In brief, the way in which people enjoy art depends on their culture.

G   In conclusion, art is a reflection of various cultures. But art also reflects the *changes* in society that take place when different cultures influence one another. As people from tribal societies move to urban areas, their values and beliefs change, and their ancient art forms begin to lose their function. For example, when most Bambara people turned to Islam, they gave up their ceremonies to make the crops grow; their new religion taught them that their headdresses were unholy, so they stopped using them. Now Bambara artists make these headdresses only for foreign tourists; the headdresses have no function. On the other hand, urban artists learn a lot from traditional art: African masks and figures had a great effect on Pablo Picasso, and Paul Gauguin was deeply influenced by South Pacific culture; many American and Canadian artists study the simplicity of Japanese painting. The result is that as the world gets "smaller," the art of each culture becomes more international.

Getting the Main Ideas

Write ___*W*___ on the lines before the statements about Western political art; ___*Ch*___ before the statements about Christian art; ___*Is*___ before the statements about Islamic art; and ___*T*___ before the statements about traditional art.

1. _____ Some of these paintings show the horror of war or express anger about social problems.

2. _____ According to the tribespeople, these decorative headdresses help their crops grow.

3. _____ Artistic figures on spears or boats are believed to help them reach their destinations.

4. _____ People learned about the Bible from the stories in this art.

5. _____ Tribe members believe that wooden figures predict the future and protect women in childbirth.

6. _____ Because of religious law, artists decorate buildings with flowered and geometric designs but no human or animal forms.

7. _____ There are no images of living things (people or animals) except on small items for daily use.

8. _____ This art serves a practical, everyday function.

Guessing Meaning from Context

A. Circle the words that give clues to the meanings of underlined words. Then answer the questions and write a definition for each word. When you finish, check your definitions in a dictionary.

1. In his well-known painting *The Third of May, 1808,* the Spanish artist Goya depicted soldiers shooting a group of simple people.

    What part of speech is depicted (noun, verb, adjective)? _____

    What kind of person might depict something? _____

    What does depicted mean? _____

2. In history books, objective information about the political life of a country is presented; that is, facts about politics are given, but opinions are not expressed. Art, on the other hand, is subjective; it reflects emotions and opinions.

    What part of speech is objective? _____

    Where might you find objective information? _____

    What is *not* part of objective information? _____

    What does objective mean? _____

    What part of speech is subjective? _____

    What does art reflect? _____

    What is the opposite of subjective? _____

3. Thus, on palaces, mosques, and other buildings, Islamic artists have created unique decoration of great beauty with images of flowers and geometric forms (for example, circles, squares, and triangles).

    What part of speech is mosques? _____

    Mosques are a kind of _____

    What kind of artists decorate mosques? _____

    What does mosques mean? _____

    What part of speech is geometric? _____

    What are examples of geometric forms? _____

    What does geometric mean? _____

Sometimes you need to see a word in several different forms or contexts before you can guess the meaning.

Examples: One of the main characteristics of art in the Middle East is its absence of human and animal <u>images</u>.

There is rich variety of functional wooden figures: Small statues of ancestors foretell the future, and <u>images</u> of a mother and child give protection to a woman as she gives birth.
   (<u>Images</u> are pictures or figures that represent people or animals.)

B. Circle the words that give clues to the meanings of the underlined words. Then write a definition on each line. When you finish, check your definitions in a dictionary.

1. This reflects the Islamic belief (from the Koran, the book of Islam) that statues are <u>unholy</u>.

   Churches and other religious buildings were filled with paintings that depicted people and stories from the Bible, the Jewish and Christian <u>holy</u> book.

   Their new religion taught them that their headdresses were <u>unholy</u>, so they stopped using them.

   What does <u>holy</u> mean? _____

2. These headdresses are certainly <u>decorative</u>, but beauty is not the reason they are made.

   For most Europeans and Americans, art serves mainly as <u>decoration</u>. It is something on a museum wall or in a glass case. It makes homes more attractive.

   What does <u>decoration</u> mean? _____

C. On the lines, write the words from the reading selection that fit these definitions. The letters in parentheses refer to the paragraphs where the words appear.

1. very important; necessary (A): _____

2. object produced by painting, etc. (B): _____

3. wrong or inappropriate use (B): _____

4. way of looking at (B): _____

5. not being present (C): _____

6. formal actions for making an important social or religious event (D):

   _____

7. a long pole with a sharp point; a kind of weapon (E): _____

8. the object that someone is trying to shoot at or reach (two possibilities) (E):

_____

9. decorative head coverings (E): _____

10. made for practical use (E): _____

11. tell in advance; predict (E): _____

12. figures (E): _____

13. have a good opinion of; respect and like (F): _____

14. influence (noun) (G): _____

D. Reread the selection carefully. Try to guess the meanings of new words from the context. Use your dictionary only when absolutely necessary.

Check your answers in the "Getting the Main Ideas" section, which follows the reading. Correct your errors.

Understanding Reading Structure

A. There are several possible ways to organize the information in the reading selection. Fill in the outline for the reading "What Can We Learn from Art?" with the following topics. (The letters in parentheses indicate paragraphs of the reading.)

  ✔ Introduction: The Study of Art History
    Traditional Art in Africa and the Pacific Islands
    Art as an Expression of Political Views
    Art as a Reflection of Change in Society
    Art as a Reflection of Religious Beliefs
    Christian Art
    Islamic Art
    The Way People View Art

What Can We Learn from Art?

I. _Introduction: The Study of Art History_ (A)

II. _____ (B)

III. _____ (C)

    A. _____

    B. _____

IV. _____ (D/E)

V. _____ (F)

VI. _____ (G)

> The reading selection contains many subtopics that serve as supporting material for the main topics of the selection.
>
> *Example:*   Over a hundred years later, symbolic images were used in Pablo Picasso's famous *Guernica* to express the horror of war. (Picasso's painting functions as a subtopic of Paragraph B, "Art as an Expression of Political Views.")

B. Refer to the outline on page 157 and write the letters of the paragraphs these subtopics would appear in. Then turn back to the reading to check your answers.

1. Goya's painting *The Third of May, 1808* (*B*)
2. the Bambara people of Mali, in Africa (*D/E*)
3. Views of art in Africa and the Pacific Islands (   )
4. Picasso's *Guernica* (   )
5. Mexican social art (   )
6. Christian images in churches (   )
7. the Bakongo people (   )
8. the Solomon Islands of Melanesia (   )
9. European and American views of art (   )
10. Islamic designs and Arabic writing (   )
11. the influence of traditional art on Picasso and Gauguin (   )
12. the effect of Japanese painting (   )
13. ceremonies to influence spiritual powers (   )

> Here are some common connecting words that indicate a summary of material will follow.
>
> | in short | in conclusion | to sum up |
> | in brief | in summary | as we've seen |
> | the result is | thus/therefore | |

C. Copy the sentences from the reading selection that begin with these connecting words. Then circle the number of the sentence that best expresses the main idea of the entire reading.

1. In short, ————————————————————————————————

   ——

   ——

2. In summary, ————————————————————————————————

   ——

3. Thus, _____

_____

_____

4. To sum up, _____

_____

5. As we've seen, _____

6. In brief, _____

_____

7. In conclusion, _____

_____

8. The result is _____

_____

Making Inferences

A. Complete each sentence by circling the letters of *all* the information that the reading states or implies.

1. _____ expressed political opinions with realistic pictures of people.

   a. the Spanish painter Goya
   b. Picasso
   c. various Mexican artists
   d. Islamic painters

2. There are examples of religious art _____ .

   a. on churches in Europe
   b. on Arab rugs and bowls
   c. in tribal ceremonies
   d. on headdresses

3. Traditional art might be used to _____ .

   a. cover walls of large buildings
   b. help hunters and soldiers
   c. improve agriculture
   d. protect women and children

B. Turn back to the beginning of the chapter and answer the questions in the "Preparing to Read" section.

Discussing the Reading

1. Tell about art in your culture. Describe typical works of art (paintings, statues, decorations on buildings, etc.). What is the function of art in your country? How do people view art?
2. Compare art in your culture with North American art. What are the similarities? The differences?
3. What kind of art do you prefer? Why?

PART TWO

FASHION: THE ART OF THE BODY

Skimming for Main Ideas

The main idea is not always clearly expressed in a paragraph. Instead, the details may *imply* the main idea, which sums up all the information in the paragraph.

Example: For various reasons, clothing of some type has been worn by human beings since the beginning of time. The Eskimos wear animal fur to protect them against the cold winter weather. Nomadic desert people wear long, loose clothing for protection against the sun and wind of the Sahara. But is clothing really essential for protection? Perhaps not. Scientists point out the absence of clothing among certain Indians of southern Chile, where the temperature is usually 43° F (7° C) and often colder. Similarly, the tribal people of Australia, where the weather is like that of the Sahara Desert, wear almost no clothing.

(The topic of the paragraph is *clothing*. The important *details* are that some groups wear clothing for protection against the weather, while others do not. Thus, the main idea of the paragraph is that protection is one function of clothing, but not an essential one.)

Read each paragraph quickly, without using a dictionary. To help you figure out the main idea, circle the letters of *all* the correct answers to the questions that follow.

Fashion: The Art of the Body

A
A lack of clothing may indicate an absence of status or social position. In ancient Egypt, for instance, children—who had no social status—wore no clothes until they were about twelve years old. In ancient times in Peru, South America, the Mohica soldiers used to take away the clothing of their prisoners of war; the Mohica believed that if the enemy had no clothes, he also had no status or power. In many societies, furthermore, only royalty could wear certain colors, styles, and types of cloth. For several hundred years in Europe, for example, fur, purple silk, or gold cloth could be used only by royal families.

1. What is the one main topic of the paragraph?

   a. Egypt
   b. clothing
   c. colors
   d. power

2. What details about the topic does the paragraph provide?

   a. Children usually wear more colorful clothes than older people do.
   b. Egyptian children and prisoners of the Mohica wore no clothes because they had no status.
   c. Soldiers in South America didn't need clothing because of the warm weather.
   d. Europeans other than the royal family were not allowed to wear certain clothing.

3. Which idea do all the circled answers have in common—i.e., what is the main idea of the paragraph?

   a. Clothing has been worn for different reasons since the beginning of time.
   b. Fur, purple silk, and gold cloth make the best kind of clothing.
   c. Clothing is an important status symbol.
   d. Ancient societies had different ideas about clothing from those of modern societies.

B

Two common types of body decoration in tribal societies are tattooing and scarification. A tattoo is a design or mark made by putting a kind of dye (usually dark blue) into a cut in the skin. In scarification, dirt or ashes are put into the cuts instead of dye. In both of these cases, the result is a design that is unique to the person's tribe. Three lines on each side of a man's face identify him as a member of the Yoruba tribe of Nigeria. A complex geometric design on a woman's back identifies her as Nuba—and also makes her more beautiful in the eyes of her people.

1. What is the one main topic of the paragraph?

    a. the Yoruba people
    b. geometric designs
    c. dirt and ashes
    d. body decoration

2. What details about the topic does the paragraph provide?

    a. Tattoos are more beautiful than scarification.
    b. Tattoos and scarification indicate a person's tribe.
    c. The dye for tattooing comes from special plants.
    d. Designs on a person's face or body are considered beautiful.

3. Which idea includes all the details circled above—i.e., what is the main idea of the paragraph?

    a. Everyone who wants to be beautiful should get a tattoo.
    b. People decorate their bodies for the purposes of identification and beauty.
    c. A tattoo is a design made by putting dark blue dye into cuts in the skin.
    d. Men more often decorate their faces; women often decorate their backs.

C

In some societies, women overeat to become plump because large women are considered beautiful, while skinny ones are regarded as ugly. A woman's plumpness is also an indication of her family's wealth. In other societies, by contrast, a fat person is considered unattractive, so men and women eat little and try to remain slim. In many parts of the world, people lie in the sun for hours to darken their skin, while in other places light, soft skin is seen as attractive. People with gray hair often dye it black, whereas those with naturally dark hair often change its color to blond.

1. What is the one main topic of the paragraph?

    a. hair
    b. skin
    c. body shape
    d. body changes

2. What details about the topic does the paragraph provide?

    a. It is unhealthy to lose or gain too much weight.
    b. Some societies consider large people attractive; others, slim ones.
    c. Some people prefer dark hair or skin; others, light.
    d. Most wealthy people try to stay thin.

3. What is the main idea of the paragraph?

    a. Individuals and groups of people have different ideas about physical attractiveness.
    b. Lying in the sun darkens the skin.
    c. In some societies, thinness is an indication that a family is poor.
    d. Dark-skinned people usually have dark hair.

D   Tattooing and scarification are only two of the methods that people use to change the appearance of their bodies. Another is foot binding: In China, wealthy families used to tightly tie up the feet of their daughters. As a result, their feet were not allowed to grow as the girls grew and, thus, remained too small to be functional. Similarly, the Maya of Yucatan and Central America used to bind the heads of their babies to change the shape of their heads. Methods of changing the body are just as common in modern Western societies: Wealthy urban people go to doctors for plastic surgery to look younger or to change the shape of their noses. Men who are losing their hair often have surgery to replace it. People pierce their ears to wear earrings or lie out in the hot sun for hours to get suntans.

1. What is the one main topic of the paragraph?
    a. binding the feet and head
    b. plastic surgery
    c. methods of changing the body
    d. getting a nice suntan

2. What details about the topic does the paragraph provide?
    a. In some societies, parts of the body are tightly bound to change their shape.
    b. Wealthy people in modern societies go through surgery to improve their bodies.
    c. Doctors can easily change the appearance of any body part.
    d. People spend many uncomfortable hours to get a suntan.

3. What is the main idea of the paragraph?
    a. Small feet, heads, and noses are generally considered beautiful.
    b. Asian people used to have different customs for improving physical appearance from those of Western people.
    c. Human beings often "pay high prices" to look better.
    d. Some methods of changing the body are dangerous, but others are safe.

Making Inferences

On the short lines, put a check by the statements that you can infer from the reading selection. Do not check the other statements, even if you think they are true. On the line after each statement that you check, write the phrases from the section from which you inferred the information.

1. ____   All people wear clothing to keep warm. _____

    _____

2. ____   Fur provides warmth, while long, loose clothing is useful in hot

    weather. _____

    _____

3. ____   Rich people wear more clothing than poor people do. _____

    _____

4. ____   In some societies, children and prisoners are examples of groups of

    people without much status. _____

    _____

5. ____   Some methods of body beautification, such as tattooing, foot binding,

    and plastic surgery, may be painful. _____

    _____

6. ____   Women are more interested in looking good than men are. _____

    _____

Discussing the Reading

1. Why are people often unhappy with their bodies? Do you agree with their reasons for changing them?
2. What do you think of the methods of body beautification that are described in the reading selection? Why?
3. What methods are common in your culture? What do you think of them?

PART THREE

BUILDING VOCABULARY AND STUDY SKILLS

Words with Similar Meanings

> Although words with similar meanings can often be substituted for one another, they may have somewhat different definitions.
>
> *Examples:*   I'm taking a geography <u>course</u>. The <u>class</u> meets twice a week, and there is a different <u>lesson</u> at each meeting. (<u>course</u> = series of lessons on a subject; <u>class</u> = a meeting of a course or the students who are taking a course; <u>lesson</u> = a separate piece of material on a subject or the amount of teaching at one time)

A. The words in each of the following groups have similar meanings, but they are not exactly the same. Match the words with their definitions by writing the letters on the lines. If necessary, check your answers in a dictionary.

1. *b*   study
2. *a*   learn
3. *c*   memorize

   a. gain knowledge or skill in a subject
   b. make an effort to learn
   c. learn to know from memory

4. ___   provide
5. ___   present
6. ___   offer

   a. show; introduce
   b. present (something) so that it may be accepted
   c. give

7. ___   depict
8. ___   indicate
9. ___   express

   a. show in the form of a picture
   b. point out; make known
   c. put (thoughts, etc.) into words

10. ___   target
11. ___   goal
12. ___   destination

   a. objective; purpose
   b. the place where someone is going
   c. an object or mark someone tries to reach or hit

13. ___   merchandise
14. ___   products
15. ___   items

   a. things that are made
   b. things that are bought and sold
   c. individual things

In some cases, the meaning of one word *includes* the meanings of many others.

Examples: Beautiful art can be found in different kinds of <u>structures</u>: <u>churches</u>, <u>mosques</u>, and <u>palaces</u>. (<u>Churches</u> and <u>mosques</u> are religious buildings, and <u>palaces</u> are buildings for royalty. The word <u>structures</u> can mean buildings, so it includes the meanings of the three other words.)

B. In each of the following items, circle the one word that includes the meanings of the others.

1. (art)   statue   painting

2. painter   designer   artist

3. actor   entertainer   musician

4. traveler   tourist   passenger

5. bus   subway   transportation

6. royalty   prince   king

7. Christianity   religion   Islam

8. murder   crime   theft

Sometimes words with similar meanings have different connotations (implied meanings: "feelings").

Examples: In some societies, women overeat to become <u>plump</u> because <u>large</u> women are considered beautiful. In other cultures, a <u>fat</u> person is considered ugly. (The words <u>plump</u>, <u>large</u>, and <u>fat</u> all mean "over normal weight." To say someone is <u>fat</u> is an insult, however, while <u>plump</u> and <u>large</u> are more polite ways of referring to the same characteristic.)

Some dictionaries provide information on usage of words in different situations and on connotations of words with similar meanings. Read the dictionary entries on page 167 and complete the following exercises.

C. Write + before the words with positive connotations and − before the words with negative ones.

1. **+**	slim	3. ___	skinny	5. ___	fat
2. **−**	emaciated	4. ___	slender	6. ___	overweight

USAGE 1 **Thin** is a general word to describe people who have little or no fat on their bodies. If someone is **thin** in a pleasant way, we say they are **slim** or (less common) **slender**, but if they are too thin they are **skinny** (*infml*), **underweight**, or (worst of all) **emaciated**: *I wish I were as slim as you!*|*She looks very thin/skinny/underweight after her illness.*|*After weeks with little or no food, the prisoners were emaciated.* The opposite of **thin** in this sense is **fat**, but this not very polite. **Plump, overweight, heavy, chubby** (esp. of babies), and **matronly** (only of older women) are all more polite ways of saying the same things. A person who is very fat is **obese**. 2 Things that are long and **thin**, in the sense of having a short distance from one side to another, are **narrow** (opposite **wide**): *a narrow country road*|*a long narrow room*.

beau·ti·ful /ˈbyuʷtəfəl/ *adj* having beauty —**beautifully** *adv*

USAGE When used to describe a person's appearance, **beautiful** is a very strong word meaning "giving great pleasure to the senses." Its opposite is **ugly** or, even stronger, **hideous. Plain** is a less *derog* way of saying **ugly. Pretty, handsome, good-looking,** and **attractive** all mean "pleasant to look at;" but **pretty** is only used of women and children, and **handsome** (usually) only of men. **Good-looking, handsome,** and **plain** are normally only used of people, but the other words can also be used of things: *a pretty garden*|*a hideous dress.*

D. Circle the words that have a polite connotation:

1. slim   3. plump   5. obese
2. emaciated   4. matronly   6. heavy

E. For each pair of words, circle the one with the stronger meaning.

1. (beautiful) / pretty   3. attractive / beautiful   5. beautiful / good-looking
2. ugly / hideous   4. ugly / plain   6. unattractive / ugly

F. Circle the letters of *all* the words that are usually appropriate for each sentence.

1. He's a very _____ man.

   a. pretty
   b. handsome
   c. attractive
   d. ugly

2. What a _____ baby!

   a. beautiful
   b. handsome
   c. pretty
   d. good-looking

3. This is a very _____ garden.

   a. good-looking
   b. plain
   c. pretty
   d. attractive

G. Write words with meanings similar to the following words. Use your dictionary for help. Write the lists of similar words on the board and discuss differences in meanings, connotation, and usage.

1. woman   3. talk   5. old
2. thief   4. believe   6. small

Increasing Reading Speed

The following exercises may help you make your eye movements faster and increase your reading speed.

A. When your teacher tells you to begin each section, look at the underlined word to the left of each line. Read across the line, from left to right. Circle the one word with the most *similar* meaning to that of the underlined word. At the end of each section, write down your time (the number of seconds it takes you to finish). Try to read faster with each section.

<u>exam</u>	culture	test	custom	identity	way
<u>region</u>	hunt	society	state	area	tribe
<u>example</u>	addition	instance	picture	difficulty	social
<u>education</u>	studies	school	memorize	requirement	hard
<u>pleasure</u>	frequent	luxurious	satisfaction	sickness	enjoy

Time: _____

<u>figure</u>	art	painting	statue	mosque	design
<u>gardening</u>	suburbs	transportation	traffic	plants	yardwork
<u>migrate</u>	move	ancestor	nomadic	language	agriculture
<u>predict</u>	therapist	bargain	tourist	organize	foretell
<u>battle</u>	fight	reservation	land	court	rights

Time: _____

<u>chance</u>	provide	offering	presentation	opportunity	allow
<u>rich</u>	various	forest	expensive	wealthy	characteristic
<u>various</u>	different	kind	exist	groups	general
<u>smog</u>	sickness	problem	theory	downtown	pollution
<u>psychologist</u>	science	prove	therapist	artist	member

Time: _____

<u>form</u>	object	fact	shape	information	express
<u>folk</u>	people	religion	hayride	songs	Indians
<u>grin</u>	image	expression	smile	depict	match
<u>discount</u>	merchandise	decoration	bargain	geometric	cheap
<u>power</u>	political	government	war	view	strength

Time: _____

B. Follow the instructions for Exercise A above, but circle the one word with the *opposite* meaning to the underlined word.

wonderful	advantageous	horror	result	terrible	luxurious
cities	suburbs	villages	continent	noise	entertainment
communal	group	desert	individual	absence	house
everyday	typical	essential	beliefs	unusual	quality
generally	specifically	result	therefore	thus	such

Time: _____

modern	marketing	traditional	value	economics	activity
birth	child	figure	anger	death	crime
objective	emotional	facts	sadness	reflect	history
criminal	soldier	faceless	symbol	victim	shoot
private	opinion	public	contrast	holy	image

Time: _____

valuable	beautiful	unique	useless	impossible	successful
elderly	young	people	senior	enthusiastic	ancestor
sour	attractive	pickle	doughnut	sweet	barbecue
worsen	produce	improve	influence	summarize	entire
plains	state	flat	mountains	desert	weather

Time: _____

PART FOUR

SCANNING FOR INFORMATION

A. Read the explanation and study the vocabulary list.

Although beauty is important in all cultures, different societies may have different ideas of beauty. The following advertisements are from an American magazine.

shape up = get into good physical condition

tan = skin browned by the sun

manicure = a beauty treatment for fingernails; the manicurist cuts the customer's nails and puts on nail polish

perm = a permanent wave; a treatment for hair that makes straight hair curly for a long time

facial = a beauty treatment for the face

passive = not active; not requiring energy

session = a meeting; a time period

whiten = make something white

straighten = make something straight

anesthetic = a drug that lets a person feel no pain

Grand Opening

Cut, Shampoo, Conditioner
$8 Reg. $18

Nexus or Zoto Perms
$30 Reg. $65

Cellophanes &
Colors Highlighting
$17 Reg. $25

Fills
$12 Reg. $17

Pedicure & Manicure
$12 Reg. $16

Porcelain Nails
Tips, Wraps, Strengthening
$22 Reg. $45

Donna's Hair & Nails
495 Benton Ave.
Hollywood, CA
241-6060
Open Daily, 10 a.m.-7 p.m.

Waxing by Larisa

European method.
Remove unwanted
hair from face & body
comfortably and quickly.

European Skincare $25

Tel. 271-6813
232 S. Beverly Dr.
Beverly Hills, 90212
Monday thru Saturday till 5 PM
Wednesday & Thursday till 8 PM

1.

2.

6.

7.

B. Scan the following advertisements. Judging from these seven ads, what do you think that North American society believes about beauty? Write T (*true*), F (*false*), or I (*impossible to know*) on the lines.

1. _____ Thin people are more self-confident than fat people.

2. _____ Body hair is not beautiful.

3. _____ Brown skin is not beautiful.

4. _____ European beauty methods are not good.

5. _____ It is usually more expensive to go to a beauty shop when it first opens than after it has been in business for a while.

6. _____ Everyone in this society likes to exercise.

7. _____ People try to get thinner before summer begins.

8. _____ White teeth are attractive.

C. Which advertisements might the following people be interested in? Write the numbers of the appropriate ads on the lines.

1. _____ A person is very pale (has very white skin) and wants to have brown skin before he goes to the beach.

2. _____ A man wants to have a haircut and a permanent.

3. _____ A woman wants to have straight, white teeth.

4. _____ A man and a woman have a son who is ten years old. He's overweight and very shy.

5. _____ A man wants to look thinner and to have stronger muscles, but he's lazy and hates to exercise.

6. _____ A woman has some hair on her face that she hates.

7. _____ A woman wants to learn about makeup.

D. Answer the following questions about the ads.

1. Is Donna's Hair & Nails open on Sundays? _____

2. How much is a beauty makeover at Fortuné Beauty Workshop? _____ Is it a special offer? _____

3. What are the hours of Perfect Body on Tuesdays? _____ How much is the first fifteen-minute session? _____ How many sessions must a person complete before the price per session is $15? _____

Going Beyond the Text

Bring to class advertisements from a local newspaper about beauty treatments and methods. Discuss new vocabulary. Tell the class about the most interesting ads and your opinions of them.

9

THE SKY ABOVE US

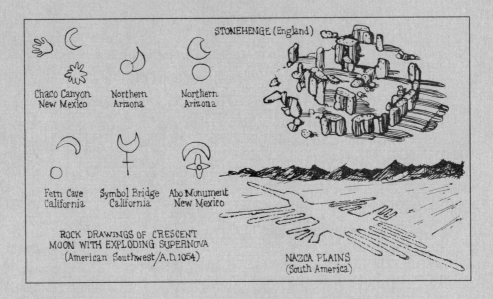

STONEHENGE (England)

Chaco Canyon
New Mexico

Northern
Arizona

Northern
Arizona

Fern Cave
California

Symbol Bridge
California

Abo Monument
New Mexico

ROCK DRAWINGS OF CRESCENT
MOON WITH EXPLODING SUPERNOVA
(American Southwest/A.D. 1054)

NAZCA PLAINS
(South America)

PART ONE

ARCHEOASTRONOMY

Getting Started

Look at the pictures and discuss them.

1. What structures and buildings do you see? What might their purposes have been?
2. Where do you see symbols? What might they have meant?
3. What might these pictures have in common?

AZTEC TEMPLO MAYOR
(equinox sunrise)

10 FT.

BIG HORN MEDICINE WHEEL (Wyoming)

AZTEC SUN SACRIFICE

Preparing to Read

In academic reading, it often helps to "survey" (get an overview of) the material before you begin to read it. Pictures provide useful first clues to the contents. In addition, some selections contain subheads, or lines that stand out, which give quick information about the reading.

A. Survey the reading selection on pages 177 to 179 quickly. Write the subheads here.

Ancient Peoples and the Sky

_____

_____

_____

_____

_____

_____

B. Look again at the pictures on the previous pages and at the subheads. Then check those topics in the following list that you believe, from your surveying, will be discussed in the reading section.

1. ✔ The Science of Astronomy

2. _____ The Science of Psychology

3. ✔ Ancient Pyramids

4. _____ The Meaning of Stonehenge

5. _____ Astronomy Courses at North American Colleges

6. _____ Indian Studies of the Sky

7. _____ Modern Astronauts on the Moon

Asking yourself questions before and during reading often helps you to understand and to remember the material.

C. In the following list, check the questions that you think, from your surveying, the reading selection might answer.

1. _____ What is archeoastronomy?

2. _____ What do scientists tell us about the compulsive behavior of ancient European tribes?

3. _____ How was Stonehenge related to the study of the universe?

4. _____ Why were the American Indians interested in the skies?

5. _____ Are there modern societies that draw pictures on stones?

6. _____ How do we know about ancient peoples' interest in astronomy?

7. _____   What was the function of the Mayan and Aztec pyramids?

8. _____   Have astronauts from other planets visited the earth?

9. _____   What problems did ancient cities have with traffic and overcrowding?

10. _____   How were the lifestyles of ancient peoples different from our modern ones?

As you read the following selection, think about possible answers to the questions that you checked above.

Archeoastronomy

Ancient Peoples and the Sky

There are many mysteries that seem to be beyond our understanding. Some of the most fascinating are those that have to do with the beliefs, customs, and knowledge of ancient peoples. We look at the circle of huge stones at Stonehenge, the mysterious images drawn on rocks in the North American Midwest, and the pyramids of Mesoamerica (Mexico and Central America), and we ask ourselves, "How did these things get here? What were their functions?" It is now clear that many ancient peoples had knowledge of, and a great interest in, the science of astronomy—the study of the sun, moon, stars, and planets. These mysterious structures were probably built for scientific reasons—to watch the skies—or they were built for religious purposes—to worship the mysterious objects in the universe as people worship in churches, mosques, and temples today. The symbols on stones and in caves were astronomical signs.

The Mystery of Stonehenge

For a long time, archeologists in England had studied the geometric circle of huge stones ("megaliths") that we now call Stonehenge and had said, "Impossible!" These experts in the study of ancient things didn't believe that the earliest inhabitants of Britain could have created such a structure on their own. They theorized that Stonehenge had been designed and built by a traveling Greek architect. Modern studies, however, have shown that Stonehenge is much older than most had believed—as old as or even older than the pyramids of Egypt. It was, in fact, built in three different time periods, and its design had nothing to do with the culture or architecture of Greece. Stonehenge is still being studied, and new theories about it have not yet been proven, but one fact is certain: The huge stone structures served as planetariums to view and study the movements of the sun and moon.

North American Astronomers

Scientists have proven that astronomy was of central importance in the lives of the North American Indians. The nomadic tribes studied the stars for directions when they migrated from place to place. Hunters, too, needed information about the changes of seasons, which they got from the skies. For farmers, the different phases of the moon and the journey of the sun across the sky foretold the time for planting crops and the season for rain. As a result, Indian tribes knew the sky well. In addition, the ancient Indians tried to explain the mysteries of the universe to their people; their folk stories, symbols, and religious beliefs are full of attempts to understand astronomy.

Proof of Indian Astronomy

Although the ancient Indians left us no written proof of their astronomical discoveries, modern scientists have been finding more and more evidence of their knowledge of the skies. Geometric forms have been discovered on cave walls, for example, which depict crescent (☽) moons near stars or circles. Furthermore, it is quite possible that some designs represent the supernova that first appeared in the sky in A.D. 1054. This exploding star was so bright that it could be seen in the daytime for about three weeks; Chinese astronomers at the time wrote about this event, and it is likely that the Indians also recorded its appearance. Another example of the Indians' astronomical studies is the "medicine wheels" that are found along the Rocky Mountains from Canada to the United States. These simple designs in the shapes of wheels may be sun symbols. They have been laid out on the ground with rocks and are all found on mountaintops or other high places with a clear view of the sky. The lines of stones at one of these, the Big Horn Medicine Wheel, points to the sunrise at summer solstice (June 21, the first day of summer) and to the place where the sun sets on the same day. Although the specific function of the medicine wheels is unknown, the well-accepted theory is that some kind of astronomical celebrations were held there.

The Mayas and the Aztecs

The Indians of Mesoamerica also paid special attention to astronomy. Ancient Mayan books include information about the appearance and movements of the planet Venus and the moon. Unfortunately, most of the Mayan records were burned by Spanish priests and soldiers, so there is little proof left of the Mayan studies. Scientists are sure, however, that Venus and the sun were very important to these Indian cultures. A sixteenth-century priest, for instance, wrote that the Aztecs killed prisoners when Venus appeared in the eastern sky. Moreover, the pyramids, it is theorized, had to do with worship of the sun or the moon.

Astronauts from Other Planets?

Some theories of ancient astronomy seem even more fascinating than those that have been proven about the Indians. According to one very popular, but highly unscientific, theory, astronauts from other planets visited South America in ancient times and were thought by the people to be gods. Erich von Däniken, a Swiss archeologist, claims that enormous drawings on mountainsides in South America were meant to be seen from the sky. He believes these forms and shapes could have been designed for visitors from other places in the universe. Furthermore, calendars, signs, and symbols that have been found by archeologists in South America contain surprisingly accurate information about the universe. Since this evidence of astronomical knowledge seems very advanced scientifically, von Däniken believes it might have been created by beings from other planets, who were expert astronomers, rather than by people in ancient societies on earth. His theories interest people with an adventurous sense of the romance of the universe; most scientists, nevertheless, disagree with von Däniken's ideas.

What Is Archeoastronomy?

Archeology is the study of prehistoric and ancient things and peoples. It has been combined with astronomy, the study of the skies, however, to create a very new science: archeoastronomy. Through objective, scientific methods, archeoastronomers are trying to uncover information and to prove facts about the knowledge of our earliest ancestors. Fortunately, they are finding out that the truth about the past can be as exciting as romantic theories.

Getting the Main Ideas

A. Write T on the lines before the statements that are *true,* according to the reading. Write F before the statements that are *false.*

1. _____   Astronomy is a very new science.

2. _____   The structures and symbols of ancient peoples present fascinating mysteries for scientists to solve.

3. _____   It has been proven that astronauts from other planets came to earth to build the pyramids.

4. _____   Archeoastronomy is the study of ancient peoples' knowledge of the universe.

B. Write s on the lines before the statements about Stonehenge; na before statements about the North American Indians (other than the Aztecs); ma before statements about the Mayan or Aztec Indians; and d before theories of the archeologist von Däniken.

1. _____ Their pyramids had to do with religion (worship of the sun and the moon).

2. _____ The geometric designs on stones and cave walls indicate their knowledge of astronomy.

3. _____ These very old structures in England were not built by the Greeks.

4. _____ Ancient peoples used the stone structures to study the skies.

5. _____ Visitors from other places in the universe may have created calendars with astronomical signs and symbols.

6. _____ Nomads, hunters, and farmers needed astronomical facts for their daily lives.

7. _____ Huge drawings on mountains might have been seen by travelers from other planets.

Guessing Meaning from Context

A. Figure out the meanings of the underlined vocabulary items by answering the questions that follow. Then check your definitions in a dictionary.

1. These structures were built for religious purposes—to <u>worship</u> the mysterious objects in the universe as people worship God in churches, mosques, and temples today.

   What part of speech is <u>worship</u>? _____

   What can be objects of <u>worship</u>? _____

   What kind of activity is worship? _____

   Where do people worship today? _____

   What does <u>worship</u> mean? _____

   _____

2. Experts theorized that Stonehenge had been designed and built by a traveling Greek <u>architect</u>.

   What part of speech is <u>architect</u>? _____

What did experts believe that an architect had done? _____

_____

What does <u>architect</u> mean? _____

_____

3. One fact is certain: the huge stone structures served as <u>planetariums</u>—to view and study the movements of the sun and moon.

What part of speech is <u>planetariums</u>? _____

What is the purpose of planetariums? _____

_____

What does <u>planetariums</u> mean? _____

_____

4. For farmers, the different <u>phases</u> of the moon and the journey of the sun across the sky foretold the time for planting crops and the season for rain.

What does the sun seem to do? _____

What does the moon seem to have? _____

How did farmers predict the time for planting crops? _____

_____

What does <u>phases</u> mean? _____

_____

5. Furthermore, it is quite possible that some designs represent the <u>supernova</u> that first appeared in the sky in A.D. 1054. This exploding star was so bright that it could be seen in the daytime for about three weeks; Chinese astronomers at the time wrote about this event, and it is likely that the Indians also <u>recorded</u> its appearance.

What expression explains <u>supernova</u>? _____

What part of speech is <u>recorded</u>? _____

What did Chinese astronomers do in the year A.D. 1054? _____

What might the Indians have done after they saw the supernova? _____

_____

What does <u>recorded</u> mean? _____

B. Reread the selection carefully. Try to guess the meanings of new words from the context. Use your dictionary only when absolutely necessary.

Check your answers in the "Getting the Main Ideas" section, which follows the reading. Correct your errors.

Understanding Reading Structure

In most reading selections, subtopics provide different kinds of support for the main ideas. *Definitions, reasons,* and *examples* are kinds of supporting information.

Follow the directions in parentheses to fill in the first part of the outline of the reading "Archeoastronomy" with the following subtopics. Then look back at the reading to check your outline.

To Help Nomads with Directions
Not Built by Ancient Inhabitants of Britain
Built by a Greek Architect
To Get Information About the Seasons for Hunters
To Get Information for Agriculture
To Study the Sky

✓ Stonehenge
✓ The Pyramids of Mesoamerica
Older Than the Pyramids of Egypt
Built in Three Different Time Periods
To Worship Objects in the Sky
✓ Images on Rocks in the Midwest

Archeoastronomy

I. Ancient Peoples and the Sky

    A. Mysteries of Ancient Peoples (Write three examples of mysteries.)

        1. *Stonehenge*

        2. *The Pyramids of Mesoamerica*

        3. *Images on Rocks in the Midwest*

    B. The Purposes of the Mysterious Structures (Write two reasons for their creation.)

        1. _____

        2. _____

II. The Mystery of Stonehenge

    A. Theories (Write two examples.)

        1. _____

        2. _____

    B. Facts (Write two examples.)

        1. _____

        2. _____

III. North American Astronomers

   A. The Importance of Astronomy (Write three reasons.)

   1. _____

   2. _____

   3. _____

   B. Attempts at Explanation Through Folk Stories and Religion

Now fill in the rest of the outline with the following subtopics. Then look back at the reading to check it.

   Astronomy = The Study of the Skies
   Enormous Drawings on Mountainsides
   Information About Venus and the Moon in Mayan Books
   Archeology = The Study of Ancient Things and People
   Writings of a Sixteenth-Century Priest
   Geometric Forms on Cave Walls
   Accurate Information in Calendars, Signs, and Symbols
   Archeoastronomy = A Combination of Astronomy and Archeology
   Theories About the Use of the Mesoamerican Pyramids
   "Medicine Wheels"

IV. Proof of Indian Astronomy (Write two examples.)

   A. _____

   B. _____

V. The Mayas and the Aztecs (Write three examples of evidence of their interest in astronomy.)

   A. _____

   B. _____

   C. _____

VI. Astronauts from Other Planets? (Write two reasons for this theory.)

   A. _____

   B. _____

VII. What is Archeoastronomy? (Write three terms and their definitions.)

   A. _____

   B. _____

   C. _____

Distinguishing Facts from Theories

In affirmative statements, certain words or expressions usually indicate the existence of facts—i.e., information that has been proven accurate. Here are some examples:

know	proof	certain
show	evidence	sure
prove	fact	positive
clear	scientific	objective

Other words can indicate theories—i.e., ideas that are believed by some people but that have not been proven to be true. Here are some examples:

think	theorize	possible
believe	claim	unscientific
suggest	(dis)agree	likely
subjective	probably	

A. On the line, write *fact* or *theory* for each statement, according to the presentation of the information in the reading selection.

1. *fact* — Ancient peoples were interested in and had knowledge of astronomy.

2. *theory* — Many mysterious ancient structures were built to study astronomy.

3. _____ — The earliest inhabitants of Britain built Stonehenge.

4. _____ — A traveling Greek architect built Stonehenge.

5. _____ — Stonehenge is as old as, or older than, the pyramids of Egypt.

6. _____ — Stonehenge was built in three different time periods.

7. _____ — Stonehenge functioned as a planetarium to study the skies.

8. _____ — Astronomy was important to the North American Indians.

9. _____ — The Indians drew symbols of the supernova that exploded in 1054 A.D.

10. _____ — The Indian designs in the shape of wheels are symbols of the sun.

11. _____ — The Indians held astronomical celebrations around the "medicine wheels."

12. _____   The purpose of the Aztec pyramids was to worship the sun and the moon.

13. _____   Astronauts from other planets visited South America in ancient times.

14. _____   The drawings on mountainsides in South America were created for visitors from the skies.

15. _____   Beings from other planets created calendars and symbols on rocks in South America.

B. Turn back to pages 176–177 and answer the questions you checked in Exercise C of the "Preparing to Read" section.

Discussing the Reading

1. Which facts in the reading make sense to you? Which theories do you believe? Why?
2. What theories do you have about the interest and knowledge of ancient peoples in astronomy?
3. Did you ever have theories about the skies, the sun, the moon, the planets, and the stars? If so, what facts did you later learn that proved or disproved your theories?
4. What theories do you have now?
5. Have you ever visited Stonehenge, the pyramids of Mesoamerica, or any other places mentioned in the reading? If so, tell about your experiences.

PART TWO

IS ANYBODY OUT THERE?

Skimming for Main Ideas

Read each paragraph quickly, without using a dictionary. To figure out the main idea, circle the letters of all the correct answers to the questions that follow. Then combine the answers to complete a sentence that expresses the main idea.

Is Anybody Out There?

A   When I was a child, back in the '50s and '60s, we used to go out into the backyard on hot summer nights and watch the sky. We'd lie on the cool grass and count the stars. Then we'd try to identify different constellations or planets. We waited and waited to see a shooting star, a supernova, or maybe a Soviet or American satellite—one with a dog or a monkey inside. Although we didn't know much about astronomy and probably couldn't have recognized a satellite if we saw one, I remember that we were fascinated by the night sky. It was enormous. Our teachers at school had told us that we could see about 2,500 stars on the very clearest night—but that there were hundreds of billions of stars that we *couldn't* see. So I began thinking about the possibilities of life out there. "Imagine!" I thought. "If the universe is so huge, maybe someone on another planet is lying on a cool green lawn and looking down at us. Is anybody out there?"

1. What is the one main topic of the paragraph?

   a. shooting stars
   b. Soviet and American satellites
   c. the universe
   d. astronomy courses in school

2. What details about the topic does the paragraph provide?

   a. The author is about 35 years old.
   b. The night sky can be fascinating.
   c. The universe is very, very large.
   d. Perhaps there is life in other places of the universe.

The main idea of the paragraph is that *the idea of life in other places in the universe is fascinating.*

B   As I grew up, I discovered that my fascination with the mysteries of the universe was certainly not unique. I read that many ancient peoples had studied the sky and believed that their gods lived there. Nowadays, science fiction books, movies, T.V. programs, and even children's toys make use of the idea of the possibility of life on other planets. Enthusiastic watchers of UFOs (unidentified flying objects) sometimes write magazine articles or appear on T.V. to tell about their experiences. Some claim they have seen spaceships from other planets, and others say they have actually met creatures that came out of these UFOs. Most of their stories have been proven inaccurate, but we human beings continue to hold onto our belief that life exists out there—somewhere.

1. What is the one main topic of the paragraph?

    a. interest in life in the universe
    b. unidentified flying objects
    c. ancient peoples
    d. beings from spaceships

2. What details about the topic does the paragraph provide?
    a. Ancient peoples believed that their gods were in the sky.
    b. Ideas about life in the universe appear in many modern forms of entertainment.
    c. The stars were used by travelers and farmers throughout the centuries to determine directions.
    d. Some people claim they have met living beings from other planets.

    The main idea of the paragraph is that _____

    _____

C   From college astronomy courses, I've learned more about the possibilities of life in the universe. I've learned that the stars and planets extend outward as far as our best telescopes can see; even with these powerful telescopes, we cannot see any sign of an end to the universe. However, life (as we know it) is possible on just a limited number of planets. Scientists say that three conditions are necessary for life to exist. A planet should have a temperature between 32 and 212 degrees Fahrenheit so that water can exist as a liquid, a suitable atmosphere (air and gas around a planet), and a sun of the right size. How many planets in the universe might satisfy these conditions? Probably millions.

1. What is the one main topic of the paragraph?

    a. the weather of planets
    b. the possibility of life in the universe
    c. the gases of the atmosphere
    d. the number of planets in space

2. What details about the topic does the paragraph provide?

    a. A sun must be very big to support life.
    b. A suitable temperature, atmosphere, and sun are essential for life.
    c. Planets near the earth must have life on them.
    d. Millions of planets in the universe have the necessary three conditions for life.

    The main idea of the paragraph is that _____

    _____

D   Most astronomers believe that life outside the earth is more than possible—it is probable. But they aren't waiting for a spaceship to land on the lawns of their planetariums so that they might talk to beings from other planets. Instead, many of these scientists believe that if we want to contact living creatures on other planets, we should use some form of electromagnetic energy—light, radio, etc.—for communication. They are suggesting that the government provide money for a well-organized center to "listen" to signals from outer space. If they succeed, we may finally find out the answer to the question "Is anybody out there?"

1.   What is the one main topic of the paragraph?

    a.   the possibility of life in outer space
    b.   the government
    c.   electromagnetic energy
    d.   methods of solving the mystery of life in the universe

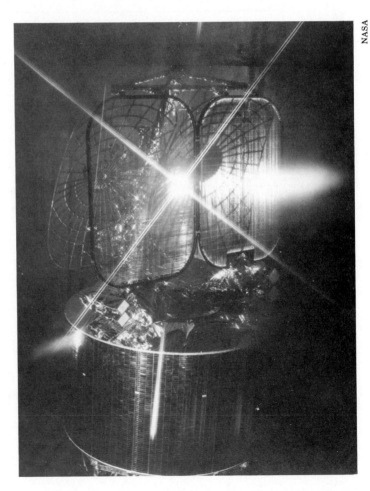

NASA

A modern-day
communications satellite

2. What details about the topic does the paragraph provide?

    a. We should send a spaceship to another planet to meet the creatures there.
    b. Communication with other beings can be in the form of electromagnetic energy.
    c. There should be a government center to try to find out about life on other planets.
    d. This center might solve some of the mysteries of the universe.

    The main idea of the paragraph is that _____

    _____

_____

Making Inferences

On the short lines, put a check by the statements that you can infer from the reading selection. Do not check the other statements, even if you think they are true. On the line after each statement that you check, write the phrases from the selection from which you inferred the information.

1. ____   All children watch the sky because they have studied astronomy in

    school. _____

    _____

2. ____   It isn't easy to recognize all the objects in the sky if you haven't studied astronomy. _____

    _____

3. ____   If the universe is so huge, then it seems possible that there is life on

    other planets. _____

    _____

4. ____   There are books and movies about creatures from outer space. _____

    _____

5. ____   People who say they have seen UFOs are crazy. _____

    _____

6. ____   No one has ever seen a creature from a spaceship. _____

    _____

7. ____   Any planet with a temperature between 32° F and 212°F, a suitable
atmosphere, and a sun of the right size has human beings on it.

_____

8. ____   A planet without these three conditions probably doesn't have life on
it. _____

_____

9. ____   Astronomers believe that a spaceship with creatures from another
planet will land on the earth in this century. _____

_____

10. ____   Modern science may help us solve the mysteries of life in the universe. _____

_____

Discussing the Reading

1. Do you believe that there is life on other planets in the universe? Why or why not?
2. If there is life, where do you think that it is? How might it look?
3. In your opinion, what should scientists do to find out about outer space? What should governments do?
4. Have you ever seen a UFO or do you know anyone who claims to have seen one? If so, describe your (his or her) experience.

PART THREE

BUILDING VOCABULARY AND STUDY SKILLS

Words with Similar Meanings

The words in each of the following groups have similar meanings, but they are not exactly the same. Match the words with their definitions by writing the letters on the lines. If necessary, check your answers in a dictionary.

1. ____   proof   a. written statement of facts
                            b. words or objects that support a belief
2. ____   evidence
                            c. a way of showing that something is true
3. ____   records

4. _____ prisoner   a. a member of an army
5. _____ enemy   b. members of the army of the other side
                               c. an enemy soldier caught and held
6. _____ soldier

7. _____ monument   a. a building or building-like object
8. _____ structure   b. a structure to honor or remember someone or something
9. _____ pyramid   c. a structure with slanted sides that meet at a point

Categories (Content Areas)

It often helps to learn words in groups (words with the same stem, words with similar meanings, words with opposite meanings, etc.). One method of grouping words is to put them together in categories, such as people, animals, buildings, and so on. One kind of category is a "content area"—i.e., the subject with which all the words are associated.

Examples: The following are words associated with the content area of astronomy: sun, moon, stars, planets.

Cross out the word in each line that does not belong. Explain your decisions: Tell the category or content area of the words that belong together.

1. stones   ~~monuments~~   rocks   caves   *(things in nature)*
2. astronomy   archeology   psychology   theory
3. satellite   planetarium   shooting star   supernova
4. architect   monkey   deer   camel
5. beliefs   knowledge   functions   customs
6. Mayas   Aztecs   Venus   Apaches
7. priests   inhabitants   soldiers   conductors
8. planet   sun   moon   pyramid
9. solstice   North Pole   South Pole   Equator

Word Roots (Stems) and Affixes (Prefixes and Suffixes)

It's often possible to guess the meanings of new words from word roots (also called "stems") and affixes (prefixes and suffixes). There is a list of many affixes on page 139. Here are more word roots and affixes and their meanings.

Prefixes	Meanings
a-, an-	no, without
ante-	before
poly-	many

Suffixes	Meanings
-ism	belief in; act or practice
-ist	a person who believes in or performs a certain action
-oid	like, similar to, resembling

Word Roots	Meanings
anthro, anthropo	man, human
aster, astro, stellar	star
ced	go, move
chrom	color
chron	time
metr, meter	measure
morph	form
scope	instrument for seeing
tele	far
theo, the	god

Without using a dictionary, guess the meaning of each word in italics. Use the list of word roots and affixes.

1. Archeologists believe that an earthquake *anteceded* the fire.

   a. caused
   b. happened after
   c. happened before
   d. put out; worked against

2. There were some *amorphous* clouds in the sky.

   a. without shape or form
   b. thick and dark
   c. beautiful
   d. related to rain

3. The ancient peoples of Mesoamerica were *polytheists*.

   a. very well educated
   b. people with many culture centers
   c. people who studied many languages
   d. people who believed in many gods

4. Movies often *anthropomorphize* creatures from other planets.

   a. study
   b. present in a terrible form
   c. give human form or characteristics to
   d. depict

5. There were *polychromatic* drawings on the cave walls.

   a. beautiful
   b. of many colors
   c. ancient; from many years ago
   d. related to the study of the sky

6. You can find a *chronometer* in one room of the planetarium.

   a. colorful chart
   b. very powerful telescope
   c. instrument for measuring the temperature of stars
   d. instrument for measuring time

7. Astronomers use *telescopes* to study the *asteroids* between Mars and Jupiter.

   telescopes:
   a. instruments for seeing distant objects
   b. satellites
   c. instruments for measuring
   d. space ships

   asteroids:
   a. satellites
   b. very bright stars
   c. small planets that look like stars
   d. unidentified flying objects

8. He used a *telemeter*.

   a. instrument for seeing something very small
   b. instrument for measuring how far away an object is
   c. instrument for measuring time
   d. instrument for finding directions

Marking a Book; Summarizing

Writing in a book often helps readers to understand and remember the information in in it. After you mark a reading selection, it may be easier to summarize it (to tell the main ideas in as few words as possible).

Example: Why do we have (day and night?) Every twenty-four hours, the earth turns on an axis, which reaches from the "top" to the "bottom" of the planet—from the North Pole to the South Pole. This regular revolution of the earth creates the time periods of day and night. The half of the world that faces the sun receives daylight while the other half is in darkness. Moreover, because the earth revolves toward the east, the sun seems to move in the opposite direction—i.e., from east to west. Thus the sun appears to "rise" in the east and "set" in the west.

   (The main topic of the paragraph is circled. The important words of the main points are underlined, and each supporting detail is numbered. Thus the important ideas can be easily summarized: The earth turns toward the east on an axis, which creates day and night every twenty-four hours.)

Mark each of the following paragraphs as shown above—with circles, underlines, and numbers. The summary that follows each paragraph will help you. Then compare your markings with those of your classmates.

1.   In addition to turning on its axis, the earth revolves around the sun. This regular journey of the planet takes 365¼ days—in other words, it takes that amount of time for the world to return to the same position relative to the sun. Because this solar year is six hours longer than our calendar year, we add one day to our calendar every four years. Thus, in "Leap Year" the month of February has 29 days.

   Summary: The earth's 365-day revolution around the sun creates a solar year of 365¼ days, but our calendar year is 365 days, except during Leap Year.

2.   Why does most of the world have seasons—usually summer, fall, winter, and spring? The earth's revolution on its axis creates day and night, while its 365¼ day revolution around the the sun creates the solar year. The reason for the seasons, however, is that the planet is tilted on its axis; that is, the earth's

axis is at an angle to the sun as the earth revolves around it. As a result, the northern hemisphere (half) of the world receives more sunlight during half the year than the southern hemisphere, while the opposite situation exists the rest of the year. Consequently, when it is summer on the northern continents, it is winter in the south, and vice versa.

Summary: It is the earth's tilt on its axis that creates the seasons because the half tilted toward the sun receives more sunlight than the half tilted away from it.

3.   Because of the tilt of the earth's axis, the sun appears to be high in the sky in summer and low in the sky in winter. Thus, in the northern hemisphere, the sun reaches its highest point around June 21, the summer solstice. This date is considered the first day of summer (the longest day of the year because it has the most hours of daylight). The winter solstice (December 21), by contrast, is the shortest day of the year—the day with the longest period of darkness. On about March 21, the "middle" of the planet—the Equator—faces the sun directly as the sun "moves north." This date, the "spring equinox," is considered the first day of spring; similarly, the autumn equinox occurs around September 23, as the sun moves south across the Equator. In the southern hemisphere, of course, the opposite situation exists.

Summary: The tilted position of the earth on its axis creates certain dividing points in the solar year: in the northern hemisphere, the summer solstice (June 21), the winter solstice (December 21), the spring equinox (March 21), and the autumn equinox (September 23). These dates are reversed in the southern hemisphere.

THE EARTH'S RELATION TO THE SUN

PART FOUR

SCANNING FOR INFORMATION

A. Read the explanation and study the vocabulary list.

> People who want to learn something about astronomy usually begin with identification of specific stars and groups of stars (constellations). The lists and the charts on pages 197–198 can serve as guides to the night sky.

mag. = magnitude; the relative brightness of a star

lt. years = light years; one light year = the distance that light travels in one year (about 5,878,000,000,000 miles)

visible = able to be seen

abbr. = abbreviation

determine = decide

orient (verb) = put something in a certain position

circumpolar = around the North Pole

pole star = Polaris, the North Star; the star in the northern hemisphere located above the North Pole, on the line of the earth's axis

select = choose

B. Scan the Sixteen Bright Stars table on page 197 and answer these questions.

1. What four kinds of information is given about each star in the list?

    _____

2. What indicates the temperature of the stars? _____

3. In which constellation can you find the star Vega? _____

    How far is it from the earth? _____

    What color is it? _____

    What is its temperature? _____

4. In what constellation can you find the star Antares? _____

    What is its magnitude? _____

    How far is it from the earth? _____

    What color is it? _____

    What is its temperature? _____

Sixteen Bright Stars

Stars	Constellations	Mag.	Distances (lt. years)	Colors*
Sirius ('see-ree-us)	Canis Major	−1.4	8.7	blue-white
Arcturus (ark-'too-russ)	Boötes	−0.1	36	yellow-orange
Vega ('vee-ga)	Lyra	+0.1	26	blue-white
Rigel ('rye-gel)	Orion	0.1	650	blue-white
Capella (kah-'pel-uh)	Auriga	0.2	47	yellow
Alpha Centauri (sen-'taw-ri)†	Centaurus	0.3	4.3	yellow
Procyon ('pro-see-un)	Canis Minor	0.4	11	yellow
Altair (al-'tare)	Aquila	0.8	16	white
Aldebaran (al-'deb-arun)	Taurus	0.8	68	orange
Betelgeuze ('bet-ul-jooz)	Orion	0.9	670	red
Antares (an-'tare-eez)	Scorpio	0.9	170	red
Spica ('spy-ka)	Virgo	1.0	150	blue-white
Pollux ('pol-uks)	Gemini	1.2	35	yellow
Deneb (den-'eb)	Cygnus	1.3	540	white
Regulus ('reg-you-luss)	Leo	1.3	85	blue-white
Fomalhaut ('foh-muh-lawt)†	Pisces Australis	1.3	22	white

*Colors indicate temperature, from blue-white (about 20,000°C) through white,
 yellow, orange to red (about 3,000° C).
†Not visible at middle and north latitudes in the United States.

5. How many stars cannot be seen from Canada? _____

6. How many stars have a temperature of about 3000° C? _____

7. Which star on the list is the closest to the earth? _____

    The farthest from the earth? _____

Major Constellations

Names	Abbr.	Pronunciations	Common Names
Andromeda	And	an-'drom-uh-duh	The Chained Princess
Aquarius	Aqr	ak-'ware-ee-uss	The Water Carrier
Aquila	Aql	'ak-wil-uh	The Eagle
Aries	Ari	'air-eez	The Ram
Auriga	Aur	oh-'rye-guh	The Charioteer
Boötes	Boo	boh-'oh-tez	The Bear Driver
Cancer	Cnc	'kan-sir	The Crab
Canis Major	CMa	'kay-niss major	The Big Dog
Canis Minor	CMi	'kay-niss minor	The Little Dog
Capricornus	Cap	kap-ruh-'kor-nuss	The She-Goat
Cassiopeia	Cas	kassee-oh-'pee-ya	The Queen's Chair
Cepheus	Cep	'see-fyooss	The King
Cetus	Cet	'see-tooss	The Whale
Corona Borealis	Cor Bor	kor-'oh-na bo-ree-'al-iss	The Northern Crown
Cygnus	Cyg	'sig-nuss	The Swan
Draco	Dra	'dray-koh	The Dragon
Gemini	Gem	'jem-uh-nye	The Twins
Hercules	Her	'herk-yoo-leez	Hercules
Hydra	Hyd	'hye-dra	The Water Snake
Leo	Leo	'lee-oh	The Lion
Lepus	Lep	'lee-pus	The Hare
Libra	Lib	'lee-bruh	The Scales
Lyra	Lyr	'lye-ruh	The Harp
Ophiuchus	Oph	off-ee-'you-cuss	The Serpent Holder
Orion	Ori	oh-'rye-un	The Hunter
Pegasus	Peg	'peg-uh-suss	The Winged Horse
Perseus	Per	'per-soos	The Hero
Pisces	Psc	'pye-seez	The Fishes
Sagittarius	Sgr	saj-uh-'tare-ee-uss	The Archer
Scorpius	Sco	'skore-pee-uss	The Scorpion
Serpens	Ser	'sir-penz	The Serpent
Taurus	Tau	'taw-russ	The Bull
Ursa Major	UMa	'er-suh major	The Great Bear (Big Dipper)
Virgo	Vir	'ver-go	The Virgin

C. Scan the Major Constellations table on page 198 to answer these questions.

1. How are the names of constellations arranged (in what order)?

   _____

2. What is the scientific name of the constellation with the abbreviation UMa?

   _____

   What is the nonscientific (common English) name for this group of stars?

   _____

3. What is the scientific name for the constellation with the abbreviation Gem?

   _____

   The nonscientific name? _____

4. What is the abbreviation for the constellation Hercules? _____

   For Orion? _____

5. What is the scientific name and the abbreviation for "The Water Carrier"?

   _____

   For "The Lion"? _____

   _____

D. Scan Diagram 1 (Circumpolar Constellations, next page), and follow these directions.

   1. Write today's date here: _____

   2. Determine the direction of north.

   3. Orient Diagram 1 so that the date corresponding to the time of year is downward.

   4. Answer these questions: If you face north tonight, (toward Polaris, the North Star), what constellation will you be able to see right in front of you? _____

_____

     Which constellation will be to the right of it? _____

     Which will be to the left of it? _____

E. Scan Diagram 2 (next page) and answer these questions. Pretend that today is January 15 and that it is 8:30 P.M. If you face south, which constellations will you see:

   1. in the Southwest? _____

   2. in the Southeast? _____

   3. directly overhead (above you)? _____

Going Beyond the Text

Bring to class the horoscope section of a local newspaper. Discuss the meanings of the signs. Find yours and read the prediction. Discuss new vocabulary, and summarize it for the class. Do you believe in astrology? Tell the class your opinions and the reasons for them.

Circumpolar Constellations

1. Northern hemisphere

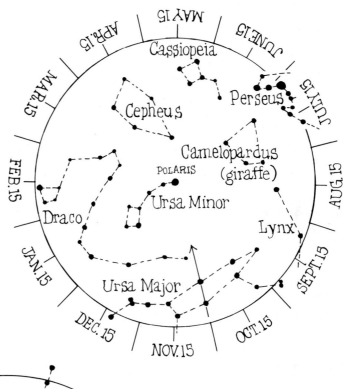

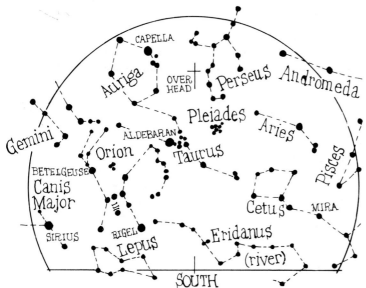

2. Northern hemisphere, looking south (January 15, 8:30 P.M.)

10

MEDICINE, MYTHS, AND MAGIC

PART ONE

THE WORK OF THE TRADITIONAL HEALER

Getting Started

Look at the pictures and discuss them.

1. What kinds of people are in the pictures?
2. Compare the pictures on the top with those on the bottom. What do all the pictures have in common? How are they different?

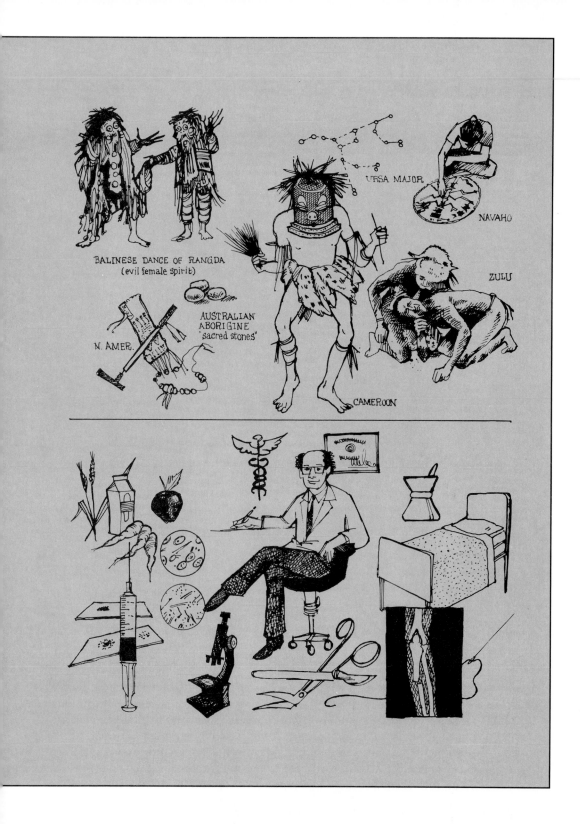

BALINESE DANCE OF RANGDA
(evil female spirit)

URSA MAJOR

NAVAHO

ZULU

N. AMER.

AUSTRALIAN
ABORIGINE
"sacred stones"

CAMEROON

Preparing to Read

A. Look again at the pictures on page 203. Then survey the reading selection on pages 204–206 by looking at the subheads. Put a check by the titles below that you believe will be discussed in the reading.

1. _____ Asian Methods of Medicine As Compared to Western Ones

2. _____ Comparison of Traditional Medicine with Modern Medicine

3. _____ Why We Get Sick

4. _____ How to Prevent Sickness

5. _____ Supernatural Methods of Treating Disease

6. _____ Ceremonies of Traditional Healers

7. _____ New Research on Astrology

B. Check the questions that you believe the reading selection will answer.

1. _____ How are the methods of traditional healers and modern doctors similar? How are they different?

2. _____ How do traditional healers view disease? How do modern scientists view it?

3. _____ What is the difference between methods of disease prevention in traditional societies and in modern urban ones?

4. _____ What are the steps in treatment of disease?

5. _____ How are tribal doctors learning the scientific methods of the West?

6. _____ What do traditional healers do in tribal ceremonies?

As you read the following selection, think about possible answers to the questions that you checked above.

The Work of the Traditional Healer

Traditional Healers and Modern Doctors

In most urban and suburban areas throughout the world, sick people are taken to a doctor's office or to a hospital for treatment. But among tribal and village people in many countries, patients are taken, instead, to a local healer. This person is a combination of a doctor, a priest, and a psychologist. Some of his or her folk methods are similar to those of a doctor, but most are very different. The difference in methods is a result of the fact that disease—to the modern, scientific mind—is viewed as something natural; it is caused by viruses, bacteria, and other small things that we can't see without a microscope. By contrast, in much of the world disease is considered to be something supernatural; in other words, sickness is not caused by something physical but instead is the result of deep anger, broken religious laws, the hatred of enemies, and so on. A physician knows how to treat a specific disease. A traditional healer, however, treats the whole person—and often the patient's family and friends as well.

Prevention of Disease

Of course, there may be no need for treatment if people know how to take care of themselves to prevent sickness. A modern physician might tell patients what to eat, how much to exercise, when and how to relax, and the like. A traditional healer, on the other hand, might tell patients to wear amulets—special necklaces for protection against bad spirits. Nevertheless, in both villages and urban societies, people do become ill and sometimes need medical help.

The Diagnosis

The first step in any treatment, of course, is the diagnosis: The doctor or the healer has to find out why the patient is ill and decide what to do about it. For the diagnosis, both ask about symptoms. (Is the patient complaining about headaches? Stomachaches? Insomnia? Skin rash?) But the similarity in methods ends there. The doctor's next step is to give blood tests, take X-rays, etc., while the healer might use supernatural methods. Healers might ask patients about their dreams, use astrology to find the cause of the problem in the stars, or go into a trance (a condition of deep concentration in which they don't function normally) in an effort to contact spirits or other beings outside the world.

The Cure

After the diagnosis comes the cure. In modern medicine, this solution usually means one or more of the following: the same methods that are used for prevention (healthful food, rest, exercise), perhaps warm baths or massage, drugs, or surgery. Likewise, folk medicine includes some of the same cures. As in the diagnosis, however, a healer also uses a wide variety of supernatural methods in his or her cures. Two of the most common are *exorcism* and *soul hunts*. Exorcism is based on the belief that disease is caused by bad spirits. Thus, in an exorcism ceremony, the healer performs a number of traditional activities to take the evil beings out of the victim's body. Songs, dances, and religious prayers are part of any exorcism, and soul hunts include them as well. In these ceremonies, the healer tries to persuade the victims' souls, which are believed to have left their bodies, to return.

A Typical Tribal Ceremony

The Ndembu people of Central Africa believe that illness is often the result of the anger of a relative, friend, or enemy. This emotion, they say, causes a tooth to enter the body of the person who is the target of the anger and to create disease. When the healer decides which body part contains the evil tooth, he calls together the victim's relatives and friends to watch a ceremony, at the end of which he "removes" it from the patient's throat, arm, leg, stomach, etc. Although the patient and the villagers know what has happened—that the tooth has been hidden inside the healer's mouth the whole time, the patient is often cured. The Ndembu ceremony is typical of treatments around the world, in which stones, insects, or small spears are taken out of sick people. Despite scientific evidence that disproves the effectiveness of such methods, the fact remains that the treatments are often successful, and many villagers prefer to be cured in this way than by a modern physician.

The Success of Traditional Healers

Scientists ask how traditional healers can actually be successful in their treatments and why they are so popular. The answers probably lie in a combination of the following reasons. First, supernatural ceremonies are symbolic, and the people who participate in them believe deeply in the symbols. Even Western physicians agree that patients with deep faith—belief in God, their doctors, the drugs they take, images, or symbols—will regain their health faster than patients with little hope. Second, ceremonies may be effective because people come together for a common goal; patients see how many people in their communities care about the cure. In addition, these communal meetings provide socially acceptable opportunities for the people of the village to express what they feel. Social and psychological problems can be solved along with the physical ones of the sick person. Fourth, scientists theorize that the trance parts of the ceremonies produce certain chemicals in the body, which then work to help cure the disease. Finally, many of the healer's natural drugs, which come from his or her surroundings (a nearby forest, jungle, or desert), have been found to be medically effective. Scientists are fascinated by what they learn from the methods of traditional healers.

Getting the Main Ideas

Write *F* on the lines before the statements about *folk* medicine and *m* before statements about *modern* medicine. In some cases, both answers are correct.

1. _____ Disease is thought to be produced by supernatural causes.

2. _____ People try to avoid getting sick by eating properly, exercising, and relaxing.

3. _____ The first step in treatment is the diagnosis of the illness.

4. _____ Spirits from other worlds are contacted through a trance.

5. _____ Rest, massage, chemical drugs, or surgery are possible cures.

6. _____ Through a ceremony, something bad is removed from the sick person's body.

7. _____ People get well more quickly if they believe they will regain their health.

8. _____ Social interaction and the help of relatives and friends are an important part of the cure.

Guessing Vocabulary from Context

A. On the lines, write words from the reading selection with similar meanings to the words listed. The numbers in parentheses refer to the number of *correct answers*.

1. doctor (1): _____

2. take care of (1): _____

3. sick (1): _____

4. disease (2): _____

5. sick person (2): _____

6. supernatural beings (1): _____

7. bad (1): _____

8. belief (1): _____

To understand the meaning of sentences or paragraphs, it is not always necessary to know the exact definitions of vocabulary items; in other words, often knowing the *general* meanings of a word is enough.

Example: Modern doctors use scientific equipment such as <u>microscopes</u> to figure out the causes of disease. (What are <u>microscopes</u>? They are a kind of scientific equipment. For this context, it is unnecessary to know exactly how they look or what they do.)

B. What is *essential* about the following vocabulary items—i.e., what do you need to know to understand their meaning in these contexts? Complete the general definitions.

1. In most urban and suburban areas throughout the world, sick people are taken to a doctor's office or to a hospital for treatment.

    A hospital is a place ___*where sick people are taken.*___

2. Disease is caused by viruses, bacteria, and other small things that we can't see without a microscope.

    Viruses and bacteria are _____

    _____

3. For the diagnosis, both the modern doctor and the traditional healer ask about symptoms. (Is the patient complaining about headaches? Stomachaches? Insomnia? Skin rash?)

    Insomnia and skin rash are _____

    _____

4. In modern medicine, the same methods that are used for prevention—healthful food, rest, and exercise—are often part of the cure (as well as warm baths, massage, drugs, or surgery).

    Exercise and massage are _____

    _____

5. Songs, dances, and religious prayers are part of any exorcism.

    Prayers are something _____

    _____

6. In these ceremonies, the healer tries to persuade the victims' souls, which are believed to have left their bodies, to return.

    Souls are something _____

    _____

7. When the healer decides which body part contains the evil tooth, he or she calls together the victim's relatives and friends to watch a ceremony, at the end of which the healer "removes" it from the patient's throat, arm, leg, stomach, etc.

   The throat is _____

   _____

8. Finally, many of the healer's natural drugs, which come from his or her surroundings (a nearby forest, jungle, or desert), have been found to be medically effective.

   Surroundings may be a forest, jungle, or desert that is _____

   _____

C. Reread the selection carefully. Try to guess the meanings of new words from the context. Use your dictionary only when absolutely necessary.

   Check your answers in the "Getting the Main Ideas" section, which follows the reading. Correct your errors.

Understanding Reading Structure

The following outline shows the organization of the comparison of the two kinds of medicine in the reading selection.

    I. Traditional Folk Medicine
        A. Theory of Disease
        B. Prevention of Disease
        C. Diagnosis
        D. Cure
   II. Modern Scientific Medicine
        A. Cause of Disease
        B. Prevention of Disease
        C. Diagnosis
        D. Cure

A. The following points are details of comparison from the reading. Show where they fit into the outline above by writing the appropriate roman numerals (I or II) and letters (A, B, C, or D) on the lines. Then look back at the reading to check your answers.

1. _____II A_____ Disease As a Result of Bacteria or Viruses

2. _____I B_____ Prevention of Illness with Amulets

3. _____ Giving Blood Tests and Taking X-Rays

4. _____   Songs, Dances, and Religious Prayers

5. _____   Illness As a Result of Bad Emotion

6. _____   Trances to Contact Supernatural Spirits

7. _____   Disease Caused by Evil Spirits

8. _____   A Tooth-Removing Ceremony

9. _____   Sickness As a Result of Broken Religious Laws

10. _____   Using Dreams and Astrology to Find Causes of Sickness

11. _____   Exorcism and Soul Hunts

Various paragraphs in most reading selections provide different kinds of supporting detail. Besides points of comparison, these might include steps in a process and reasons.

B. Complete the following paragraph outlines of the reading selection by adding the kinds of details asked for in parentheses.

A Typical Tribal Ceremony

(Write four steps in a process.)

I. *The healer decides which body part a tooth is in.*

II. *He or she calls together friends and relatives for a ceremony.*

III. _____

_____

IV. _____

_____

The Success of Traditional Healers

(Write five reasons.)

I. _____

_____

II. _____

_____

III. _____

_____

IV. _____

_____

V. _____

_____

Distinguishing Facts from Theories

A. Which of the following statements have been scientifically proven, and which are only beliefs that some people hold? On the line, write *fact* or *theory* for each statement, according to the presentation of the information in the reading selection.

1. _fact_   In most parts of the world, patients are taken to doctors or hospitals if they get sick.

2. _theory_   If people take care of themselves physically, they won't get ill and won't need doctors or healers.

3. _____ Disease is caused by something supernatural.

4. _____ Doctors should treat the whole person, not only the specific symptoms of the disease.

5. _____ Amulets protect people against disease.

6. _____ Blood tests and X-rays are ways to discover the cause of some illnesses.

7. _____ The Ndembu people of Central Africa have a ceremony in which the healer pretends to remove a tooth from a sick person's body.

8. _____ Many people get better after tribal ceremonies.

9. _____ Going into a trance will help patients get better.

10. _____ Some natural medicines from forests and jungles are effective.

B. Turn back to the beginning of the chapter and answer the questions you checked in Exercise B of the "Preparing to Read" section.

Discussing the Reading

1. Which facts in the reading make sense to you? Which theories do you believe? Why?
2. In what situations might a traditional healer help more than an urban physician can? In what situations might modern medicine be necessary? Why?
3. What are your personal theories about health, illness, and cures?

PART TWO

SUPERNATURAL HEALING: TWO CASES

Skimming for Main Ideas

Read each paragraph quickly, without using a dictionary. Mark the information in any way that helps you to understand it. (For example, you could circle the main topic, underline the important words of the main points, and number the supporting details.) Then use the information that you marked to complete the summarizing statement.

Supernatural Healing: Two Cases

An Eskimo Ceremony

A
It was early in the morning. In an Eskimo village, a woman named Nanoraq was so sick that she could hardly stand. All of the villagers were called together, and Angutingmarik, the healer, began to treat her. He walked back and forth for a long time before he called on the healing spirit for help.

When an Eskimo woman got sick, _____

_____ .

B
Angutingmarik began by diagnosing the cause of the illness. He asked the spirit about the cause of the woman's pain. Had he or his wife broken a *taboo* (a tribal law against a specific action)? Or had Nanoraq herself caused her illness? Finally, the sick woman told the truth: She had had evil thoughts and had broken many taboos.

To diagnose the illness, the healer _____

_____ .

C
The rest of the healing ceremony consisted of one confession after another. Nanoraq said that she had eaten a piece of meat at a time when it was taboo for her. She had combed her hair after giving birth to a child—and this, too, was a taboo. She had once stolen and eaten a salmon, taken a lamp that had belonged to a dead person, and touched a small bird at a time when she shouldn't have. The list of broken taboos went on and on. After each confession, the villagers all cried, "Such a small thing! Let her be forgiven!" or "That is a serious crime, but it doesn't matter. Let her get well!"

During the healing ceremony, _____

_____ .

D   Finally, the woman ended her confessions. The exorcism was repeated at noon and again in the evening. Then the villagers left her house. They believed that her evil acts had been forgiven and that she would regain her health soon. In addition, they felt that cultural values had been strengthened in her.

The woman was cured when _____

_____ .

Adapted from Knud Rasmussen, "Report of the Fifth Thule Expedition"

A Malay Ceremony

E   In a Malay village 180 miles from Kuala Lumpur, Pak Long Awang was a powerful healer. He put his patients into a trance that the people called "forgetfulness" to cure both physical and mental pain. Cultural objects, prayers, songs, and stories helped the patients fall into the healing state. Music was important in the ceremony—especially the regular sound of a drum.

Pak Long Awang was _____

_____ .

F   One village woman had always wanted to be a dancer. Although she was a wife and a businesswoman, she felt a deep need to entertain others and was very upset about her inability to perform in the Malay opera. She functioned well in society most of the time, but once a year her emotion became so strong that she lost all her energy, became ill, and had to go to bed.

The problem of one village woman was that _____

_____ .

G   At these times, Pak Long Awang was called. He and his helpers played music of the Malay opera to help the woman make the journey from the normal world into the mysterious state of a trance. In this supernatural world, she would get up and dance the role of a princess before her audience of friends and relatives. Afterwards, her symptoms disappeared. She was cured.

The woman was cured after _____

_____ .

Adapted from Carol Laderman, "Trances That Heal"

Making Inferences

Write T before the statements that are *true,* according to the information that is stated or implied in the reading. Write F before those that are *false.* Write I (*impossible to know*) before the statements that are not proven, disproven, or implied by the reading.

AN ESKIMO CEREMONY

1. __T__   Eskimos used to have ceremonies to heal patients.

2. __I__   Eskimo communities still call on healers when villagers become ill.

3. ____   Angutingmarik believed that Nanoraq herself had caused her illness.

4. ____   To the Eskimos, eating certain foods and touching certain things at the wrong time were taboos.

5. ____   Eskimos never comb their hair because they are afraid this action will lead to illness.

6. ____   Eskimo villagers forgive all the crimes of their people.

7. ____   The Eskimo ceremony included a kind of exorcism.

8. ____   The ceremony was a part of Eskimo culture that had more functions than just healing a patient.

A MALAY CEREMONY

9. ____   Pak Long Awang was the best healer in the history of Malaysia.

10. ____   Music is against the religion of the Malay people.

11. ____   It was the trance of the ceremonies that cured the patients, not the prayers or song.

12. ____   The Malay woman who wanted to entertain was an excellent singer and dancer.

13. ____   Her problem was more emotional than physical.

14. ____   Pak Long Awang's method had no basis in psychology or science.

Discussing the Reading

1. How can you explain the success of the ceremonies described in the readings?
2. What kinds of supernatural ceremonies have you heard about or participated in? Describe them and tell your opinions of them.

PART THREE

BUILDING VOCABULARY AND STUDY SKILLS

Categories

Circle the words in each item that belong in the underlined category.

1. <u>body parts</u>:

   target   (tooth)   exorcism   (throat)

2. <u>emotions</u>:

   anger   sadness   effect   cure   hatred

3. <u>symptoms of illness</u>:

   insomnia   blood   trance   rash

4. <u>things that cause disease</u>:

   patient   virus   bacteria   supernatural

5. <u>methods of diagnosis</u>:

   blood test   relaxation   X-ray   stomachache

6. <u>groups of people</u>:

   organization   tribe   community   society

7. <u>places to live</u>:

   suburbs   village   mosque   solstice

8. <u>kinds of structures</u>:

   pyramid   amulet   cave   monument

9. <u>kinds of meetings</u>:

   evil   spirit   ceremony   celebration

10. <u>words in medicine</u>:

    patient   priest   physician   treatment

11. <u>words in astronomy</u>:

    planet   universe   drug   space

12. <u>words in religion</u>:

    prayer   soul   faith   worship

Word Forms

Complete the sentences with the appropriate forms of these base words.

diagnose	nature	tradition
✓treat	be	accept
combine	effective	

1. In most urban and suburban areas of the world, sick people go to a doctor for
   treatment .

2. The healer is a _____ of doctor, priest, and psychologist.

3. In _____ village societies, disease is viewed as something
   outside the world—something _____ .

4. During the _____ , a doctor asks about symptoms.

5. While he or she is in a trance, the healer tries to contact spiritual _____
   _____s.

6. Folk medicines are often successful, and scientists are trying to find out the
   reasons for their _____ .

7. At communal ceremonies, villagers can express their feelings in a socially
   _____ way.

Word Roots and Affixes

Here are more word roots and prefixes and their meanings.

Prefix	Meaning
hyper- hypo-	above, beyond beneath, under

Word Root	Meaning
corp derm gam mort ortho spir	body skin marriage death straight, correct breathe

Without using a dictionary, guess the meaning of each word in italics. Use the list of word roots and prefixes. (Look back at the list in Chapter 9, Part Three, for additional help.)

1. He went to a *dermatologist* for help with his problem.

    a. person who studies bones
    b. eye doctor

    c. skin doctor
    d. person who helps people with mental problems

2. The *mortality* rate is very high in that village.

    a. birth
    b. death

    c. marriage
    d. divorce

3. The child began to cry when the doctor took out a *hypodermic* needle.

    a. large
    b. for use in the stomach

    c. for use on the skin
    d. for use under the skin

4. The little girl is *hyperactive*.

    a. very quiet, shy
    b. more active than is normal

    c. less active than is usual
    d. having difficulty with breathing

5. He's in the hospital on a *respirator*.

    a. strict diet
    b. special bed to help his back problems

    c. machine to help him breathe
    d. machine that pumps blood (as the heart does)

6. The physician looked at the *corpse*.

    a. dead body
    b. amulet

    c. ceremony
    d. rash

7. People in that village believe in *polygamy*.

    a. many gods
    b. marriage

    c. marriage to more than one person
    d. the necessity of marrying someone from a different village

8. They took their child to an *orthodontist*.

    a. doctor
    b. dentist

    c. dentist who straightens teeth
    d. doctor who helps people with breathing problems

Improving Reading Skills: Predictions

> Because good reading requires an active mind, fluent readers make use of "predictions" about the material they are reading. They try to guess quickly—without thinking about it—what is going to come next.

A. In each of the following sentences, complete the last word. Work as fast as you can and write your time (the number of seconds it takes you to finish) on the line. Try to work faster with each section.

1. You should take care of yourself to prevent ill_____*ness*_____ .

2. A healer might give an amulet to his or her pat_____ .—

3. A trance is a condition of deep concen_____ .

4. Many patients prefer to be cured by traditional methods rather than by a modern physi_____ .

5. Some scientists think that the trance produces healing body chemi_____ .

   Time: _____

6. Some natural cures for pain are warm baths and mass_____ .

7. Some people believe that illness is the result of the hatred of a friend or rela_____ .

8. The healer thought that the patient had broken a tab_____ .

9. The woman told the truth, and the villagers listened to her confess_____ .

10. At the end of the exorcism ceremony, all the victim's evil acts were for_____ .

    Time: _____

11. A dancer likes to entertain an aud_____ .

12. The patient felt weak; he didn't have any ener_____ .

13. The patient was cured and his symptoms disapp_____ .

14. Some illnesses are emotional and some are phy_____ .

15. This is a difficult problem; is there any sol_____ ?

    Time: _____

B. In these sentences, fill in the last word. (There may be more than one correct answer.) Work as fast as you can and write your time (number of seconds) on the line. Try to work faster with each section.

1. Disease is usually caused by _____ .

2. In a tribal society, if a man is sick, he may believe that he has broken a

    _____ .

3. Both healers and physicians treat _____ .

4. The patient has been feeling terrible; she has bad _____ .

5. Some people believe deeply in _____ .

    Time: _____

6. The earth turns on its axis every twenty-four _____ .

7. While half the world is in darkness, the other half receives _____ .

8. Because the earth revolves toward the east, the sun seems to move in the

    opposite _____ .

9. When it is summer in the North, it is winter in the southern _____ .

10. When I was a child, I used to watch the sky and try to see _____ .

    Time: _____

11. If we want to contact creatures on other planets, we should use _____ .

12. For life to exist, a planet must have a suitable _____ .

13. Do you believe that the universe has _____ ?

14. When I want to look at the stars, I go to the _____ .

15. Many ancient peoples had knowledge of _____ .

    Time: _____

PART FOUR

SCANNING FOR INFORMATION

A. Read the explanation and study the vocabulary list.

There has been a lot of study in the field of folk medicine. One part of folk medicine, as we've seen, is faith healing. The following index is from a book on the subject.

An *index* is a section in a book, usually toward the end, that helps you to find information in the book quickly because it gives page numbers. Items are not always listed according to the first word of a phrase; instead, last names appear first, and the most important words of a phrase may appear before the first word (e.g., if you want information about the "Society for Psychical Research," you look under the words "Psychical Research").

paralysis = loss of the ability to move

shrine = a religious place; a structure where people worship

synonym = a word that has the same meaning as another word

miracle = a very unusual event that some people believe is caused by God

B. Scan the index on the next two pages and answer these questions.

1. On what pages of the book can you find information about:

   a. paralysis? _____

   b. prayer? _____

   c. the use of massage? _____

   d. the interaction of body and mind? _____

   e. the healing shrine at Pompeii? _____

   f. the attitude of the Roman Catholic Church toward miracles? _____

   g. the healing beds of Pistoia? _____

2. How many last names are listed in this index that begin with the letter *n?* ___

   What name is listed in two sections? _____

3. What first names belong with these last names?

   a. Nightingale, _____

   b. O'Connor, _____

   c. Pio, _____

INDEX

4. What titles did these people have?

   a. William Osler: _____

   b. George May: _____

5. On what pages can you find information on medical practice:

   a. in ancient Middle-Eastern culture? _____

   b. in Judaism? _____

   c. in the folk medicine of Western Europe? _____

6. On what two pages is there information about mental illness? _____

   If you want more information on this, which two other topics can you look up

   in this index? _____

   Look up these two topics. What pages do they lead you to? _____

7. Where can you find information on paranormal healing? _____

   What is paranormal healing? _____

   Where else can you look in this index to find more information on this subject?

   _____

8. Which topic in this book might you really look up—i.e., which one interests
   you?

   _____

Going Beyond the Text

Look at the index of another book. How is it similar to the index from the book on
faith healing? How is it different?

   What is the book about? Name some subtopics that might be discussed in the
book. Look them up. Read the information and summarize it for the class.

11

THE MEDIA

PART ONE

MOVIE MAGIC

Getting Started

Look at the pictures and discuss them.

1. What is happening in each scene?
2. Which scene happened the furthest in the past? Which happened the most recently? How do you know?

224

Preparing to Read

Look again at the pictures and then survey the following reading selection. In addition to the subheads, look quickly at the first and last sentences of each paragraph. Then check the following questions that you believe will be discussed in the reading.

1. _____ When did the earliest movies appear?

2. _____ Were there illusions in the first movies?

3. _____ How was the movie business different from television?

4. _____ How did people become movie stars?

5. _____   What is the history of film lighting?

6. _____   Why is there so much crime in movies?

7. _____   What was used for blood in black-and-white movies, and what is used now in color ones?

8. _____   How is the computer used in making movies?

9. _____   How much do actors in Western films get paid?

10. _____   What are some substitutions that have been used in movie illusions?

11. _____   Who are the most famous directors of modern films?

12. _____   Where can you learn about the best films to see?

13. _____   How do movie makers these days create believable special effects in science-fiction films?

14. _____   How many musical films will be made in the next few years?

As you read the following selection, think about the possible answers to the questions that you checked.

Movie Magic

The Birth of the Motion Picture Industry

The enormous film industry of today had a relatively simple beginning. The first public showing of a motion picture—on May 22, 1891, at Thomas Edison's workshop in New Jersey—consisted of a polite man who bowed to the audience, smiled, waved, and took off his hat. Then in 1895, the Lumière brothers presented their first film; it depicted workers as they left the Lumière factory in France. Soon afterward, in 1896, three films were shown at Koster and Bial's Music Hall in New York City: one of a man walking his dog, another of a train arriving at a station, and a third of a balloon flying in the air. Each film was only about 30–90 seconds long; the quality was poor, and the images were jumpy, but these early moving pictures were a great success. They soon led to the creation of longer films (of about ten minutes each), such as George Méliès' *A Trip to the Moon* and Edwin S. Porter's *The Life of an American Fireman* and *The Great Train Robbery,* made between 1902 and 1905. These films, for the first time, told a story, and the motion picture industry was born.

The First Movie Illusions

Since its birth, the movie industry has been filled with illusion—i.e., things that seem to be real but actually aren't. The early movie makers and their audiences were as fascinated by the creation of illusions as film viewers are today. George Méliès, for example, was excited about the camera's ability to create "supernatural" images. He surprised his audience by showing people disappearing or objects flying through the air. His art seemed to be magic! Although the methods used then were very simple, the viewers accepted the images on the screen and believed them. In *The Great Train Robbery,* for instance, there was a lot of shooting; smoke came out of the guns, and men "dropped dead." There was no sound at the time. (The first "talking" motion picture—*The Jazz Singer*—didn't appear until 1927.) But even so, women in the audience of *The Great Train Robbery* put their fingers in their ears to shut out the "noise" of the guns. The imagination of the viewers, added to the pictures on the screen, made the illusion seem real.

Film Lighting

The reason why the American film industry moved to southern California early in the twentieth century was simple: the good weather. In the East, it rained, snowed, or was cloudy for several months every year, but in the West it was sunny year-round. "Inside" scenes were filmed outdoors in "rooms" with only two or three walls, so that the sun could light the scene. Unfortunately, this illusion was a poor one; the light looked exactly like what it was—sunlight—and not like the light inside a building. Nevertheless, when powerful lights came into existence and indoor scenes were actually shot inside, not all problems were solved. On the one hand, good weather was no longer essential, and movie makers could decide how to use the lighting in a scene. On the other hand, the heat of the huge lights made actors very uncomfortable. Among other problems, it caused ice cream to melt very quickly. Thus, film producers began looking for new solutions to create illusion. In this case, mashed potatoes, which didn't turn to liquid, were used instead of ice cream.

The Appearance of Blood

One of the most common illusions throughout the history of film has been the use of "blood." Because of the popularity of murder mysteries, war stories, horror movies, and westerns, there has always been an enormous amount of blood on the screen. Movie producers were challenged by two problems: *what* to use and *how* to use it. When movies were filmed in black and white, it was possible to use chocolate syrup as a substitute for real blood. These days, in color films, "blood" is a combination of Karo syrup, food dye Red. No. 33, and food dye Yellow No. 5. "How?" is a more difficult problem. In old westerns, when the "bad guy" was shot by the "good guy," he used to hit the place where he had been shot, say, "You got me," and drop to the ground. Though not very realistic, it was essential for the actor to hit himself in this way because "blood" was hidden in a small packet under his shirt. When he did this, the packet would break, and blood would come out through his fingers. These days, however, "bleeding" is a matter of technology. Sometimes, as in *The Godfather,* a performer may be shot over a hundred times! In such cases, the many packets hidden on the victim's body are attached to thin wires which, in turn, are connected to a computer. The computer causes each packet to explode at exactly the right moment.

Substitutions

Movie illusions include a wide variety of substitutions. Instead of letting actors or actresses fall off a building, producers use dummies (large dolls). Stunt people usually take the place of movie stars for the action of dangerous scenes. Instead of paying thousands of people to appear in a scene, movie makers have often made use of miniature figures to create the illusion of a huge crowd. Once, during the filming of *The African Queen,* tea leaves in clear water were even substituted for mosquitoes when the little insects couldn't be persuaded to perform. Some of the most creative substitutions can be found in sets from war movies. In one very early film, *The Battle of Santiago Bay,* miniature ships were put into inch-deep water. Smoke was essential to the scene, so the artist's wife offered to smoke a cigarette, and an office boy added a cigar. The film was a great success.

Special Effects

Today, of course, such simple methods of creating special effects would not be accepted by audiences who are used to seeing very believable action. Nowadays, especially in science-fiction films, very realistic-looking scenes are made possible by modern technology. Spaceships zoom through the universe, supernovas explode, and human (as well as not-so-human) astronauts fight each other for power and wealth. Viewers who are fascinated by this "movie magic" often ask how it is produced. Most of the illusions in these scenes combine the *real* (live performers) with the *imagined* (e.g., miniatures and painted scenes). The actors and actresses are often filmed separately from a picture of a spaceship; then a view of the stars and planets is shot. After that, miniature figures of creatures from outer space might be filmed, and so on. Afterwards, these separate elements are all combined on the same piece of film. In one "simple" 5- to 10-second piece of action, as many as eighteen different elements might be required. In addition, computers make possible new kinds of movement. The use of technology has led many viewers to believe that special effects—not live performers—are the true modern "movie stars."

Getting the Main Ideas

Write T on the lines before the statements that are *true,* according to the reading. Write F before the statements that are *false.*

1. _____ The motion picture industry began many hundreds of years ago.

2. _____ The first movies had many interesting sound and special effects.

3. _____ Even early movies included illusion.

4. _____ The lighting in early films came from the sun.

5. _____ In early movies, there was no blood, but now western and crime films use real blood.

6. _____ To create illusions, movie makers have used dolls, miniatures, and substitutions.

7. _____ Combinations of "special effects" are an important part of modern space movies.

Guessing Vocabulary from Context

A. On the lines, write words or expressions from the reading selection that fit these definitions.

1. a small package: *packet* _____

2. people or things taking the place of other people or things: _____

3. large dolls used in movies: _____

4. people who do dangerous things in movies: _____

5. very small: _____

To understand sentences or paragraphs, it is often enough to know only the general meaning of vocabulary items, rather than the exact definitions.

B. On the lines, write the items from the reading that correspond to these general meanings. The number in parentheses indicates the number of possible answers.

1. moving pictures (3): _____

2. words that describe things that seem real but aren't (3): _____

3. kinds of weather (4): _____

4. kinds of food (3): _____

5. people in movies (4): _____

6.   a kind of insect (1): _____

7.   things to smoke (2): _____

C. Reread the selection carefully. Try to guess the meanings of new words from the context. Use your dictionary only when absolutely necessary.

   Check your answers in the "Getting the Main Ideas" section, which follows the reading. Correct your errors.

Understanding Reading Structure

Time words often show the relationships between events and their order in time. Here are just a few examples:

first	next	after that
beginning	later	finally
at present	until now	

A. List the time words from the reading selection.

_____

_____

_____

B. Number the important events of the reading selection in order.

1.   _____   The motion picture industry moved to California.

2.   _1_   With the first films that told stories, the movie industry began.

3.   _____   A variety of substitutions were added to scenes for the purpose of illusion.

4.   _____   Audiences were surprised by simple illusions of flying or disappearing objects.

5.   _____   Through technology, separate elements were combined to create special effects.

C. Match each of the following lists with a paragraph from the reading selection by writing the paragraph's subtitle on the line. Then number the events of the list in order.

1. *film lighting* _____

   a. __3__   Objects were substituted for other objects to solve the problems of hot lights.

   b. __1__   Inside scenes were filmed in sunlight.

   c. __2__   Powerful lights were invented.

2. _____

   a. ____   Movies added sound.

   b. ____   Smoke came out of guns.

   c. ____   "Supernatural images" of objects seemed magical to the audiences.

3. _____

   a. ____   George Méliès made a film about a trip to the moon.

   b. ____   A man walked his dog, a train arrived, and a balloon flew into the air on film.

   c. ____   A film showed workers as they were leaving a factory.

   d. ____   A man in a film bowed to the audience and took off his hat.

4. (two subtitles) _____

   a. ____   Miniatures and painted scenes were filmed.

   b. ____   Different elements were combined on the same piece of film; new kinds of movements were created.

   c. ____   Dolls were used for stunts instead of people.

D. Turn back to the beginning of the chapter and answer the questions you checked in the "Preparing to Read" section.

Discussing the Reading

1. What is the oldest movie that you can remember seeing? How was it different from movies today?
2. What are some movie illusions other than those talked about in the reading? Can you guess how they are created?
3. Which do you prefer—old movies or modern ones? Why?
4. Are there theaters in your city that mainly show old movies?

PART TWO

MOVIE REVIEWS: THE CRITICS' CHOICE

Skimming for Main Ideas

Readers often glance at material quickly before they read it, to get a general idea of what it is about.

A. As quickly as you can (try to do this in about 30 seconds), look over the following four newspaper articles. Then write the appropriate article number next to the corresponding description.

1. _____   a positive review of a science fiction movie

2. _____   a negative review of a mystery film

3. _____   a negative review of a science fiction movie

4. _____   a positive review of a mystery film

B. Quickly read each paragraph again, without using a dictionary. Mark the information in any way that helps you understand it. Then use the information that you marked to write a summarizing statement.

Movie Reviews: The Critics' Choice

1.
A CLASSIC

Murder, She Says is a classic mystery that will be received most enthusiastically by people who enjoy folk culture. The film is like a traditional folk story, one that has been told and retold through the centuries by expert storytellers. Like a folk story, *Murder, She Says* contains little that is new or surprising. Instead, it has all the elements of the best whodunits — predictable elements, to be sure, but the beauty of this movie lies in the *way* the story is presented. The photography is good, the music is exciting, and the special effects are realistic but do not overpower the film itself. Best of all, the acting is wonderful. The stars succeed in being believable and in making their art look easy

2.
MUSEUM PIECE

It's easy to predict the ending of *Murder, She Says* within the first fifteen minutes of the movie. In fact, nothing in this film is surprising. It is, of course, a whodunit. An archeologist is murdered deep inside a Mesoamerican pyramid, and absolutely everyone in the film—his assistant, his wife, his brother, another archeologist, as well as the traditional healer of a nearby village—has a good reason to want him dead. A well-known detective is asked to come and solve the mystery, and, in the end, the murderer is found to be the only person who did not act like a killer. Every character in *Murder, She Says* is a stereotype from the old-fashioned movies of the '40s. We've seen it all before, again and again. This film belongs in a museum, not a theater. There is nothing unique or creative about it—no reason for even making

3.

PIX EFX WOW 'EM

Astrostation XZ901 is the latest science-fiction film to come out of Zonar Studios. It presents a fascinating view of the universe in the year 2103, when spaceships are as common as jet planes, solar power is the only kind of energy, and science is the only religion. Scientists are the priests of this future world, and satellites are their churches. Human beings have enormous physical strength and mental power, but they have lost the ability to feel any emotion. All feelings—sadness, happiness, nostalgia, excitement, fear, etc.—are considered to be taboo and are carefully exorcised in ceremonies which include the use of chemicals and X-rays. More important than the story, however, is that *Astrostation XZ901* offers the most exciting, believable effects that have ever been seen on a movie screen. Spaceships zoom realistically toward the audience, human beings melt before our eyes, and rays turn creatures into dust within a few seconds. The audience is pulled into this future world and given an opportunity

4.

XZ901 DISAPPEARS IN EFX

The biggest disappointment of the year is Zonar Studios' *Astrostation XZ901*. A huge amount of money has been spent on technology, but the movie is still not a success. It offers almost no acting, no story, and no ideas. The performers cannot move the audience emotionally because they have nothing to say and no ability to say it. The main character (played—badly—by Kurt Cute) is laughable and his co-star, Suzanne Slick, has the personality of a mosquito. With its total absence of value, the whole film consists of special effects that have no purpose; these shots cannot affect the audience in any way because there is no *reason* for them. This enormous failure is another typical case of the issue of expensive film illusion to try to hide the fact that the film makers have nothing to say.

Distinguishing Facts from Opinions

Even in readings that are *fiction* (not real), there is information that can be considered *fact* (true according to what is stated or implied) and statements that are the *opinions* of the writer.

Example: *Astrostation XZ901*, made by Zonar Studios, is a purposeless film consisting of nothing more than badly presented special effects.

(*Facts:* The movie *Astrostation XZ901* was made by Zonar Studios. It contains special effects. *Opinions:* The film has no purpose. It contains nothing of value, and the special effects are badly presented.)

On the short lines, write F before the statements that are *facts*, according to what is stated or implied in the reading. Write O before the statements that are (or may be) the *opinions* of the writers of the articles.

MURDER, SHE SAYS

1. _F_   *Murder, She Says,* is about an archeologist who is murdered.

2. _O_   This film belongs in a museum.

3. _____   In the movie, the archeologist's assistant was one person who had a good reason to want the archeologist to die.

4. _____   The elements of this mystery have appeared in many other films.

5. _____   The movie has music and special effects.

6. _____   Because there is nothing new or surprising in it, audiences will be bored.

ASTROSTATION XZ901

7. _____   *Astrostation XZ901* is a science fiction film.

8. _____   There are spaceships, scientists, and X-rays in the movie.

9. _____   The characters in the film have lost the ability to feel emotion.

10. _____   The actors and actresses who starred in the film have lost the ability to think or express their ideas.

11. _____   The film has no meaning because feelings cannot be exorcised in ceremonies.

12. _____   The special effects are fascinating.

13. _____   The stars of the film are not very effective.

14. _____   Special effects are expensive.

15. _____   Movie studios should not spend much money on special effects.

Discussing the Reading

1. Do you watch movie reviews on T.V. or listen to them on the radio? Do you read them in the newspaper? Why or why not?
2. What effect do you think the reviews have on the success of the movies they describe?
3. If you see the movie, do you usually agree or disagree with the opinions of the reviewer?
4. Do you think that movie reviews are good or bad for the motion picture industry? Why?

PART THREE

BUILDING VOCABULARY
AND STUDY SKILLS

Hyphenated Words

> Hyphens (-) have several meanings. For instance, a hyphen can replace the word *to*.
>
> *Example:*   Each film was only 30-90 seconds long. (30-90 = 30 to 90; i.e., between 30 and 90 seconds)
>
> Hyphens often connect word parts, especially of adjectives.
>
> *Example:*   In the West there is <u>year-round</u> sunshine. (<u>Year-round</u> means "throughout the year.")

Complete the sentences with the missing hyphenated words. Choose from these:

part-time	inch-deep	up-to-date
self-discipline	one-third	well-known
X-rays	old-fashioned	realistic-looking

1.   This mystery takes place in a hospital. A doctor kills patients by taking
     X-rays .

2.   When performers become famous, they do not forget their difficult pasts. One
     _____ actor friend of mine, for example, remembers that he
     used to spend about _____ of each day looking for work. He
     had to take many _____ jobs in fields other than entertain-
     ment. Acting is difficult work that requires a lot of _____ .

3.   In the past, illusions were created simply; in one war movie, for instance, mini-
     ature ships were put in bowls of _____ water. Nowadays,
     however, audiences expect that _____ special effects will be
     created by _____ technology. They are no longer satisfied
     with simple, _____ stories and good acting.

Figurative Language

All words have at least one *literal* (basic, usual) meaning. Many words, more-over, have additional meanings that are *figurative*; that is, when they are used nonliterally, they may produce various images in the minds of the readers.

Example: Audiences are <u>pulled</u> into the film by the fascinating special effects.
(<u>Pulled</u> in this context does not mean "physically moved by something in front of them." Rather, it means "attracted.")

A. Complete this selection by filling in the blanks with words (or parts of words) used figuratively. Choose from the underlined words that appear elsewhere in the selection with their literal meanings.

Soon after the ____*birth*____ of the motion picture industry, producers began looking for ways to create illusion. Because ice cream <u>melted</u> under the hot lights of movie sets, they substituted mashed potatoes, and they _____ scenes with chocolate <u>syrup</u> instead of blood. Through the years, <u>Western</u> <u>science</u> and technology have developed these illusions into special _____s.

I find these developments unfortunate. Personally, _____ fiction films bore me. Again and again, spaceships zoom through the universe, and planets <u>explode</u> in wars. I hate modern motion pictures because they don't have an emotional <u>effect</u> on me. I much prefer old-fashioned films: the kinds of _____s, for instance, in which a cowboy _____ dead after he had been <u>shot</u>. I miss the _____y emotion of traditional love stories, in which the starring actress _____d with anger at her male co-star, or a tear <u>dropped</u> from her eye in a particularly moving scene, or she _____ into the arms of her lover when he returned alive from a war. Eventually, of course, these films had predictable happy endings—marriage and the <u>birth</u> of babies—yet I still look back at them with nostalgia.

B. In this book and other sources, find examples of words used in figurative ways. Copy the sentences and write the most interesting on the board. Discuss the literal and figurative meanings of the words.

Improving Reading Skills

To be a good reader, it is not necessary to understand every word or even every sentence of a selection, exactly. In fact, good readers usually accept some amount of uncertainty when they read; i.e., they decide which words and sentences are essential for understanding the main ideas and important details. Instead of worrying about the other elements of the selection, they then go on to other, more important material.

> ★ **JEAN DE FLORETTE** (PG, Royal). This film is like good peasant bread: honest, chewy, unsurprising and heavily satisfying. A tragicomedy of time and place— 1920s southern France, where various interests are fighting over a lone natural spring—"Jean de Florette" is zestfully well acted by Gerard Depardieu, Yves Montand and relative newcomer Daneil Auteuil.

Example: What is important about a movie review? Perhaps the name of the film, the director, the main actors, the type of film (comedy, drama, tragedy, romance, science fiction, or adventure), and something about the story. In the review above, we find the following information:

title: *Jean de Florette*
theater: Royal
type of film: tragicomedy
actors: Gérard Depardieu, Yves Montand, Daniel Auteuil
story: various people fight over a natural spring (a small river) in France in the 1920s
opinion of the critic: honest, unsurprising but satisfying; well-acted

Because they were written for a big-city newspaper, the following movie reviews contain vocabulary that may seem difficult to nonnative speakers. Nevertheless, it is not necessary to understand every word or sentence to get the meaning of the reviews.

Underline the words and phrases that seem important. Then answer the questions about each movie.

> **NADINE** (PG, citywide). This little sweet nothing from writer-director Robert Benton—concerning a recently divorced couple who (sort of) get back together again—benefits so much from the chemistry between its two stars, Kim Basinger and Jeff Bridges, that you many not mind its thinness. Benton's loving look at yet another offbeat, tenacious Texas woman—Bonnie Parker and the sisters of "Places in the Heart"—is pretty much the light beer of movies, but enough happens to you that you may not mind so very much !

1. What is the name of the film reviewed on the previous page? _____

    Who is the director? _____

    Who are the main actors? _____

    What is the film about? _____

    What is the critic's opinion of the film? _____

    _____

> **EAT THE PEACH** (Times-rated: Family; Cineplex and Westside Pavilion). This easy-tempered Irish comedy is based on a real-life episode: an unemployed machinist, inspired by the Elvis Presley movie ''Roustabout,'' erects a ''Wall of Death'' cylindrical motorcycle track near his house; as he follows Elvis' dream, reality chastens him. Writer-director Peter Ormrod gives the movie lots of nice, naturalistic touches—and Eamon Morrissey and Niall Toibin are excellent as a sidekick and would-be entrepreneur—but the movie needs more obsessiveness and drive from its central character, more psychological levels.

2. What is the title of this film? _____

    Where is it playing? _____

    Who is the director? _____

    Who are the main actors? _____

    What is the film about? _____

    What is the critic's opinion of the film? _____

    _____

> **BACK TO THE BEACH** (PG, citywide). After 20 years, Frankie Avalon and Annette Funicello return to Malibu—to visit their grown-up daughter (Lori Loughlin). A deft, funny movie that's nostalgic without being embarrassing and knowing without being either cruel or cynical. With Connie Stevens, Tommy Hinkley and many guest stars, including Pee-wee Herman. The feature directing debut of Australian Lyndall Hobbs.

3. What is the name of this film? _____

    Where is it playing? _____

    Who is the director? _____

    Who are the main actors? _____

    What is the film about? _____

    What type of movie is it? _____

> ★ **ROXANNE** (PG, citywide). It's hard to recall a current movie in which every element is in such balance as it is here, in a modern retelling of the Cyrano story that becomes a warm, nimble, utterly contemporary modern romance. There's a tenderness to writer/star Steve Martin's performance as C. D. Bales that's magnetic, and Darryl Hannah's Roxanne, an astronomer, is smart and sublimely beautiful all at once. What's interesting is to discover that the essence of the original play's love triangle—a beautiful woman finding out just who she loves, and why—is as as strong in sunshine as in shadow.

4. What is the name of this film? _____

Who are the main actors? _____

What type of movie is it? _____

What is the critic's opinion of it? _____

PART FOUR

SCANNING FOR INFORMATION

A. Read the explanation and study the vocabulary list.

Before viewers go to the movies, they often check the entertainment section of a newspaper to find out what is available. Besides names of movies, theaters, producers or directors, and performers, this guide from an urban newspaper contains "mini-reviews" of the films.

language (in this context) = "bad" language; vulgar words

mature = thinking and understanding like an adult

immature = thinking and understanding like a child

nudity = being without clothes

teens = teenagers; people thirteen to nineteen years old

sci-fi = science fiction

suitable = correct, proper, right

appropriate = suitable

earthy = concerned with things of the body, not of the mind

spy = a person who steals secrets from another country

wed = to marry

rebukes = expressions of strong disapproval

district attorney = a lawyer for the government

struggle = fight; work hard

nerd = an unpopular, boring, unattractive person (slang word)

B. Scan the movie reviews to find the answers to the questions that follow them.

Rating symbols in parentheses after movie title:

G = for general audiences; a good movie for children

PG = "parental guidance"—parents should decide if this movie is good for their children; there might be something in it that is unsuitable for small children

PG-13 = "parental guidance" is suggested for children under thirteen

R = restricted; children and teenagers under seventeen may enter the movie theater only with an adult

X = no one under seventeen may enter the theater

1. Look at the parental film guide below. Then, in the following chart, fill in the ratings for each movie and check all the items that apply.

PARENTAL FILM GUIDE

As a guide for family viewing, Calendar indicates areas of content (theme, language, sex, violence) that may be inappropriate for the very young or impressionable. MPAA or The Times' ratings are in parentheses.

FAMILY
BACK TO THE BEACH (PG). Wholesome family film.

DISORDERLIES (PG). Some distant and discreet glimpses of nudity; appropriate for entire family.

THE GARBAGE PAIL KIDS MOVIE (PG). A G-rating seems more appropriate for this children's movie.

INNERSPACE (PG). A mild profanity here and there.

MAID TO ORDER (PG). A few blunt words but suitable family fare.

THE MONSTER SQUAD (PG-13). Despite cautionary rating, suitable children's fare.

SUPERMAN IV: THE QUEST FOR PEACE (PG).

MATURE
May be too intense in themes, language, violence and/or sexuality for immature or younger teen-agers.

ADVENTURES IN BABYSITTING (PG-13). Some language and some violence.

BEVERLY HILLS COP II (R). Language, violence and nudity.

THE BIG EASY (R). Nudity, sexual situations, violence, language

BORN IN EAST L.A. (R). Seems unduly severe rating, some earthy talk and situations but suitable family fare.

CAN'T BUY ME LOVE (PG-13). Some toilet humor and sexual innuendo.

DIRTY DANCING (PG-13). Adult themes and situations; perfectly appropriate for teens.

DRAGNET (PG-13). Language

FULL METAL JACKET (R). Violence, bloodshed, much too intense for children.

HAMBURGER HILL (R). Typical war movie bloodshed and strong language; not for small children

JAWS THE REVENGE (PG-13). Violence, bloodshed, shark attacks.

JEAN DE FLORETTE (PG). Two bits of violence that might upset children; OK for teens.

LA BAMBA (PG-13). Language, adult situations

THE LIVING DAYLIGHTS (PG). The usual Bondian comic-book mayhem, nothing really objectionable

MY LIFE AS A DOG (Times-rated: Mature). Too intense for children, but teens should identify and benefit from it.

NADINE (PG). Some low-intensity sexual situations

NO WAY OUT (R). Nudity, sexual situations, language, violence

RITA, SUE AND BOB, TOO! (R). Sex, nudity, language.

ROBOCOP (R). Extreme and graphic violence, language.

ROXANNE (PG). Frank (but not indecent) discussions of love and desire; OK for teens.

STAKEOUT (R). Language, brief nudity, violence.

SUMMER SCHOOL (PG-13). Teen comedy with language stronger than rating would suggest

TAMPOPO (Times-rated: Mature). Sexual situations, adult themes.

THE UNTOUCHABLES (R). Graphic violence and foul language

THE WHISTLE BLOWER (R). Some violence, too downbeat and convoluted for pre-teens

WISH YOU WERE HERE (R). Nudity, language, sexual situations

WITHNAIL AND I (R). Strong language, adult situations; not for the very young.

| Movie | Rating | Has some: | | | Suitable for: | |
		Sex or nudity	Bad language	Violence	Children	Teens
The Big Easy	——	——	——	——	——	——
Born in East L.A.	——	——	——	——	——	——
Dirty Dancing	——	——	——	——	——	——
Disorderlies	——	——	——	——	——	——
Full Metal Jacket	——	——	——	——	——	——
The Garbage Pail Kids Movie	——	——	——	——	——	——
Maid to Order	——	——	——	——	——	——
My Life As a Dog	——	——	——	——	——	——
No Way Out	——	——	——	——	——	——

2. Look at the list of movies below. Then, in the chart on page 244, check each film's type.

CALENDAR

MOVIES

CONTINUING

Ratings are by the Motion Picture Assn. Categories: (G) for general audiences; (PG) parental guidance urged because of material possibly unsuitable for children; (PG-13) parents strongly are cautioned to give special guidance for attendance of children under 13; (R) restricted, under 17 admitted only with parent or adult guardian; (X) no one younger than 17 admitted. Opinions are by Times reviewers Sheila Benson, Kevin Thomas, Michael Wilmington, Patrick Goldstein and Charles Solomon. Especially noteworthy movies are designated with a ★.

BACK TO THE BEACH (PG, citywide). After 20 years, Frankie Avalon and Annette Funicello return to Malibu—to visit their grown-up daughter (Lori Loughlin). A deft, funny movie that's nostalgic without being embarrassing and knowing without being either cruel or cynical. With Connie Stevens, Tommy Hinkley and many guest stars, including Pee-wee Herman. The feature directing debut of Australian Lyndall Hobbs. (Thomas)

BEVERLY HILLS COP II (R, citywide). Fifteen minutes of this careening, screaming experience and you begin to know how a tenderized flank steak feels, even though—to his credit—Eddie Murphy avoids the trappings of infallibility that the screenwriters would lumber him with. And when the trademark Murphy scatology is mixed with gratuitous nudity, the effect is not worldly fun but childish crudity. (Benson)

THE BIG EASY (R, selected theaters). This film has several methods of establishing its authority over your attention: one is the palpable electricity between Dennis Quaid (as the faintly corrupt, smooth-talkin' New Orleans police lieutenant) and Ellen Barkin (as the post-strait-laced, mid-'80s-uptight assistant district attorney investigating police corruption). Another is the feeling of New Orleans that goes beyond the familiar iron filigree and the ''N'Awlins'' lilt of the voice. Add to these some delectable supporting bits (most particularly by the late Charles Ludlam as the lieutenant's attorney) and stir with knee-bending sexuality. (Benson)

BORN IN EAST L.A. (R, citywide). An across-the-board winner, an exuberant crowd-pleaser from writer-director-star Cheech Marin, who casts himself as a third-generation American who nevertheless finds himself deported to Tijuana. Amidst the hilarity, Marin makes his points about about the second-class nature of U.S. citizenship for minorities and about the desperate plight of illegal aliens. With Daniel Stern, Kamala Lopez. (Thomas)

CAN'T BUY ME LOVE (PG-13, citywide). Another gimmick movie—excuse us, "high concept"—in which a high school nerd pays a gorgeous cheerleader to date him for a month, later discovering that coolness and the in-crowd are no bed of roses. This feeble script doesn't really deserve the sometimes charming performances of its young leads, Patrick Dempsey and Amanda Peterson, or Steve Rash's sometimes lively direction; the moral here—you can't buy popularity—is something the moviemakers should take to heart themselves. (Wilmington)

THE CARE BEARS' ADVENTURE IN WONDERLAND (G, citywide). Another formula adventure for the determinedly cute teddy characters that reduces bits of Lewis Carroll's classics, "The Prisoner of Zenda," "Androcles and the Lion" and the Three Stooges to so much saccharine mincemeat. The minimal plot, sappy songs, limited animation and smarmy message are virtually indistiguishable from many other recent cartoon features. Small children deserve better. (Solomon)

DEATH SHADOWS (Times-rated: Mature; Little Tokyo Cinemas). Master samurai director Hideo Gosha's highly stylized, gorgeously photographed saga about a woman warrior, a member of the Shogunate secret police, and her struggle to bring down a corrupt lord. Convoluted plot yields a strong sense of fatalism, tempered with dark humor. Mariko Ihihara, Masanori Sera and Mari Natsuki star. (Thomas)

⭐ **DIRTY DANCING** (PG-13, selected theaters). Smart and funny, touching and unabashedly sensual, this musical love story set in the Catskills in the early '60s is the sweet sleeper of a hot season. Because director Emile Ardolino comes from a background in dance films (including "He Makes Me Feel Like Dancin'"), he doesn't insult us with the impossible, the too-easily achieved. Instead, the dancing is smart and sympathetic and, as a musical, "Dirty Dancing" is one of the most significant fusions of drama and dance since "Saturday Night Fever"—and more involving. (Benson)

DISORDERLIES (PG, citywide). Good-natured but exceedingly slight comedy starring the Fat Boys, one of the hottest rap groups in music today, and Ralph Bellamy as an ailing tycoon given a fresh lease on life by their antics. Disappointingly, the Fat Boys—Mark Morales, Damon Wimbley and Darren Robinson—have only one big musical number. With Anthony Geary, Tony Plana. (Thomas)

DRAGNET (PG-13, citywide). It's a shame that decisions were made to interrupt this fond recollection of the old show with slam-bang car-crashes, silly pagan rituals and other Big Movie-isms. A double shame, because there are patches of bright dialogue in the script by Dan Aykroyd, Alan Zweibel and the movie's director, Tom Mankiewicz. And Aykroyd and Tom Hanks play off each other to great effect. It makes the film seem absolutely schizophrenic. (Benson)

EAT THE PEACH (Times-rated: Family, Westside Pavilion). This easy-tempered Irish comedy is based on a real-life episode: an unemployed machinist, inspired by the Elvis Presley movie "Roustabout," erects a "Wall of Death" cylindrical motorcycle track near his house; as he follows Elvis' dream, reality chastens him. Writer-director Peter Ormrod gives the movie lots of nice, naturalistic touches—and Eamon Morrissey and Niall Toibin are excellent as a sidekick and would-be entrepreneur—but the movie needs more obsessiveness and drive from its central character, more psychological levels. (Wilmington)

THE FOURTH PROTOCOL (R, citywide). Based on Frederick Forsyth's novel, the film concerns the construction of a miniaturized atom bomb and how the device could topple NATO. Stars Michael Caine, Pierce Brosnan and Ned Beatty. Directed by John Mackenzie.

⭐ **FULL METAL JACKET** (R, selected theaters). In this film, director Stanley Kubrick brings his rigorous artist's eye to Vietnam to create a powerful and centered statement of outrage. Although its two sections—observing the antiseptic madness of Parris Island and the too-mortal chaos in Vietnam proper—are not perfectly balanced, it is a muscular return to form for the man who made "Dr. Strangelove" and "A Clockwork Orange." And in a superb cast of mostly unknowns, Vincent D'Onofrio and ex-Marine drill instructor Lee Ermey are exceptional. (Benson)

THE GARBAGE PAIL KIDS MOVIE (PG, citywide). They should have kept the lid on this one, a limp morality tale for children about the folly of judging by appearances and featuring those gross but friendly critters featured on bubble gum cards. Anthony Newley is a kindly antiques dealer whose 14-year-old assistant (Mackenzie Astin) gets help from the garbage pail kids in pursuit of a hard-bitten type (Katie Barberi). (Thomas)

GAUGUIN: WOLF AT THE DOOR (R, selected theaters). Henning Carlsen's biographical drama on Paul Gauguin (played by Donald Sutherland) focuses on the painter's 18-month stay in Paris and Brittany before his final departure for Tahiti, like Carlsen's 1966 "Hunger," it's a chronicle of an artist *in extremis*, enduring and severing all the rebukes that society can inflict. Sutherland's Gaugin skimps a bit on the savagery, but the film is shot beautifully and sensitively. And it has a lovely performance, by Sofie Graboel, as the young girl who loves the libertine artist upstairs. (Wilmington)

HAMBURGER HILL (R, citywide). Standard issue patriotic Vietnam War movie centering on one the war's bloodiest battles and marred by a heavy dose of rabble-rousing preachiness. A little subtlety would have greatly enhanced the film's potential for tragic irony. Featuring 14 newcomers, the most prominent of which are Courtney Vance and Dylan McDermott. (Thomas)

JAWS THE REVENGE (PG-13, citywide). With this latest installment in the seemingly never-ending "Jaws" saga, the very notion of the escapist summer movie bottoms out with a joyless gurgle. Dumb beyond belief, hollow, bloody and nonsensical, it's Universal Pictures' vanity movie, a way of providing employment once again for its Great White icon. (Benson)

⭐ **JEAN DE FLORETTE** (PG, Royal) This film is like good peasant bread honest, chewy, unsurprising and heavily satisfying. A tragicomedy of time and place—1920s southern France, where various interests are fighting over a lone natural spring—"Jean de Florette" is zestfully well acted by Gerard Depardieu, Yves Montand and relative newcomer Daniel Auteuil. (Benson)

LA BAMBA (PG-13, citywide). Although this film of the tragically brief life of Latino rocker Ritchie Valens has its strengths—especially the fine turn by the unknown Lou Diamond Phillips—the wonder is that the movie isn't full of raw energy, that it's for the most part polite melodrama, no more electrifying than the ordinary '50s musical bio-pic. There is the honesty, however, great dollops of '50s songs, and it lifts the movie when the dialogue and the earnest-but-uninspired direction (by Luis Valdez) keeps it earthbound. (Benson)

THE LIVING DAYLIGHTS (PG, citywide). Yes, the new Bond—Timothy Dalton—is splendid, and everything Bondish is back in force: hurtling cars, parachutes, ski troops, paratroops, troops of toy soldiers, troops of Afghan freedom fighters, missives, missiles, heroin and heroines. Is it possible that, with this Bond chapter, the 15th, audiences have outgrown the gizmos? It feels that way. (Benson)

LIVING ON TOKYO TIME (Times-rated: Mature; Westside Pavilion and Los Feliz). Steven Okazaki's minimalist comedy about two lovers who can barely communicate or connect—a Japanese-American janitor, an aspiring rock guitarist of pumpkin-like passivity and a tourist from Tokyo who weds him for a green card. It's the cinematic equivalent of a bass guitar's dirty fuzztone rubbing aurally against the strummed zithery plonks of a Japanese koto. If you ignore its low-budget austerity and occasionally awkward performances, it has its own special rewards—the laughter bubbling out from a near-limbo: curious silences, quirky dead spots, deadpan speeches with their own incongruous wait of atonal, blocked-off absurdity. (Wilmington)

MASTERS OF THE UNIVERSE (PG, citywide). A sword-and-sorcery epic based on the famous toy line and syndicated TV cartoon series; in this case, it might have worked better with the cartoon characters in the leads. Or even the toys. Dolph Lundgren, as the redoubtable "He-Man," gives a nearly incomprehensible, polyethylene performance—and the plot has the legions of Eternia invading Colby, Calif.: a town so blase that nobody shows up for the intergalactic war on Main Street. But three cheers for Billy Barty as the Yoda-clone, Gwildor: He's the only actor who gives this movie any real fairy-tale fervor. (Wilmington)

THE MONSTER SQUAD (PG-13). Delightful horror comedy aimed at youngsters, about a group of small-town boys who take on Count Dracula and other beloved baddies in a struggle for an amulet that controls the balance between good and evil in the universe. Andre Gower is the boys' leader, Duncan Regehr is Dracula. With Leonardo Cimino, Stephen Macht and Stan Shaw. (Thomas)

★ **MY LIFE AS A DOG** (Times-rated: Mature; Music Hall). Somehow, director Lasse Hallstrom has caught all the perils and delights of treading that knife edge between pain and delight that is childhood blending to adolescence. A sterling film whose style sits between the light moments of his Hallstrom's fellow Swede, Ingmar Bergman and the darker moments of Francois Truffaut's childhood films. (Benson)

NADINE (PG, citywide). This little sweet nothing from writer-director Robert Benton—concerning a recently divorced couple who (sort of) get back together again—benefits so much from the chemistry between its two stars, Kim Basinger and Jeff Bridges, that you many not mind its thinness. Benton's loving look at yet another offbeat, tenacious Texas woman—Bonnie Parker and the sisters of "Places in the Heart"—is pretty much the light beer of movies, but enough happens to you that you may not mind so very much. (Benson)

★ **NO WAY OUT** (R, citywide). Abetted by director Roger Donaldson's main strengths—bedrock believability, solid, self-effacing technique and the bristling tension of his sexual relationships—this cracklingly fine thriller plumbs the depths of deception in the federal government. The action is whizzingly fast but the performances are lovingly fleshed out. The greatest prize is Kevin Costner as the youngish Navy officer around whom the baroque plot unwinds; he's fiercely good, intelligent and appreciatively sensual. (Benson)

★ **ROBOCOP** (R, citywide). This comic book-style sci-fi actioner about an automated cop—in a futuristic Detroit where private industry has taken over the police—has been assembled with ferocious, gleeful expertise. It's crammed with humor, cynicism and jolts of energy. The script nastily parodies everything from vacuous TV commentators to dope dealers to cut-throat corporate warfare; it satirizes a society—an exaggeration of our own—where every tendency toward dehumanization and centralization has gone hellishly out of control; and it suggests that Robocop Murphy's private struggle between humanity and his programming is a noble one. Dutch Director Paul Verhoeven—aided by top-notch Hollywood pros—does a sensational job here; this may be the best action movie of the year. (Wilmington)

★ **ROXANNE** (PG, citywide). It's hard to recall a current movie in which every element is in such balance as it is here, in a modern retelling of the Cyrano story that becomes a warm, nimble, utterly contemporary modern romance. There's a tenderness to writer/star Steve Martin's performace as C. D. Bales that's magnetic, and Darryl Hannah's Roxanne, an astronomer, is smart and sublimely beautiful all at once. What's interesting is to discover that the essence of the original play's love triangle—a beautiful woman finding out just who she loves, and why—is as as strong in sunshine as in shadow. (Benson)

★ **TAMPOPO** (Times-rated: Mature: Fine Arts). Japanese films have commented before on the intrinsic connection between food and sex, but not with the erotic gusto of director Juzo Itami's "Tampopo" and rarely with the comic lustiness of this broad-scale satire. What's delightfully unsettling about the film is its lubricious mix of the sensual and the satiric—no sooner do we settle ourselves for one when the other comes along to knock the props out from under our expectations. (Benson)

THE WHISTLE BLOWER (R, selected theaters). A taut, understated British spy thriller that develops striking parallels with Costa-Gavras' "Missing." A notably bitter expression of Britain's decline of power and of the helplessness of the individual when confronted with an implacable, monolithic government agency. Marvelous performances by Michael Caine, Nigel Havers, John Gielgud, Barry Foster and others. Directed by Simon Langton (of "Smiley's People") and adapted by Julian Bond from the John Hale novel. (Thomas)

Movie	Science fiction	Comedy	Drama	Musical	Spy
Dirty Dancing	——	——	——	——	——
Disorderlies	——	——	——	——	——
Gauguin: Wolf at the Door	——	——	——	——	——
The Living Daylights	——	——	——	——	——
Living on Tokyo Time	——	——	——	——	——
Robocop	——	——	——	——	——
The Whistle Blower	——	——	——	——	——

3. What country is each of these films probably from?

   a. *Tampopo:* _____

   b. *My Life As a Dog:* _____

   c. *Nadine:* _____

   d. *The Whistle Blower:* _____

   e. *Eat the Peach:* _____

4. Match the following movies with their stories. Write the letters on the lines.

   1. ____   *Born in East L.A.*

   2. ____   *Can't Buy Me Love*

   3. ____   *Robocop*

   4. ____   *The Fourth Protocol*

   5. ____   *The Big Easy*

   6. ____   *Gauguin: The Wolf at the Door*

   7. ____   *The Monster Squad*

   8. ____   *Living on Tokyo Time*

   a. A famous painter suffers from society's rebukes.

   b. A small atom bomb is constructed that could destroy NATO.

   c. A third-generation American is deported to Tijuana, Mexico.

   d. A police lieutenant meets an assistant district attorney in New Orleans.

   e. An unpopular high school student pays a beautiful girl to date him.

   f. A group of boys struggle for an amulet that controls the balance between good and evil in the universe.

   g. A policeman who is part human and part robot fights crime in the future and struggles between his humanity and his programming.

   h. A tourist marries a Japanese-American janitor (who wants to be a rock guitarist) because she wants a green card.

5. List three films that the critics liked very much. _____

    _____

    List three films that the critics disliked. _____

    _____

    Which film did the critics not express an opinion about? _____

    _____

6. Have you seen any of these films? _____

    If so, which ones? _____

    What did you think of them? _____

    _____

    _____

    Do you agree or disagree with the critics? _____

    _____

    _____

7. Who are Thomas, Benson, Wilmington, and Solomon? _____

8. Which of these films would you like to see? _____

    _____

    Why? _____

Going Beyond the Text

Bring to class the movie section of a local newspaper. Discuss the new vocabulary. Then choose one film that interests you and summarize the review for the class. Go to see the movie and tell the class about it.

12

PREJUDICE, TOLERANCE, AND JUSTICE

PART ONE

THE CONCEPT OF LAW

Getting Started

Look at the picture and discuss it.

1. What is the scene? Who are the people and what are they doing?
2. Make up a story about the scene. What might have happened before this scene began? Why might the people be in this situation? What might happen next?
3. Would a comparable scene in your culture be similar? Why or why not?

Preparing to Read

If you ask questions before and during the reading process, and then think about the answers, your reading will be more active; you will probably understand and better remember the material you have read.

A. Look at the picture again and then scan the reading selection that follows. List questions that you think the reading might answer.

1. _____

2. _____

3. _____

4. _____

5. _____

6. _____

B. As you read the following selection, think about possible answers to the questions that you wrote above.

The Concept of Law

The Idea of Law

The idea of "law" exists in every culture. All societies have some kind of law to keep order and to control the interactions of people with those around them. The laws of any culture tell people three things: what they *can* do (their rights), what they *must* do (their duties), and what they may *not* do (illegal actions). In addition, there are usually specific types of punishment for those who break the law.

What Prevents Crime?

Although all societies have laws, not all have the same idea of justice—which is "right" and "wrong" and how "wrong" should be punished. In most Western cultures, it is thought that punishing criminals will prevent them from committing other crimes. Also, it is hoped that the fear of punishment will act as a deterrent that prevents other people from committing similar crimes; in other words, people who are considering a life of crime will decide against it because of fear of punishment. In most non-Western cultures, by contrast, punishment is not seen as a deterrent. Instead, great importance is placed on restoring balance in the situation. A thief, for example, may be ordered to return the things he has stolen instead of, as in Western societies, spending time in prison.

Kinds of Law

Another difference in the concept of justice lies in various societies' ideas of what laws are. In the West, people consider "laws" quite different from "customs." There is also a great contrast between "sins" (breaking religious laws) and "crimes" (breaking laws of the government). In many non-Western cultures, however, there is little separation of customs, laws, and religious beliefs; in other cultures, these three may be quite separate from one another, but still very much different from those in the West. For these reasons, an action may be considered a crime in one country but be socially acceptable in others. For instance, although a thief is viewed as a criminal in much of the world, in a small village where there is considerable communal living and sharing of objects, the word *thief* may have little meaning. Someone who has taken something without asking is simply considered an impolite person.

Civil Law and Society

Most countries have two kinds of law: criminal and civil. People who have been accused of acts such as murder or theft are heard in the criminal justice system, while civil justice deals with people who are believed to have violated others' rights. The use of the civil system reflects the values of the society in which it exists. In the United States, where personal, individual justice is considered very important, civil law has become "big business." There are over 600,000 lawyers in the United States, and many of them keep busy with civil lawsuits; that is, they work for people who want to sue (bring legal action against) others. If a man falls over a torn rug in a hotel and breaks his arm, for instance, he might decide to sue the hotel owners so that they will pay his medical costs. In a country like Japan, by contrast, there is very little use of the civil justice system. Lawsuits are not very popular in Japan, where social harmony (peaceful agreement) is even more important than individual rights, and where people would rather reach agreements outside court.

The Judgment of Disputes

In most cultures, when people cannot reach agreement on their own, a judge might be called on to make a decision. In North America, a case might be heard in a court of law before a judge chosen by the government and, perhaps, a group of citizens in a jury. In some tribal societies, however, a man or a woman who is thought to have special supernatural power might be chosen by the people to judge disputes. In the 1950s, among the Gisu people of Uganda, the inhabitants of a village had great faith in a man who was believed to have the ability to cause smallpox, a serious disease. On Sundays, they went to his "court," where he charged a fee for his judgments of cases. Although the Ugandan government considered this practice illegal, he was very popular with the people.

Social Justice

In societies where courts and judges simply don't exist, self-help is necessary and socially acceptable in disputes. If a cow has been stolen, the owner's friends and relatives may get together and help him get the animal back. In small villages, everyone, in a sense, becomes a judge; in such societies, where people's neighbors are also friends, members of their families, or co-workers, the opinions of the villagers are very important. Social disapproval of people's activities can serve both as powerful punishment for and as strong deterrent to crime.

Modern and Traditional Justice

In some countries, traditional and modern justice exist side by side. A good example of this combination can be found in Tanzania, where people usually take their legal disputes first to family leaders or the representatives of their village "age-set," a group of people of about the same age. If the disagreement cannot be settled by these leaders, then the case is taken to a modern court. The people who are part of the dispute will argue until both sides agree, for the goal is to restore a situation of balance and social harmony.

Getting the Main Ideas

A. Write T on the lines before the statements that are *true,* according to the reading. Write F before the statements that are *false.*

1. _____ The concept of law and justice is the same in every culture.

2. _____ Punishment serves to bring back balance to situations or to prevent other crimes.

3. _____ Every country's laws are based on historical customs and religious beliefs.

4. _____ In urban societies, crimes are usually judged in the criminal law system, while personal disagreements are resolved by other methods.

5. _____ In every society, it is illegal and socially unacceptable to solve conflicts without lawyers and courts.

B. The reading selection gives examples of concepts of justice in the United States and other Western countries, Japan, and traditional village societies. Choose the important ideas about these systems and write them on the lines, without mentioning the specific society. Then exchange books with a classmate. Write _US_ in the parentheses before the statements about the United States, _J_ before those about Japan, and _tr_ before those about traditional societies. Exchange books again to check the answers.

1. (*US*) *Punishment is considered a deterrent to crime.*

2. (   ) _____

3. (   ) _____

_____

4. (   ) _____

_____

5. (   ) _____

_____

6. (   ) _____

_____

7. (   ) _____

_____

8. (   ) _____

_____

Guessing Vocabulary from Context

A. Here are some vocabulary items that might be new from the reading. Try to determine the definition of each item from the context and write it on the line. Then
check your answers in a dictionary.

1. concept = _____
2. punishment = _____
3. justice = _____
4. deterrent = _____
5. commit = _____
6. restore = _____
7. balance = _____
8. order = _____
9. prison = _____
10. sin = _____
11. lawsuit = _____
12. sue = _____
13. harmony = _____
14. dispute = _____

B. Are there other vocabulary items in the reading that are new to you? If so, write them in a list on the left-hand side below. Then try to determine their meanings from the context, write definitions, and check your answers in a dictionary.

C. Now reread the selection carefully.

Understanding Reading Structure

A. Write your own outline for each paragraph of the reading selection. (There may be several correct possibilities.) Then compare your outlines with those of your classmates and explain the reasons for your organization of the information.

   I. The Idea of Law

       a. *What People Can Do*

       B. *What People Must Do*

       C. *What People May Not Do*

   II. What Prevents Crime?

III. Kinds of Law

_____

_____

_____

_____

_____

_____

IV. Civil Law and Society

_____

_____

_____

_____

_____

_____

V. The Judgment of Disputes

_____

_____

_____

_____

_____

_____

VI. Social Justice

_____

_____

_____

_____

_____

_____

VII. Modern and Traditional Justice

_____

_____

_____

_____

_____

B. Turn back to the beginning of the chapter and answer the questions you wrote in the "Preparing to Read" section.

Discussing the Reading

1. In Exercise B of the "Getting the Main Ideas" section, which follows the reading, you listed statements about various systems of justice. In your opinion, what other cultures or countries do these statements refer to? Why?
2. What else do you know about the system of law and justice in the United States or Canada? Compare it with the system in your culture.
3. What kind of justice system seems most advantageous to you? Why?

PART TWO

MY LAWSUIT THAT WASN'T

Skimming for Main Ideas

Read the following selection quickly, without using a dictionary. Then list the main ideas (the important events) of the story.

1. *A friend talked to the writer about lawsuits.*

2. _____

3. _____

4. _____

5. _____

My Lawsuit That Wasn't

A few weeks ago, I went to a party at my friend Carl's house. I hadn't really wanted to go. I had a backache and would have preferred to stay home, but I knew that if I didn't show up, Carl would be disappointed.

I decided not to stay very long, so I explained to Carl about my back and told him that I wanted to go home early. That was my first mistake. Carl immediately looked interested.

"How did you get that backache?" he asked.

"Well," I said, "I'm not sure. Maybe I just need to buy a new bed; the mattress on mine might be too soft. Or—oh, I don't know—it doesn't hurt very badly. Maybe it happened when I fell down."

"Aha!" he said with enthusiasm. "When did that happen?"

"As I was coming out of Anita's Health and Beauty Place."

"That's it!" Carl shouted. "I'm sure you hurt your back when you fell. I have just one word of advice for you: *sue.*"

"What?" I said. "Why? Perhaps all I need is a good massage and a little rest. Then I'll be fine."

"Don't miss this opportunity," he said excitedly. "My cousin Michael was in a traffic accident a few years ago, and he sued the driver who caused the accident. He won the lawsuit, and the driver not only had to take care of all of Michael's medical treatment, but he also had to pay Michael $10,000 in cash."

"You're kidding," I said.

Carl shook his head. "No. It's true."

My second mistake was letting Carl persuade me to see his lawyer, whom I'll call "Harvey."

"This will be a great case," Harvey told me after I had explained the situation. "Your backache began when you fell over something just outside the door to Anita's. It seems clear that this was Anita's fault. Probably the entrance to the shop was slippery or was in bad condition."

"I'm not sure about that," I answered. "I don't think that's exactly what happened."

Harvey smiled. "But that's the best way to present the case to the judge."

To me, Harvey seemed a little too enthusiastic. This made me uncomfortable because I wanted to settle this problem without "stretching the truth."

Going to the next lawyer, "Scott," was my third mistake. As soon as he had heard my story, he grinned from ear to ear.

"This will be a challenging case," Scott said. "But I think we can win. First, you have to learn one basic fact about lawsuits: If you want to win a lot of money, you have to choose the right person to sue."

"What?"

"Sure. In this situation, for example, we won't even try to sue Anita. Her beauty shop is small, so she can't be very wealthy. Instead, we'll have to find some evidence that you fell on the city sidewalk—not on private property. The city government," he smiled, "has lots of money. The possibilities are limitless."

I did not want to get into a long conflict with the city government; I just wanted to solve the problem of my aching back. So I visited a third lawyer, who had successfully helped another friend of mine settle his case out of court.

At first, this lawyer seemed helpful. "Hmmm," said "Louise" after she had heard the facts, asked a lot of questions, and thought about the problem for a long time. "You probably won't want to go through a long lawsuit—that can take years. But after we begin filing our papers, we can probably settle this case out of court, and get some money for you."

"That sounds reasonable," I said. "What do we do first?"

"About my fees," Louise continued, "of course you will have to pay direct costs—there's the cost of filling out forms, secretarial time, the price of copying, mail, parking at the courthouse, and so on. I charge an hourly rate—some now, some later. Now if you will just write out a check, and sign here. . ."

"Uh . . . ," I answered, as I reached for my coat. "Let me think about it a little more, and I'll call you. . . ."

"Don't forget," said Louise as I was on my way out. "You mustn't talk about the case to anyone—anything you say could be held against you later on. And of course, don't go to Anita's until this is settled. You can do your own hair, and . . . ."

Finally, I did something right. I went to "Richard," a lawyer who didn't say much, but who seemed very certain about his opinions. After he had listened to my story, he looked at me across his desk and shook his head.

"You may not appreciate my advice," he said, "but here it is. If I were you, I'd get some rest and then a good massage. Then, if I had a few hundred dollars, I'd buy a new bed with a very good mattress. Of course, I'm not a doctor, but I think this could be a very effective cure for your backache. In short, I see no basis for a lawsuit."

I grinned. "Thanks for your opinion," I answered, "but you're wrong about one thing. I do appreciate your advice very much!"

Making Inferences

What can you infer about the American legal system from the reading? List the possibilities.

_____

_____

_____

_____

_____

Discussing the Reading

1. In your opinion, what are the author's feelings about the American legal system? Do you agree or disagree? Why?
2. Have you or someone you know ever been involved in a lawsuit? If so, what happened?
3. In what situations would you go to a lawyer? In what situations would you sue? Why?
4. How do you usually solve disagreements? Are you usually satisfied with the solutions? Why or why not?

PART THREE

BUILDING VOCABULARY
AND STUDY SKILLS

Categories (Content Areas)

A. What categories (content areas) are the following words usually connected with?
Write ___*ed*___ on the lines before the words about education;
___*rel*___ before the words about religion; ___*med*___ before words about
medicine; ___*l*___ before words about law; and ___*bus*___ before words about
business and money. In a few cases, more than one answer may be correct.

1.	*ed* classroom	17.	___ bargain	33.	___ credit
2.	*l* jury	18.	___ crime	34.	___ sin
3.	___ virus	19.	___ disease	35.	___ worship
4.	___ budget	20.	___ advertise	36.	___ physician
5.	___ justice	21.	___ worship	37.	___ prison
6.	___ blackboard	22.	___ instructor	38.	___ salesclerk
7.	___ courtroom	23.	___ judge	39.	___ faith
8.	___ sue	24.	___ lesson	40.	___ charge
9.	___ priest	25.	___ dispute	41.	___ exam
10.	___ account	26.	___ assignment	42.	___ cash
11.	___ symptoms	27.	___ punishment	43.	___ deterrent
12.	___ prayer	28.	___ lecture	44.	___ consumer
13.	___ ceremony	29.	___ memorize	45.	___ hospital
14.	___ treatment	30.	___ marketing	46.	___ graduate
15.	___ patient	31.	___ cure	47.	___ surgery
16.	___ merchandise	32.	___ illegal	48.	___ discount

B. Divide into groups. The class chooses a content area, such as astronomy, travel, city
life, work, art, geography, movies, etc. Within a given time limit, each group writes
a list of as many words as possible connected with the content area. Then the class
discusses the words. The winner is the group with the most correct words. Then
repeat the activity with another content area.

Improving Reading Skills: Prediction

Fluent readers often make use of prediction when they read; they try to guess, without thinking about it, what is going to come next. The following exercises may improve your ability to predict.

A. Fill in the words missing from the following paragraphs. There may be several correct answers. When you are finished, discuss the reasons for your choices.

In disputes in which a reasonable _agreement_ seems impossible,

it may be _____ to get the help of a lawyer.

_____ a good one is not easy. You might want to ask friends for

_____ , but their suggestions may help only if their cases were

_____ to yours. There may also be _____

in your area that provide lists of _____ with their specialties.

It is important to choose a lawyer who _____ a lot about the

particular _____ that you are worried about.

Your first _____ is to call the lawyer and

_____ an appointment to see him or her. During this first

_____ , you may not get answers to specific legal

_____ , but you can find out about the lawyer's

_____ and fees, and you can see if you get a positive

_____ from the conversation. If you ask, you may not have to

pay _____ for this first meeting. Its purpose is to

_____ whether or not this lawyer is the best one to take care of

your _____ .

Lawyers make most of their money by _____ for their time.

They usually charge by the hour, and add up _____

_____ for phone calls, writing _____ ,

filling out legal _____ , and so on. To save yourself

_____ , always be prepared before you call or

_____ your lawyer: Write a _____ of your

questions and _____ before you begin your discussion. Then,

during the session, listen _____ , take notes, and

_____ organized. Always be honest with your

_____ and tell him or her all the _____ .

In addition , provide the lawyer with all the written _____ you

have on the case.

B. Find sections from reading selections at the level of the class. Rewrite the material, but leave out every eighth word. Have copies made for everyone in the class. You and the other students try to figure out the missing words from clues in the reading. Then discuss the reasons for your choices.

PART FOUR

SCANNING FOR INFORMATION

A. Read the explanation and study the vocabulary list.

Some people try to avoid lawyers whenever possible. They may not have the money to pay high legal fees; if there is no disagreement, they might want to take care of simple matters on their own. If there is a dispute, moreover, these people may prefer to settle matters out of court, if possible. Although many situations in North American society require legal knowledge, more and more people are trying to get as much information as they can and complete as much of the work as possible themselves. One possibility for them is a Do-It-Yourself Legal Action Workshop. The brochure on the next page is from such an organization.

vs. = versus; against; in conflict with

attorney = lawyer

consultation = discussion with a lawyer, usually in person

retainer = large fee paid to a lawyer at the beginning of a case

rate = hourly fee

exceed = be bigger than

client = customer; person who needs legal help

salary = the money that a person is paid for his or her work

analyze = study each part and its relationship to the whole situation

B. Scan the brochure. Which of the following activities happen in a traditional law office (or legal clinic)? Which happen in the Legal Action Workshop? Check the appropriate column in the chart on page 262.

LET'S COMPARE
Traditional Law Office or Legal Clinic
vs.
Legal Action Workshop "PROGRAM METHOD"

In a traditional Law Office or Legal Clinic, you meet their attorney who may request a minimum retainer against an hourly rate which means the fee can greatly exceed the retainer—**ALL PAID FOR BY YOU, THE CLIENT!**

VS.

At the Legal Action Workshop, in most programs, we give you private consultation with our L.A.W. attorney where a one time, low cost program fee is requested of you, the client. **YOU SAVE MONEY!**

At a traditional Law Office or Legal Clinic additional consultations with their attorney, including telephone calls and face to face meetings, each increase their fee to you substantially. **TIME PAID FOR BY YOU, THE CLIENT!**

VS.

Using the Legal Action Workshop "Program Method," you receive unlimited consultations with an L.A.W. attorney at workshop sessions at no additional fee. Quality! Service! Efficiency! **YOU SAVE TIME AND MONEY!**

At a traditional Law Office or Legal Clinic, their attorney obtains information from you, the client, by asking you questions and gathering needed facts to begin your case. **ATTORNEY TIME PAID FOR BY YOU, THE CLIENT!**

VS.

At the Legal Action Workshop, specially designed client questionnaires accompanied by our attorney's clearly presented cassette tape provide our L.A.W. attorney all information needed to handle your legal matter. **SAVE ATTORNEY TIME—YOU SAVE MONEY!**

At a traditional Law Office or Legal Clinic, their attorney dictates information to a legal secretary who prepares and types the paperwork. (APPROXIMATELY 75% MORE TIME SPENT IN TYPING COMPARED WITH L.A.W. COMPUTER PREPARED DOCUMENTS.) Legal Secretary salaries are rising. **THESE COSTS ARE PAID FOR BY YOU, THE CLIENT!**

VS.

At the Legal Action Workshop, the L.A.W. computer analyzes your questionnaire information, prepares your legal paperwork for review by our L.A.W. attorney and L.A.W. files your papers with the Court. **NO LEGAL SECRETARY NEEDED! FEWER ERRORS! GREATER EFFICIENCY! YOU SAVE TIME AND MONEY!**

At a traditional Law Office or Legal Clinic, their attorney may not receive a large number of similar cases or may not be prepared to offer you, the client, rapid service. Your paperwork may take longer than necessary to complete because it is not computerized and your case may be delayed. **TIME WASTED! PAID FOR BY YOU, THE CLIENT!**

VS.

At the Legal Action Workshop, experienced attorneys are knowledgeable in a wide variety of legal matters and can meet your needs in an effective, cost saving, fast and efficient way. L.A.W. attorneys handle a great volume of similar cases and our computer is programmed to handle volumes of paperwork. **YOU REMAIN IN CONTROL OF YOUR LEGAL MATTER! YOU SAVE TIME AND MONEY!**

What happens?	Traditional law office	Legal Action Workshop
The client pays a one-time fee.	_____	_____
The client pays an hourly fee.	_____	_____
Additional consultations are paid for by the client.	_____	_____
The client pays for the time spent on the telephone with the lawyer.	_____	_____
There are no additional fees.	_____	_____
The attorney asks the client questions and gets facts to begin the case.	_____	_____
The case begins with a questionnaire and a cassette tape.	_____	_____
A computer analyzes the information from the client's questionnaire.	_____	_____
A computer prepares the client's legal paperwork.	_____	_____
The attorney gives information to a legal secretary, who types the paperwork.	_____	_____
The attorney handles many similar cases.	_____	_____

C. Write T before the statements that are *true,* according to the brochure. Write F before those that are *false.* Write I before those that are *impossible to know* from the brochure.

1. _____ All areas of the law can be handled by the "Program Method" of the Legal Action Workshop.

2. _____ At the workshop, attorneys are never necessary.

3. _____ You can easily sue someone through the "Program Method."

4. _____ Fees at the Legal Action Workshop will probably be lower than fees paid to a private attorney.

5. _____ The client makes all decisions at the Legal Action Workshop.

6. _____ Attorneys in a law office make all the decisions for their clients.

D. Write *F* before the statements that are *fact.* Write *O* before the statements that may be the *opinions* of the writers of the brochure.

1. _____ Some attorneys request retainers for their legal work.

2. _____ Consultations at the Legal Action Workshop give clients better information than visits to a private attorney.

3. _____ Questionnaires are a good way to get information from a client.

4. _____ A lawyer can give clients a lot of the information they need with a cassette tape.

5. _____ Law offices and clinics have legal secretaries.

6. _____ All law work can be computerized.

7. _____ Clients should have control over all steps in the legal process.

Going Beyond the Text

Do you have any contracts or legal papers that you don't understand? Bring them to class. Discuss new vocabulary and the meaning of the important points.